Fresh From the Word
the Bible for a change
2014

IBRA
International Bible Reading Association

FRESH from the WORD

the Bible for a change

Foreword by Archbishop Desmond Tutu

Edited by Nathan Eddy

Fresh From the Word aims to build understanding and respect for different Christian perspectives through the provision of a range of biblical interpretations. Views expressed by contributors should not, therefore, be taken to reflect the views or policies of the Editor or the International Bible Reading Association.

The International Bible Reading Association's scheme of readings is available in English, French and Spanish, and may be downloaded from the Christian Education website at www.christianeducation.org.uk/about-ibra

Cover design by Christian Education Publications
Typography designed by Stephen Raw www.stephenraw.com

Editor: – Nathan Eddy

Published by:
The International Bible Reading Association
1020 Bristol Road
Selly Oak
Birmingham B29 6LB
United Kingdom

Charity number 211542

ISBN 978-1-905893-61-4
ISSN 2050-6791

Typeset by Wordsense Ltd, Edinburgh: www.wordsense.co.uk
Printed and bound in the UK by Mosaic Print Management

Contents

Foreword

by Archbishop Desmond Tutu

Welcome to *Fresh From the Word*. Whether you are a new or returning reader, whether you are young or old, may God bless you and inspire your reading of the Bible this year, guided by this book.

The Bible is not some dry and dusty list of rules. It is the story of how we are created good in God's eyes, how that goodness was damaged, and how wholeness is ours with God. Depravity came into the world through individual choices, drip by drip. The Bible is an invitation to wholeness instead of brokenness. We can choose wholeness and a life of beauty. We can choose to work for peace in the small choices that face us each day. Each of us has the dignity of these choices, whether we are rich or poor, from the global North or South, in prison or not. The Bible shows us how. It is about peace and reconciliation. It is about social justice in your neighbourhood. It is about joy and laughter.

The International Bible Reading Association has a rich history. It goes all the way back to the evangelical revival in the nineteenth century and the creation of Sunday schools and public education for all. IBRA has always been an association, not just a publisher of Bible reading notes. To be an association means we learn from one another, wherever we are in the world. We can be human only together – we have too much to learn from one another to be divided. In South Africa our word for this is 'ubuntu' – we are whole together, and all are diminished if one of us is diminished. We must be an association! Despite all the horrors of life I have seen in my work for reconciliation, I am still struck by how wonderful people are. We are created by God to be a blessing, and we need one another to become this. *Fresh From the Word* carries on the founding vision of IBRA for our generation to be this kind of global association for good.

In the words of the psalmist, the Bible is 'lamp for my feet'. May the 'Word for Today' found in this book be a 'Light for our Path'. I pray that this book and its writers will guide us in our efforts to make peace, and in our laughing and loving. Life is too precious for anything less.

I hope you are ready for the adventure. Day by day as you read, I hope you are aware of the gracious, peaceful, and hopeful presence of God, and are changed by it!

God bless you

Archbishop Emeritus D M Tutu

How to use *Fresh From the Word*

How do you approach the idea of regular Bible reading? It may help to see daily Bible reading as spiritual exploration. Here is a suggestion of a pattern to follow that may help you develop the discipline but free up your mind and heart to respond.

- Before you read, take a few moments – the time it takes to say the Lord's Prayer – to imagine God looking at you with love. Feel yourself enfolded in that gaze. Come to scripture with your feet firmly planted.

- Read the passage slowly before you turn to the notes. Be curious The Bible was written over a period of nearly 1000 years, over 2000 years ago. There is always something to learn. Read and reread.

- 'Read' yourself as you read the story. Be attentive to your reactions – even trivial ones. What is drawing you into the story? What is repelling you? Observe yourself 'sidelong' as you read as if you were watching a wild animal in the forest; be still, observant and expectant.

- What in the scripture or in the notes is drawing you forward in hope? What is closing you down? Notice where the Spirit of Life is present, and where negative spirits are, too. Follow where life is leading. God always leads into life, even if the way feels risky.

- Lift up the world and aspects of your life to God. What would you like to share with God? What is God seeking to share with you?

- Thank God for being present and offer your energy in the day ahead, or in the day coming after a night's rest.

Introduction from the Editor

Welcome to *Fresh From the Word*, a new resource for daily Bible reading. We really do mean 'welcome'. We aren't just publishers – the International Bible Reading Association (IBRA) is an association of readers of the Bible around the world, in many different churches. Wherever you have come from, we are glad to share this journey with you.

For returning IBRA readers, it's you who are welcoming me as Editor, as well. I come to *Fresh From the Word* from parish ministry, university chaplaincy, journalism and creative writing, and I've enjoyed working with the editorial team on this new venture.

Our mission is simple. *Fresh From the Word* aims to help you read the Bible daily. There are notes here for every day of the year, followed by prayers and questions to stimulate your imagination and prayer. You will need to have a Bible to hand to engage with the notes – the notes are meant to take you deeper into scripture, not to stand alone.

Our writers were also given the challenging brief of reaching out to new Christians, to Christians involved in social action, and to Christians involved in Fresh Expressions worship contexts – all the while maintaining the same international and ecumenical perspectives which were hallmarks of IBRA notes in recent years. I think they've done that – and I'll be interested in hearing your views.

We hope this new title is familiar to returning readers, but there are new features for *Fresh From the Word*, as well. All these notes are written using the 2011 New International Version of the Bible, the bestselling English language translation. The 2011 NIV uses inclusive language where its previous incarnations did not.

One last word – you might find it interesting to visit our Facebook page (http://www.facebook.com/freshfromtheword) to share your views and join discussions on notes. The site is updated regularly by me and the IBRA team and we hope you'll join the discussion on the themes this year, including The greening spirit, Journeys, War and Peace, and God in translation.

Every blessing on your journey with these writers and, in faith, with readers around the world.

Nathan Eddy

Acknowledgements and abbreviations

We are grateful to the following copyright holders for permission to use quotations from the New International Version of the Bible in the following territories:

Within the UK, EU and EFTA
Scripture quotations taken from the Holy Bible, New International Version Anglicised. Copyright © 1979, 1984, 2011 Biblica, formerly International Bible Society. Used by permission of Hodder & Stoughton Ltd, an Hachette UK company. All rights reserved. 'NIV' is a registered trademark of Biblica. UK trademark number 1448790.

Within the US and Canada
Scriptures taken from the Holy Bible, New International Version®, NIV®. Copyright © 1973, 1978, 1984, 2011 by Biblica, Inc.™ Used by permission of Zondervan. All rights reserved worldwide. www.zondervan.com The "NIV" and "New International Version" are trademarks registered in the United States Patent and Trademark Office by Biblica, Inc.™

Within all other territories worldwide and for all electronic versions of this text
Scriptures taken from the Holy Bible, New International Version® Anglicized, NIV® Copyright © 1979, 1984, 2011 by Biblica, Inc.® Used by permission. All rights reserved worldwide.

Note
Some writers use the abbreviation CE and BCE to indicate Common Era/before the Common Era according to modern convention. No disrespect is intended.

Voices

This week's notes are by **Nathan Eddy**

 Nathan is editor of *Fresh from the Word* and minister at North Lowestoft United Reformed Church, Suffolk, UK. His poetry and prose have appeared in magazines and scripture commentaries and he has worked as a journalist near Boston, USA. Nathan's wife Clare is a full-time Anglican vicar and they have two young daughters. After university, Nathan spent a year living in monasteries in Ghana, Israel, Egypt, India, China and Japan. He has noticed that, the less time he spends riding his mountain bike, the more money he spends on it. He is ordained in the United Church of Christ (USA).

Wednesday 1 January
A fresh start

Psalm 119:129-136

Direct my footsteps according to your word; let no sin rule over me.
(verse 133)

Well, you've done it. You've got hold of *Fresh From the Word* and a Bible and you've started. Whether you are a new or returning reader, welcome.

Psalm 119 is a good place to begin, because this psalm shows us what a discipline like Bible reading can be. This psalm – the longest one – is written in a demanding form called 'acrostic': each verse begins with the same letter, in sets of eight. In new New International Version Bibles, you'll see all twenty-two letters of the Hebrew alphabet reproduced next to their English sound. Alphabets were invented in this part of the world, the Ancient Near East. In fact, if you look at the start of the psalm, you'll see the first two letters 'aleph' and 'beth', which are related to the English word itself, through Greek.

Reading the Bible is a discipline. It takes effort. The Bible is old and it can be strange. We are all busy. But this disciplined psalm is not grim. It is like a dance between two people who have been partners for years: direct my footsteps …

The psalmist belongs to God. There is no anxiety, just trust that God will be there. Through your disciplined reading this year, may that trust grow and grow as God directs your footsteps in your dance together.

† Lord of the dance, direct our footsteps in ways of peace and life this year, and help us persevere when we stumble.

Thursday 2 January
Committed and complete

1 John 1:1-4

We proclaim to you what we have seen and heard, so that you also may have fellowship with us. And our fellowship is with the Father and with his Son, Jesus Christ. We write this to make our joy complete. (verses 3-4)

You might know the most famous passage from 1 John, the one often used at weddings: 'God is love' (4:8b). Like a wedding or union, the point of the opening verses of John is togetherness. The point is to be drawn together into fellowship, which will complete the joy that the writer's community seeks. In other words, reading the Bible is good for nothing unless we are drawn into community. To be Christian means to share what you have in fellowship – as partners promise to do in a wedding ceremony!

Like all committed relationships, Christian community takes work. It can involve real pain and suffering. There are indications in this book of a painful split in John's community. (In 2:19 we read, 'they went out from us, but they did not really belong to us'. Ouch.) Perhaps these opening verses reflect a disagreement over Jesus – other Christians at the time believed that he only appeared to suffer, or came only as a spirit, not flesh and blood that could be seen and touched. But our author is clear: Jesus, the Word of life, was real – someone whose body and wounds could be touched.

You don't need me to tell you that our relationships and faith communities are as fragile as Jesus' human body. Churches, like John's, can be torn apart. But the bonds of God's love (the bonds that *are* God, according to 1 John!) are stronger even than death. In that love all creation is called into committed fellowship. And we are called to build it up, relationship by relationship – not just read about it.

† Gracious God, thank for you sharing everything you have with us. Give us your commitment and generosity to share with others, to complete your joy.

For further thought

- What community will you be building up this year as you read the Bible?

Friday 3 January
Hearts on fire

Luke 24:25-32

Were not our hearts burning within us while he talked with us on the road and opened the Scriptures to us? (part of verse 32)

We will be reading a lot of the Bible this year together. In particular, we will be reading a lot of the Old Testament, or Hebrew Bible – Joshua, Ecclesiastes, Amos and Habbakuk, to name a few. The scriptures that Jesus was opening to his discouraged followers on the road would have been like these; the New Testament hadn't been written yet.

As he did for those followers, Jesus helps us re-imagine the Old Testament. And the relationship works the other way, too. The Old Testament in its own right helps us understand Jesus. If you persevere in your reading of the Hebrew Bible, it will enlarge and challenge your understanding of Jesus, his teaching, and his people.

Nothing looks quite the same with the living Jesus at our side, including the Bible. The two people on that road thought their world had ended with Jesus' death. It was only after the fact that they understood what God was up to.

About 20 years ago we had a fire in the sanctuary of my church. The organ was a write-off, and smoke damaged much of the front wall. It was awful at the time. But today, after generosity and hard work, the sanctuary feels fresh and contemporary. I'm not sure things would have changed without that fire.

At the start of a New Year we tend to think about the future. I wonder what in your past will be seen in different perspective this year as Jesus opens the scriptures among us. I wonder what part of the Bible might come alive for you – and what aspect of Jesus you might see in new light.

† Living Lord, unsettle what we think we know about you. Illuminate the scriptures again. Set our hearts alight.

For further thought

• If you have a chance to read the Bible in person with Jews or Muslims and have an open and friendly discussion, don't hesitate. You'll be amazed and challenged.

Saturday 4 January
Signs of life

John 20:30-31

But these are written that you may believe that Jesus is the Messiah,
the Son of God, and that by believing you may have life in his name.
(verse 31)

One of the challenges of following Jesus is that he is not here physically on earth as he was in the Gospels. Christians believe that Jesus will come again – but for now we are in-between times. I wonder if the church is in-between times, too. Things are changing about the way we worship, the way we engage with young families and young adults, and the way we live out our mission in diverse societies. We are in-between times, building a church that does not fully exist.

John assures us that Jesus leads us even though absent. He has written down these signs of Jesus so that we, too, can have life in his name (verse 31) even though Jesus isn't around in the same way. By listening to the voices we've looked at over the past few days – voices of discipline and trust, voices calling you to a shared life, and voices calling you to hope with a living Jesus – we can be guided by the presence of Jesus into life.

Recently a long-time member of my church died. She had been a Sunday school teacher and preacher in local churches and was an inspiration to many people. She kept all her sermons, and we read some at her funeral. Although many missed her, and felt upset, in the sermons we read we were comforted by her trust that death was not the end for her. Her words, and her presence, were in a sense still with us.

Although we live in-between times, by reading, listening and imagining together, we, too, will be led by Jesus into life. He is not anxious or afraid.

† Lead us into life, Lord of life, one sign at a time.

For further thought
• Take some space somewhere on this page to record some hopes for that life in your life this year, and for your community.

Readings in Matthew 1 – 4
1 The birth of Jesus, the Messiah

This week's notes are by **Jennifer Smith**

The Revd Dr Jennifer Smith is a Methodist minister serving in West London. She is originally from Boston, Massachusetts, but has lived in the UK since 1993. Before ordination, she was a lecturer, and has regularly taught in Nigeria. Jennifer cares passionately about teaching as part of church life, so faith can stand up to hard questions and give a good account of itself in the modern world. She enjoys bluegrass, gospel and blues music, is married to an Anglican priest and has two adult stepdaughters.

Sunday 5 January
A very human birth

Matthew 1:18-25

This is how the birth of Jesus the Messiah came about: his mother Mary was pledged to be married to Joseph, but before they came together she was found to be pregnant through the Holy Spirit. (verse 18)

There were no bodyguards or team of doctors for the birth of this king, that's for sure. But Joseph had already made up his mind to protect Mary before he knew what was going on, even when he thought she had been unfaithful. That is righteousness! The older scripture saying – that she should be put to death (Deuteronomy 22:23-27) – was no longer enforced in their day, but Mary still would have lost everything had Joseph exposed her. Readers across time have cheered to see Joseph do the right thing rather than what others would have told him was necessary. This baby would need the strong protection of both his mum and his dad, in addition to his heavenly Father.

God performed a miracle in Mary's pregnancy, and would come into the world as a normal human baby. The prophecy to which verse 23 referred (Isaiah 7:14), about a virgin bearing a son, was not written in its own time as a prediction of Jesus' birth. However, that does not mean Matthew was making anything up by referring to it; he was simply giving his readers a head start in understanding how significant this baby would be. The way Matthew told this story and the others we shall read this week leaves no doubt that Jesus is the Messiah.

† Pray today for people finding out about a pregnancy. Pray for new babies and their parents. In Jesus' name. Amen

5

Monday 6 January (Epiphany)
A confused and threatened king

Matthew 2:1-8

When King Herod heard this he was disturbed, and all Jerusalem with him.
(verse 3)

The irony was that Herod had nothing to worry about. At least, nothing among the things he thought he should be worried about. He was worried that a resentful population, whom he ruled on Rome's behalf, would unify behind a new ruler to unseat him. He was worried that a Bethlehem child could legitimately claim King David's crown, as referred to in the verse at Micah 5:2, which his priests and teachers had quoted to him. All his worries seemed to be coming true at once with the arrival of the blissfully ignorant magi.

We know, and Matthew's earliest readers would have known, that Jesus had rejected the possibility of being an earthly ruler. Whatever else his followers claimed for him, they knew he had gone to the cross and died instead of leading a rebellion against Rome. He wanted nothing so small and temporary as any king's position. Many of his own followers would pin hopes for earthly power on him, but he would resist them all in turn. Herod was only the first in a long line of friends and foes to be confused about the nature of Jesus' kingship.

Fear among oppressive rulers is not new. Secrets and lies are not new. The kind of kingship offered by this baby was and is and always will be new in a world where the strongest army wins and money buys public opinion. Herod was right to be worried. He was just too blinkered to know what about.

† Lord, on this Epiphany day we pray for those who travel, those who seek, those who have not yet found. We pray for people of all cultures and times who retell the gospel story, that it may be for ever new. In Jesus' name. Amen

For further thought
• Many cultures have celebrations for Epiphany, the traditional 'twelfth night' end to the feast of Christmas. Consider having friends round to put decorations away, making a party of it.

Tuesday 7 January
Overjoyed amidst the cardboard crowns

Matthew 2:9-12

When they saw the star, they were overjoyed. On coming to the house, they saw the child with his mother Mary, and they bowed down and worshipped him. Then they opened their treasures and presented him with gifts of gold, frankincense and myrrh. (verses 10-11)

I will for ever associate these verses with church nativity plays: three medium-sized children, in dressing gowns and sandals with glitter-glue crowns, make their way down the aisle carrying boxes covered in tinsel and kitchen foil. The congregation sings something to do with kings and the Orient. Up on the platform there is by now some pushing among the child-sheep who have had to stand still since the shepherds' bit from Luke 2 was read a few minutes ago, and the 'company of angels' (also from Luke) have begun to get itchy in their wings and are making faces at each other. This is usually in a city church, with a background of sirens from the police station across the street. Into such a gathering do our kings arrive, overjoyed to have found the Christ child.

Matthew was the only Gospel writer to include these 'magi', not literally kings, but wise men or astrologer/scientists. And the fact that they gave three gifts appropriate to a king (including spices for embalming a body) does not mean there were only three in the party. But how many there were does not matter as much as who they were: as non-Hebrew witnesses to the coming of the Messiah, they show that this king was *for* the whole world, if not *of* the world as Herod feared. By the time Matthew's readers were hearing about magi, they already knew the story of Jesus. Matthew wanted to leave no doubt that Jesus was and is good news for all people. That is surely worth being overjoyed about.

† Gracious God, we pray for churches who faithfully tell your story year on year. Give us new ears to hear the old stories; surprise us with joy. In Jesus' name. Amen

For further thought

• Write a brief thank-you note to someone whose work usually gets taken for granted at Christmas, in church or out of it.

Wednesday 8 January
How ecumenism came to Lake Woebegon

Matthew 2:13-18

When Herod realised that he had been outwitted by the Magi, he was furious, and he gave orders to kill all the boys in Bethlehem and its vicinity who were two years old and under, in accordance with the time he had learned from the Magi. (verse 16)

It is not surprising that nice, friendly churches usually stop their nativity plays before reaching this point in chapter two of Matthew's Gospel. American humorist Garrison Keillor tells a story about the year a zealous nun at 'Our Lady of Perpetual Responsibility' in the fictitious Minnesota town of Lake Woebegon extended things beyond verse 12 in a bid for scriptural authenticity. Keillor left the congregation's response largely to be imagined. But if we were to do so, the nun's extra scene could explain why, the following year, the Roman Catholics decide to forgo their own nativity and join in the Lutheran 'Christmas songs of praise' – an unexpected show of ecumenical warmth not wholly reciprocated nor understood.

Tragically, massacre to remove political opposition remains a tool of tyrants. A sure way to remove a political minority is to kill and displace its children. If power can justify massacre with the rationale that the minority poses a threat to the well-being of the society, so much the easier.

However, in the scripture, Herod was not so calculating. Matthew says that he killed the Hebrew babies in fury when he realised the magi had avoided his first trap. Although scripture is silent, I can almost hear a self-justification that would blame the departed visitors for the massacre: 'See, if they had given him up, all these lives would have been saved. I had no choice, because of them!' Jesus' life would always pose a threat to power, from the first to the last.

† Pray for the work of reconciliation in countries that have suffered genocide, for refugees and those who are displaced by violence. Pray for all who are tempted by fury. In Jesus' name. Amen

For further thought

• Find out more about a situation of civil violence in the news today, or in recent history. What has happened in the aftermath?

Thursday 9 January
Joseph, just another dreamer

Matthew 2:19-23

Having been warned in a dream, [Joseph] withdrew to the district of Galilee, and he went to live in a town called Nazareth. So was fulfilled what was said through the prophets, that he would be called a Nazarene. (verses 22b-23)

An important part of Matthew's telling of the stories of Jesus' birth is that Jesus really was that vulnerable, really was as dependent on his mum and dad as any baby. And yet, Mary and Joseph had help from the start in the shape of dreams. Let's count:

1   *Joseph reassured Mary can be his wife*
2   *The Magi warned not to return to Herod*
3   *Joseph warned to flee to Egypt*
4   *Joseph told it is safe to return as Herod is dead*
5   *Joseph warned to settle in Nazareth*

We could treat dreams as a simple literary device on Matthew's part to get the important characters to the right place and doing the right thing without breaking the narrative. Or we could treat dreams as a window into mystery. We don't need a literal belief in angel voices to consider that in dreams we may realise things we have been afraid to know or feel. In dreams our rationality meets our more basic instincts and desires, and God holds their communion.

What distinguished the folk in Matthew's Gospel is how much attention and authority they gave to dreams. They respected and discerned amongst the internal urgings of which they are aware, humbly willing to accept that their first rational thought might not be the final word.

† Gracious God, we pray for those whose sleep is broken by pain, or fear, or care. We offer thanksgiving for Joseph, who loved the child Jesus as his son, and dreamed of his safety. In Jesus' name. Amen

For further thought

• Consider keeping a dream journal, and jotting down images or what happens, however odd. Do you have 'special' dreams you remember from different times in your life?

Friday 10 January
John, voice in the wilderness

Matthew 3:1-6

In those days John the Baptist came, preaching in the wilderness of Judea and saying 'Repent, for the kingdom of heaven has come near.' ... People went out to him from Jerusalem and all Judea and the whole region of the Jordan. Confessing their sins, they were baptised by him in the River Jordan. (verses 1-2 and 5-6)

So far, so good for John the baptiser – he was a popular minor celebrity, the latest fad to hit the headlines. Move over Botox, move over low-carb lifestyle, let's head to the desert!

Of course, those who came to John would be genuine seekers, in addition to spiritual sightseers. But seekers for what? Power, happiness, spiritual fulfilment? What did they think they would find, coming to this unconventional hermit in the desert? What are we looking for, as we look for guides and teachers in our faith?

Matthew does not give his readers any biographical explanation about John, in contrast to Luke's elaborate backstory in preparation of Jesus' own baptism and public ministry. In each of the Gospels, John the Baptist is identified one way or another with the prophecy from the prophet Isaiah 40:3, that the way of the Lord will be prepared by a voice of one calling in the wilderness. The details about his food and dress are entirely realistic. He eats insects and wild food, as desert dwellers do today.

This week we have been reading in depth Matthew's narrative of Jesus' birth and first years. In the third chapter, Jesus himself becomes the central actor and speaker in the text as he begins his public ministry. But, for now, we are left with the longings of the crowd, not sure what they are asking from John, and accepting his baptism, call for repentance and declaration of God's forgiveness. John's message will not long remain popular, and the political implications of his teaching will make him a martyr.

† Lord, we pray for ourselves, in our spiritual longing. We pray that we may form good questions and risk the journey into the wilderness. In Jesus' name. Amen

For further thought

- What spiritual trends have you been aware of? (These are not necessarily bad things!) What new way of prayer, or study might you try?

Saturday 11 January
Imagine the scene ... a modern parable

Matthew 3:7-12

The axe has been laid to the root of the trees, and every tree that does not produce good fruit will be cut down and thrown into the fire. (verse 10)

A minister comes in late one evening to find several new messages on the answerphone. This afternoon has seen the annual ladies' outing to a 'place of spiritual interest', this year a coach trip with packed lunch to the Judean wilderness:

Beep! [A woman's voice]: Um, Jen, I am sure you did not know what that abusive man would be like. 'Why not give the Baptist a try', you said. I for one do not blame you. You could not have known, whatever anyone else says. You are always so loving, so inclusive in your preaching! Well, I tell you ... *[machine cuts off].*

Beep! [Another woman's voice, with a man in the background]: What?! Yes, I'm calling now – hello, Jen? Hello? No, she's not home. Jen, we got some good preaching today, the *'full gospel'* kind Gerald wants to see more of. Gerald feels very strongly that ... *[scuffle, sound of phone dropping, machine cuts off].*

Beep! [A man's voice]: Hello? This is John Appleby from Appleby Coaches. I don't usually turn away business, but I'd ask you not use us in the future. Sick in the back, honey on the windows and big hopping bugs in the luggage compartment. It is not what I expect. No need to come back to me, we'll send a bill for the clean. *Beep! [The sound of sighing, as the minister presses 'erase all messages'.]*

† Lord, we pray for ears to hear hard teaching, and spirits of repentance. Challenge us in love, but preserve us from too many trips to the Judean wilderness. In Jesus' name. Amen

For further thought

• When was the last time you were distinctly uncomfortable with a sermon or church teaching? Why, and what did you do?

Readings in Matthew 1 – 4

2 Then Jesus came from Galilee

This week's notes are by **Catrin Harland**

Catrin is the Methodist Chaplain to the University of Sheffield, discussing life and faith with students and staff, usually over coffee and cake. She is passionate about equipping young adults to live out their calling in the church and the world. She is engaged in research into the New Testament and the early church. In her spare time, she enjoys drumming and climbing (badly), watching comedy, cricket and Formula 1, and playing with Lego, usually with her three children.

Sunday 12 January
What if God were one of us?

Matthew 3:13-17

Then Jesus came from Galilee to the Jordan to be baptised by John. But John tried to deter him, saying, 'I need to be baptised by you, and do you come to me?' Jesus replied, 'Let it be so now; it is proper for us to do this to fulfil all righteousness.' Then John consented. (verses 13-15)

I grew up in Birmingham and it will always be 'home', in a particular and unique way, especially now that I'm a Brummie in exile!

Patriotism is a powerful thing. Many have even been willing to die for their bond with those who share their place of origin. In this, Jesus was no exception. His home was Galilee and, when he needs a place of refuge, that is where he can be found.

But Galilee has a broader significance, representing his genuine humanity. In Christ, we see a unique and glorious occurrence – God enters time and space, taking on vulnerable humanity. John is shocked that the Messiah should come to him for baptism but, for Jesus, this is crucial. He shares in the full human experience, including this ritual by which God's love for us is revealed. What happens at the Jordan marks him out as the representative of human relationship with God – receiving God's full and unconditional love.

Matthew's Gospel tells the story of Christ as our representative, beginning with his human lineage, and including his very human temptation, suffering and death. He is even willing to die for his shared bond with us – and we share in his resurrection and new covenant relationship with God.

† God, who shared our humanity, strengthen our love for all humanity, that we may be your hands, feet, voice, heart and life in your world.

Monday 13 January
Starting as you mean to go on

Matthew 4:1-11

Jesus answered, 'It is written: "Man shall not live on bread alone, but on every word that comes from the mouth of God."' Then the devil took him to the holy city and set him on the highest point of the temple.
(verses 4-5)

As a university chaplain, I always enjoy freshers' week. Thousands of new students arrive in their new home, desperate to make friends, eager to begin their study, resolving to work hard, and determined to play hard, too. The week is a whirlwind of socialising, registration, orientation, meeting new flatmates and coursemates. And the pressure is immense – to fit in, to make the most of freedom from parental scrutiny, to find out all they need to know. And it is not unusual to feel vulnerable, alone, unprotected, away from home, fearing 'failure', before there's been any possible chance of 'success'.

Jesus is also away from home. He's alone in a strange, hostile environment. He's vulnerable. He's left behind all that's familiar. Fresh from his baptism and its revelation, he must now be wondering what he's let himself in for. And then he's offered all sorts of temptations – not the cheap alcohol and fun of freshers' week, but still things that many new students might dream of: free food, success without effort, glory and achievement.

Perhaps if Jesus had succumbed, if he'd taken the easy route to his own glory, we'd never have heard of him. But like (most of) the students I meet, he recognises an empty promise when he sees one. He knows that the path before him will be a hard one, but one that must be trodden. He's retreated into the wilderness to seek strength, and strength is precisely what he finds. Strength to serve, to do right, to glorify God – strength to be himself.

† God of the vulnerable, who accepted weakness and knew temptation: in our frail humanity, let us know your presence and comfort and, through our human vulnerability, make us strong.

For further thought

- When do you feel most vulnerable or afraid? Next time you find yourself there, reach out for the God who became vulnerable for our sake.

Tuesday 14 January
A prophet in his own home

Matthew 4:12-17

Land of Zebulun and land of Naphtali, the Way of the Sea, beyond the Jordan, Galilee of the Gentiles – the people living in darkness have seen a great light; on those living in the land of the shadow of death a light has dawned. (verses 15-16)

I love to travel, see new places, meet new people, learn new things. And I love coming home again. If travel broadens the mind, perhaps it's back home that we can process all we've seen and learned, and take stock of our new breadth of understanding. We see the familiar through new eyes and acquire a different perspective on what we have never questioned.

Jesus, dealing with the frightening reality of what John's ministry, and his, might cost, does what any of us might do – he goes home. Back to the familiar, the comfortable. But even home feels different; he sees it in a new way. Elsewhere, Jesus discovers that a prophet is rarely recognised at home. I suspect that it also works the other way – it's easy to miss what's special or significant about the place where you've grown up. But now Jesus sees his home region of Galilee in the light of his new self-understanding and his growing understanding of God's plans. Galilee, seen by many as a rural backwater, inhabited by simple fishermen and colonised by enterprising Greeks, has become the focus of a fulfilled prophecy. What seems normal, familiar, unexciting, safe, perhaps backward and stuck, is suddenly to be seen as the location of God's transformative power.

The God who takes us to exciting new places also brings us home. The God who shows us who we are, does so through the new and the familiar. But home or away, God is there, with us, as we engage in the adventure of discovering what it means to be God's children.

† Give thanks to God for those places that have been 'home' and have helped to shape you in positive ways: the place of your roots, of your birth, where you grew up, where you live.

For further thought

• Practise recognising God at work in the place you call home. How might God be calling you to be prophetic there?

Wednesday 15 January
Charity begins at home

Matthew 4:23-25

Jesus went throughout Galilee, teaching in their synagogues, preaching the good news of the kingdom, and healing every disease and sickness among the people. News about him spread all over Syria, and people brought to him all who were ill with various diseases. (verses 23-24a)

Charity begins at home. Not as an excuse for limiting our caring support to our own family, friends or compatriots – of course we are called to put the needs of others before our own love of luxury, regardless of national boundary.

But it can also be tempting to focus so much on faraway needs that we miss those beneath our own noses. It's much easier to feel complacent about our giving when the ongoing need isn't forced into our notice. As joblessness increases, wages are frozen, more people depend upon benefits and food banks become indispensable, we can end up feeling guilty and helpless, and look to blame others, especially those suffering. Compassion compels us to act, so where action is hard, we find ways of avoiding compassion.

Charity does begin at home because, unless we care about those at home, we can never care truly about those we never meet. Seeing need daily around us should prompt us into active campaigning, genuine engagement, or simply recognising the humanity of the vulnerable. Jesus' care, compassion and love were inspired in Galilee. He shared, in word and deed, what God's love for creation really means. But his charity did not begin and end at home. He was ready to go where he was sent, where he was needed, to show to the stranger and foreigner the love he showed first to his fellow Galileans. Think how many of his encounters were with 'outsiders'.

Charity does indeed begin at home, but it is boundless, because the love of God is boundless.

† Pray for the places you thought about yesterday, and places you've visited or that you don't know, but which are in the news. Pray for them, for people who live there, for their leaders.

For further thought
• How do you show the love of God in your neighbourhood and further afield? How might you – in your giving, volunteering, or general outlook?

Thursday 16 January
Who do you think you are?

Matthew 1:1-11

This is the genealogy of Jesus the Messiah the son of David, the son of Abraham: Abraham was the father of Isaac, Isaac the father of Jacob, Jacob the father of Judah and his brothers, Judah the father of Perez and Zerah, whose mother was Tamar. (verses 1-3a)

Since the success of the BBC2 television series *Who Do You Think You Are?* Britain has become a nation of amateur family historians, fascinated by the details and stories of our ancestors' lives. So far, unlike some of those featured on the programme, I have discovered no royalty in my lineage, and no very scandalous skeletons in my cupboard. But I live in hope!

Matthew's Gospel begins with a list of names designed to tell us who Jesus is and where he has come from, and his family includes both royalty and scandal. An Israelite's lineage was a serious matter, and was described through the male line. Yet, intriguingly, today's passage contains four women and, tomorrow's, one more. Their stories are worth a read.

Tamar pretended to be a prostitute to seduce her father-in-law and produce an heir to his line (Genesis 38:6-30). Rahab, who was a prostitute living in Jericho, risked her life to conceal some Hebrew spies (Joshua 2, and 6:17-25). Ruth left her own home in Moab, to remain with her Israelite mother-in-law (Ruth 1 – 4). Uriah's wife, Bathsheba, willingly or otherwise bore a son for David, who then had her husband killed (2 Samuel 11).

These women are variously brave, ill-used, disreputable, outsiders, loyal, independent. But they all – whether by design or circumstance – do what is necessary to keep the messianic line going. So often, the place of women is 'merely' to bear children, but here 'merely' becomes 'crucially'! Jesus' forefathers are listed for who they were but his foremothers are identified for what they did – Matthew's champions of the holy lineage.

† Father and Mother God, we thank you for the determination, the self-giving and the willingness to be different shown by so many of those by whom your purposes have been fulfilled. Amen

For further thought

• Who in your family or church deserves recognition for unconventional creativity in their service of God? When did you last acknowledge it to them?

Friday 17 January
Expected Messiah, or unexpected king?

Matthew 1:12-17

... and Jacob the father of Joseph, the husband of Mary, and Mary was the mother of Jesus who is called the Messiah. Thus there were fourteen generations in all from Abraham to David, fourteen from David to the exile to Babylon, and fourteen from the exile to the Messiah. (verses 16-17)

I remember, in a school history lesson, being asked to examine various portraits of Elizabeth I. It was a very valuable lesson in how to interpret propaganda, for what we learned was less about the Queen herself than about how she was viewed by the artists, how she viewed herself and how she wished to be viewed by others.

I suspect that no portrait – drawn, painted, photographed or written – is entirely impartial. The clothing, the stance, the expression, the details, all contribute to the impression, positive or negative, that we are supposed to take away. Matthew's pen-portrait of Jesus is no different, and his genealogy, which opens the account, is designed to establish Jesus, from the beginning, as the Messiah.

Whoever, or whatever, the expected messiah might be, he would stand, genealogically or symbolically, in the royal line of David, who represented the ideal leadership of an idealised Israel – one, great, godly ruler of the united kingdom and reunited people of God. Matthew demonstrates this descent not just by locating David in Jesus' family tree, but also by the symbolic sets of fourteen generations. Hebrew script used letters for numbers, and the values of 'DVD' (David: Hebrew uses only consonants) add up to fourteen. The number therefore took on powerful messianic significance.

All that follows, for Matthew, flows from Jesus' identity as a Davidic king – a messiah. He didn't come from nowhere but from a tradition of expectation and prophecy, looked for and longed for. Yet his leadership is not what we might expect: he is a preacher, teacher, miracle-worker, executed criminal. What kind of king is this?

† Jesus Christ, Messiah, you came to lead your people in ways not of war, but of peace. Give us the courage to be a kingdom in the pattern of your kingly rule.

For further thought

• Jesus stands in a kingly tradition, and transforms it. What one thing will you do today to show that you follow in his messianic lineage?

Saturday 18 January
To arrive where we started …

Matthew 28:16-20

Then the eleven disciples went to Galilee, to the mountain where Jesus had told them to go … Then Jesus came to them and said, 'All authority in heaven and on earth has been given to me. Therefore go and make disciples of all nations.' (verses 16, 18-19a)

If home is where the heart is, it is also where we expect to find comfort, familiarity and reassurance. Once again, Galilee becomes the place of retreat when things are difficult – in this case, for Jesus' disciples, following Jesus' instructions. They go back home, back to where it all began. The circle is completed.

T S Eliot wrote, in Section V of 'Little Gidding' (1942) from his *Four Quartets*:

We shall not cease from exploration
And the end of all our exploring
Will be to arrive where we started
And know the place for the first time.

Matthew began his Gospel with Jesus' messianic, Israelite identity, and ends it with Jesus' eternal significance for 'all nations'. Here, too, the circle is completed: this man is truly of all the divine importance that his lineage is meant to suggest. But Matthew has so transformed the understanding of messianic kingship that it is now embodied, not in earthly pomp, but precisely in a self-giving, crucified healer.

To learn, grow, have our preconceptions about God challenged: this is the essence of discipleship. A disciple is one who learns. It is not merely the eleven mentioned in this passage who have grown in understanding – we are expected to learn with them. And discipleship is a lifelong journey in which we learn to see the familiar through new eyes, and to expect to encounter God in unexpected places.

† Jesus Christ, come to us in strange and familiar places. Surprise us, comfort us, unsettle us, challenge us, change us. And, having changed us, send us out through your world, to do your work.

For further thought

• Consider how your understanding of God has changed or grown over the last year. Pray for wisdom and humility, to expect to be divinely surprised!

IBRA ebooks

Do you know someone who would prefer to use Bible reading notes on their eReader or computer?

Fresh From the Word 2014 is available as Kindle, ePub and PDF files.

Priced at £7.49 inc VAT they can be purchased from our website: shop.christianeducation.org.uk

Please contact the IBRA office for more details:

International Bible
Reading Association
1020 Bristol Road, Selly Oak,
Birmingham B29 6LB

0121 472 4242

sales@christianeducation.org.uk

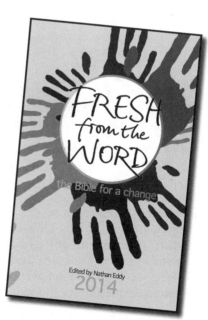

History of IBRA and the International Fund

The International Bible Reading Association (IBRA) was founded by the Sunday School Union (SSU) committee under Charles Waters in 1882. At the time Waters was the manager of a bank in King's Cross. As a devout young man and Sunday school teacher, Waters had arrived in London in 1859 to further his career and had encountered the brilliant and inspirational teaching of Charles Spurgeon. He threw himself heart and soul in to working with Spurgeon and the Sunday School Union. In 1882 the SSU wrote to all members in Britain and overseas inviting them to join the newly formed International Bible Reading Association, circulating lists of daily Bible readings, supported by brief commentary notes.

The response was amazing. Readers appreciated that each day they were provided with a portion of scripture that was thoughtfully brief, selected with the utmost care to link to the week's topic. There was a living personal touch which was seemingly the secret of its success.

Charles Waters at his desk

By 1910 the readership had exceeded a million people and was touching the lives of soldiers fighting wars, sailors on long voyages to Australia, colliers in the coal mines of Wales, schools in Canada, Jamaica and Belfast, prisoners in Chicago – people all over the world, alone or in groups, felt comforted and encouraged by the idea of joining other Christians throughout the world in reading the same Bible passages. And they still do!

Today, over 130 years later, this rich history lives on, touching the lives of hundreds of thousands of people across the world. IBRA is now part of the Birmingham-based charity Christian Education and is working to continue the legacy, providing support to our global community of IBRA readers. Our aim is still to enable Christians from different parts of the world to grow in knowledge and appreciation of each other's experience of God through our international contributors and writers.

The original mission continues today and on in to the future!

Foolishness

1 The wise and the foolish in the Old Testament

This week's notes are by **Jules Gomes**

The Revd Canon Dr Jules Gomes is Canon Theologian at St German Cathedral, Peel, and Vicar of Castletown, Arbory and Santon parishes on the Isle of Man. He earned his doctorate in Old Testament from the University of Cambridge and taught biblical studies at the United Theological College, Bangalore, the London School of Theology and Liverpool Hope University. He served as Canon at Liverpool Cathedral and as a journalist in Bombay. He now contributes regularly to Manx Radio and has written five books. Jules enjoys literature, art, classical and jazz music, target shooting, walking, and golf.

Sunday 19 January
Fools of a feather flock together

Psalm 14:1-7 (end)

The fool says in his heart, 'There is no God.' They are corrupt, their deeds are vile; there is no one who does good. (verse 1)

In Dostoevsky's novel *The Brothers Karamazov* (1880) it is the atheist Ivan who utters the famous phrase, 'Without god, everything is permitted'. In this Psalm, it is not the atheist who is labelled a fool. It would have been difficult, if not impossible, to find an atheist in the cultural world of Israel and her neighbours. If anything, most people believed in a multiplicity of gods. The folly of denying God referred to here is not metaphysical but moral, not intellectual but existential. Fools live as though there is no god. They may affirm God's existence theoretically, but deny God's existence by their practical choices. They do not deny God's existence, but God's governance.

From his initial reference to a single fool, the psalmist switches to denounce the morality of the majority. The psalm is not a prayer. It is a form of instruction – calling upon the listener to eavesdrop upon the psalmist's extensive grasp of human experience and make the right choice by noting the dire consequences of folly. Even though we claim to believe in God, do we make our choices as if God does not exist?

† Forgive our foolishness, Lord, for confessing you with our lips while in the same breath often denying you by our lives. We ask this in the name of one who became our Wisdom. Amen

Monday 20 January
Wisdom and wit

Proverbs 1:1-7

For receiving instruction in prudent behaviour, doing what is right and just and fair; for giving prudence to those who are simple, knowledge and discretion to the young. (verses 3-4)

I first discovered the power of proverbs when I served as University Chaplain in London. Students from all backgrounds would come to me for counselling. However, Asian and African students, unlike their Western counterparts, had a fund of proverbs they brought with them. In counselling sessions, the student would suddenly beam and exclaim, 'I've found a solution.' He or she would then recite a proverb from his or her culture. When I was growing up in Bombay, my father constantly used English proverbs to instruct me. 'A stitch in time saves nine,' he would say when it came to studying regularly, rather than cramming a day before the exam. 'Little things please little minds,' he would say when I came home with local gossip. Now I live in a culture where children know very few proverbs. What they do know are advertising slogans!

What makes proverbs tick, stick and click? Proverbs are nuggets of experience refined and handed down by tradition. A proverb is the wisdom of many, articulated by the wit of one person. This is what gives a proverb its punch. But are most proverbs even remotely religious? A proverb is not 'revelation from above' but 'revelation from below'. God speaks to us through human experience. Proverbs are used to teach, to advise, to console, to encourage socially acceptable behaviour and shape character. What makes the biblical proverbs unique is that the compiler of this marvellous collection roots it all in the 'fear' of or 'reverence' for Yahweh. For us, God is surely the pioneer and perfecter of all human life and all we say and do.

† Almighty God, we thank you for sending your Son to live among us as a human being. Help us not to despise the wisdom that comes from below, but to see your hand in human experience. Amen

For further thought
• Love a proverb? Share it! www.facebook.com/freshfromtheword

Tuesday 21 January
The taming of the tongue

Proverbs 12:15-23

Fools show their annoyance at once, but the prudent overlook an insult.
(verse 16)

The book of Proverbs makes nineteen references to the 'tongue', forty-eight references to 'lips' and over fifty references to right and wrong ways of speaking. Such emphasis is not unique to the Bible. Instruction on right speech was part of the wisdom of Israel's neighbours: the Egyptian wisdom books extolled the virtues of right speech. If wisdom is the ability to make the right choices, we would be wise to choose the right word at the right time and speak it in the right tone of voice. Or else we would be wise to remain silent.

The prudent choice of words is what distinguishes the wise person from the fool. Here, the 'fool' is not necessarily 'godless' or 'immoral' as in Psalm 14, but thick as a brick – stupid and a simpleton. The problem, of course, is that such a person is too proud and insolent to accept instruction and discipline. He is wise in his own eyes. This section encloses such instruction by repeating (in the Hebrew) the words 'fool', 'prudent', 'folly' and 'overlook/keep to themselves' in verses 16 and 23. Our words reveal to the world who we are. The proverbs here call for speech that is temperate (verses 16, 18, 23), truthful (verses 17, 19, 22), constructive, restorative, healing and reconciling (verses 18 and 20).

† Lord God, I surrender my undisciplined tongue to you. Let my 'yes' be 'yes' and my 'no' be 'no'. Help me to speak the truth in love and to love the truth, for Jesus' sake. Amen

For further thought
• For one week, make a list of the number of times you lost your temper. Could you have restrained yourself on those occasions?

Wednesday 22 January
The incorrigible fool

Proverbs 26:1-12

As a dog returns to its vomit, so fools repeat their folly. Do you see a person wise in their own eyes? There is more hope for a fool than for them. (verses 11-12)

Is there really no hope for a fool? It depends on the Hebrew word used for 'fool'. *Kesil* is the word used to describe the incorrigibly foolish. It occurs seventy times in the Old Testament and recurs in eleven of the twelve verses here, in both singular and plural forms. *Peti* describes the 'naïve' or 'simple' fool. It occurs fifteen times in Proverbs. *Ewil* describes persons who are not innately stupid, but who resist instruction. It occurs twenty-seven times in the Old Testament. *Nabal* describes someone who scoffs at instruction and is therefore unteachable.

What parallels the detailed description of the fool's behavior here is the striking use of analogies from nature. Seasons – summer, harvest; natural phenomena – snow, rain; birds – sparrow, swallow; animals – horse, donkey, dog; and plants – thorn bush. Wisdom literature is rooted in the theology of creation. It not only asks us to learn lessons from human experience, but delights in God's order in creation and asks us to observe and learn from God's revelation in nature. If God created all there is in nature, and if God created human beings to be the crown of his creation, in his very image and likeness – how foolish and utterly shameful would it be to live worse than the birds and animals? In an honour-based culture, the purpose of such analogies is to shame fools into recognising their folly and returning to the right path. But the *kesil* just won't listen! In such a situation, it is for the wise to take heed, recognise such a person and make right choices in dealing with the fool of this category.

† Lord, help me to be wise in recognising the stubbornness of the human heart. Help me to learn from my mistakes and not to persist in returning to them. Amen

For further thought

• How often have you kept returning to commit a sin or do something you had resolved not to do?

Thursday 23 January
Simpson or Solomon?

Ecclesiastes 2:12-23

For the wise, like the fool, will not be long remembered; the days have already come when both have been forgotten. Like the fool, the wise too must die! (verse 16)

Homer Simpson is a fool. Yet he is the world's most loved cartoon character. Every week 60 million people in 60 countries watch *The Simpsons*. Solomon is the antithesis of Simpson. If Simpson is TV's biggest fool, Solomon is history's wisest man. Simpson has nothing. Solomon had it all: wealth and wisdom, power and prosperity. And yet, his words betray an unfathomable existential emptiness. 'I have seen it all! Nothing makes sense!' What's the best way out? Knowledge? Pleasure? Wine? Work? Shopping? Music? Entertainment? Sex? But all this is merely chasing the wind. The author's verdict is devastatingly candid. Wisdom may have its advantages – the wise man has eyes in his head while the fool walks in darkness – but they are few and far between.

In the ultimate analysis there is no difference between Homer Simpson and King Solomon. The foolish and the wise both meet with the same fate: death. Both are forgotten. Both rot in their graves. Even the most powerful king has no option but to leave his work and wealth to a successor who may build on it or blow it up! The king despairingly asks, in verse 15, 'Why have I been *so very* wise?' The clue lies in the term 'so very', which is missing in the NIV. It occurs seven times in Ecclesiastes. It is possible to overindulge even in the pursuit of wisdom and to lose the balance between wisdom and other aspects of life! After all, wisdom is about making the right choices so as to live a balanced and wholesome life.

† Almighty God, you give wisdom to those who ask for it. Help us to seek it in the power of the Holy Spirit and through Jesus who became wisdom for us. Amen

For further thought

• Watch an episode of *The Simpsons* and ask yourself how the cartoon characters offer a commentary and critique on contemporary society.

Friday 24 January
Careless words, vows and whispers

Ecclesiastes 5:1-7

Do not be quick with your mouth, do not be hasty in your heart to utter anything before God. God is in heaven and you are on earth, so let your words be few. (verse 2)

The author frames this section with two attitudes worshippers approaching God need to possess: 'guard your steps' (verse 1) and 'fear God' (verse 7). Within this framework of attitudes he offers three injunctions concerning the use of words in worship: do not be quick to speak (verse 2); fulfil quickly what you promise to do (verse 4); and don't be led into sin by what you say (verse 6). Worship the Lord in the beauty of holiness, not in the banality or frivolity of careless words. God's presence is not trite or trivial. There can be no easy intimacy, cuddly communion or cosy chat with an awesome God.

Despite his scepticism, the author regards Temple worship as essential to meaningful existence. He assumes that his audience goes regularly to the 'house of God'. He assumes that Torah will be read there. What will give meaning to worship and to life is listening to Torah rather than incessant chatter. Superficial and superfluous words are wasted words. In the culture of the ancient Near East, pagan worship often consisted of formulae that were supposed to have a magical outcome by twisting the arm of the gods into granting favours. Similarly, divination through the interpretation of dreams was common. The author wants worship to be rooted in reality and in rationality, not in the mumbo-jumbo of myth and superstition.

The God of Israel cannot be manipulated or domesticated. Any attempt at doing so is worse than meaningless. It is hazardous. Above all, words signify commitment. In worship we give our word to God. Failure to keep our word can be disastrous.

† Lord Jesus, we recall the parable of the Pharisee who used many words in worship and the tax-collector who beat his breast and pleaded for mercy. Help us to reflect on words we use in worship. Amen

For further thought

• Read Luke 18:10-14. How do you think Luke's Gospel might have developed this parable based on Old Testament wisdom literature?

Saturday 25 January
The weakest link

Ecclesiastes 9:13-18

The quiet words of the wise are more to be heeded than the shouts of a ruler of fools. (verse 17)

In cultures where power is an addictive aphrodisiac, the survival of the fittest is the only prevailing worldview. *Homo homini lupus est.* Man is wolf to man. The author of Ecclesiastes uses a parable to subvert the doctrine of 'might is right'. His parable is an illustration of a surprising principle in verse 11: it is not always the swift who win the race or the strong who win the battle, because time and chance may very well trip up the strong or swift or powerful or prosperous or learned! Let the powerful not boast, because life is often a lottery with no certainties and no guarantees. The weak, small and insignificant might have surprisingly subversive force. For example, wisdom is mightier than military might. It is the poor, wise man who by his wisdom can pull the rug from beneath the feet of an attacking king with a powerful army. But, given human pride and the class system, would those in power even bother to take the wise words of a poor man seriously? The author of Ecclesiastes is a realist to the core. Undoubtedly, wisdom is better than might. But it is precisely because the poor man is poor and insignificant that his contribution is disregarded and forgotten. What an irony! What a tragedy! Yes, how often do we find ourselves despising and disregarding the power and potential of the powerless? Do we really believe that it is the meek who will inherit the earth? Can we believe that one person plus God can really be a majority?

† Lord God, we thank you that you chose the foolish to shame the wise and the weak to shame the strong. We thank you that your Son became powerless on the cross that he might conquer all powers. Amen

For further thought

• Who are the people you tend to greet first when you go to church? Try greeting at least one stranger each week and welcoming them.

Foolishness

2 Wise, foolish or both?

This week's notes are by **Ann Conway-Jones**

Ann Conway-Jones lives in Birmingham with her husband and two teenage sons. She worships at the local Anglican church, where she occasionally preaches. She combines the academic study of Jewish and Christian biblical interpretation with active involvement in Jewish–Christian relations. She is on the Advisory Board of the Council of Christians and Jews. She recently completed a PhD on mystical understandings of the heavenly temple, and is now working to turn the thesis into a book. Where her life goes next, she has no idea.

Sunday 26 January
Abram ventures into the unknown

Genesis 12:1-5

Go from your country, your people and your father's household to the land I will show you. (verse 1)

Abram, Sarai, Lot and their households are called to leave everything that is familiar and venture out into the unknown. All they take with them is the promise that God will bless Abram, and make him a blessing to others. Our theme this week is wisdom and foolishness. As we shall discover, it is not always easy to tell the difference. Wisdom is not a matter of clever thoughts, but of making the right choices in life. And yet, is there always such a thing as the 'right' choice? Where to live, whom to love, how to cope with disaster: such matters are never simple. Decisions made in good faith can have unintended consequences. The Bible sometimes portrays people with complex personalities, or who are caught in impossible situations, and it doesn't necessarily pass judgement. Discovering what God requires was no more straightforward then than it is now. So read this week with an open mind, and be prepared to look at things from several different points of view. Don't expect there always to be easy answers. And as we ask ourselves 'what does God require of me?' let us pray for God's blessing, not only for ourselves, but also for all those affected by our decisions.

† Hold in your prayers those who take the step of leaving home and family to seek a better life elsewhere.

Monday 27 January
Samson and Delilah

Judges 16:15-22

Then she said to him, 'How can you say, "I love you," when you won't confide in me?' ... With such nagging she prodded him day after day until he was sick to death of it. (verses 15a, 16)

Samson's birth may have been announced by an angel, and he may possess legendary strength, but he is a fool when it comes to women. To make matters worse, he approaches every problem with impetuous brute force, leaving a trail of destruction in his wake. His first wife is given away to Samson's companion by her father, and ends up being burnt to death (Judges 15:6). Now he is besotted with Delilah. Given what the Philistines will do to him (see verse 21) it is ironic that love makes him blind. He has been given plenty of opportunity to realise what Delilah is up to. His first wife coaxed a secret out of him by weeping copiously and saying that he didn't love her (Judges 14:16-17). And three times he has given Delilah false information, only to find himself bound, and the Philistines upon him (16:6-14). But he is remarkably dense, and just doesn't learn. He shows no self-awareness and no intuition about other people. He can't resist the nagging, and gives in to her manipulation.

Neither Samson nor Delilah comes out of the story well. Their relationship is thoroughly compromised by greed, stupidity and tribal conflict. The Bible doesn't always deliver what we expect. Samson is a most ambiguous judge of Israel. What we seem to have here is an entertaining folktale about a deeply-flawed hero, rather than any simple moral message.

† Hold in your prayers those caught in abusive relationships.

For further thought
• How do you cope with people you can't trust?

Tuesday 28 January
David and Michal

2 Samuel 6:12-23

And Michal daughter of Saul had no children to the day of her death.
(verse 23)

In order to understand the end of the relationship between Michal and David, we need to go back to the beginning. We first meet Michal in 1 Samuel 18, where we are told that she loves David (verses 20 and 28). This is the only time in the Bible that a woman is explicitly said to love a man. Of David's feelings we know nothing: she is simply a pawn in his power struggle with Saul. In 1 Samuel 19:11-17 she stands up to her father and saves David's life. There are no words of gratitude as he escapes through the window. During David's years on the run, she is once again pushed around by men, as she is first given in marriage to Paltiel, and then taken from him (1 Samuel 25:44; 2 Samuel 3:12-16). Now, at David's moment of triumph, Michal's frustration boils over.

After the public celebration comes private conflict. Michal cannot share in David's religious ecstasy; all she sees is shameful behaviour – a mere linen ephod doesn't leave much to the imagination. The biblical text doesn't take sides; it simply reports Michal's sarcasm and David's biting reply. She may be Saul's daughter, but he is now king. He will be the judge of what is honourable, and there is nothing she can do about it. Is Michal's childlessness some kind of punishment, simply the inevitable result of the end of intimacy, or a bitter coincidence?

† Hold in your prayers those whose marriage or long-term partnership has died.

For further thought
• Are there long-standing resentments undermining any of your relationships?

Wednesday 29 January
Job foolishly dares to challenge God

Job 13:13-24

Why do you hide your face and consider me your enemy? (verse 24)

Job's life is in tatters. He has lost everything. The friends who come to comfort him assume that he must have done something to merit such punishment (chapter 8). They tell him not to complain and urge him to repent: 'if you put away the sin that is in your hand ... then, free of fault, you will lift up your face' (Job 11:14-15).

But Job clings on to the one thing he has left: his integrity. He refuses to confess to offences he has not committed, and insists on giving voice to the unfairness of life: 'Why do the wicked live on, growing old and increasing in power?' (21:7). In today's passage he challenges God to let him speak, to listen to his case for, despite everything, he still has faith in God's justice: 'yet will I hope in him' (13:15). And the reward for Job's honesty, his struggle and long wait, is God's answer to him out of the whirlwind (38:1). God neither reproves nor comforts him, giving him instead a sweeping panoramic vision of creation's beauty. God's presence is overwhelming. Job is caught up into the divine mystery, and all arguments fade away.

† Hold in your prayers those who cannot understand what is happening to them.

For further thought
• What questions would you like to put to God?

Thursday 30 January
The folly of prophecy

Hosea 9:5-9

Because your sins are so many and your hostility so great, the prophet is considered a fool, the inspired person a maniac. (part of verse 7)

Much Hebrew prophecy has come down to us in the form of poetry. It uses dense allusive language, capable of more than one interpretation. Here in Hosea, the prophet seems to be anticipating a reverse exodus: the people will be returning to Egypt, their current dwellings left to be overtaken by briars and thorns. Suddenly, in the middle of talk of the days of reckoning, come five words in the original Hebrew: fool – the prophet – lunatic – the man – of the spirit. The NIV translation understands them to be the insults hurled at Hosea by his contemporaries. It is a reasonable possibility, but there are others. Is Hosea maybe talking about people he considers to be false prophets, who dole out false hope? Or is he reflecting on the lunacy of his own mission? The beauty of poetry is that the different possibilities can be held in tension: we can't be sure who is the fool.

The words of verse 8 are even more difficult to decipher. But there is something about the prophet being a watchman – standing on the ramparts looking out into the far distance, and then having to report back on what he has seen. Maybe the reference to snares is because he is treated like a wild animal, with traps set to catch him. Warning people of the dangers ahead is a thankless task, and finding the right words at times seems impossible.

† Hold in your prayers those who are mocked.

For further thought
• When is it difficult for you to find the right words?

Friday 31 January
Jonah and the people of Nineveh

Jonah 3:10 – 4:11

The LORD replied, 'Is it right for you to be angry?' (verse 4)

Jonah's problem is the opposite of Job's. Job feels that God is making him suffer for something he didn't do; Jonah thinks that God is being merciful to people who don't deserve it. The words of 4:2 are a kind of refrain that, with slight variations, punctuates the Old Testament (see, for example, Exodus 34:6, Nehemiah 9:17, Psalm 86:15). The prophet Joel uses them to try to persuade the Israelites to return to God (Joel 2:13). But Jonah turns them into an accusation: God is a 'soft touch', taken in by the extravagant superficial show of repentance in 3:5-8. Is he right to be angry? He has prophesied that in forty days Nineveh will be overthrown (3:4). If it doesn't happen, he will be considered a fool. The Ninevites may well go back to their evil ways. He builds himself a shelter and waits to see what will happen.

God provides a leafy plant, which withers after less than a day. Maybe it is symbolic of Jonah's achievements: yes, Nineveh has repented, but will it last? Jonah, who feels no compassion for the Ninevites, feels very sorry for himself. God again repeats the question: is it right for him to be angry? The question is given more bite when we remember that an army from Nineveh, the capital of Assyria, will destroy northern Israel only decades after this story seems to be set. We never do know how Jonah responds.

† Hold in your prayers those who feel that it would be better to die than to live.

For further thought
• For whom do you need to feel compassion?

Saturday 1 February
Micah challenges extravagant worship

Micah 6:6-8

What does the LORD require of you? To act justly and to love mercy and to walk humbly with your God. (verse 8b)

Micah has some devastating criticism for the political rulers of his time. He sees that profit is taking precedence over anything else: leaders judge for a bribe, priests teach for a price, prophets tell fortunes for money (3:11). In his most shocking language, he describes the exploitation of the poor using images of butchery: the people are being flayed, dismembered and chopped up for the pot (3:2-3). And what about worship? There is an assumption that God too has a price and will be impressed by extravagant sacrifices. Even human sacrifice is being contemplated, as a show of costly devotion. This is a fundamental misunderstanding of who God is. Micah is not attacking Temple worship as such – all ancient peoples took animal sacrifice for granted – but the idea that it can be used to manipulate God, and that God is impressed by human wealth.

The name 'Micah' means 'Who is like God?' It encapsulates an attitude of gratitude, love and awe. God is not like greedy human beings. What God requires is very simple: to treat others with justice and compassion, to live a life of humble service. This, in a sense, is a sacrifice more costly than material offerings: it demands a radical reorientation, a renunciation of status based on power and wealth. In human terms, Micah is no doubt foolish to challenge the powers that be, but then, as the next verse reminds us, they would be wise to fear God's name.

† Hold in your prayers those whose lives are based on extravagant displays of wealth.

For further thought
• How can you fight for justice in your community?

Foolishness

3 Human foolishness and the foolishness of God

This week's notes are by **Lynne Frith**

Lynne Frith is a writer, poet, and Methodist presbyter in a central and inner city parish in Auckland, Aotearoa, New Zealand. Her pleasures in life include her adult children and her young grandchildren, listening to and playing music, going to movies and theatre, walking along the many beautiful beaches in the Auckland region. Lynne's creative inspiration comes from daily encounters with all kinds of people, time away from the city streets, and a lifelong passion for justice.

Sunday 2 February
The good life

Luke 12:13-21

Then [Jesus] said to them, 'Watch out! Be on your guard against all kinds of greed; life does not consist in an abundance of possessions.' (verse 15)

Most of us know someone who lives so cautiously that they seem afraid to live. They're anxious about every possible mishap and wrap themselves in emotional bubble wrap as a protection against the unexpected but too vividly imagined calamity.

Living in the light of the Jesus story contains its challenges and opportunities.

The readings for this week both describe and invite us to consider a way of life that is contrary to the dominant culture and values of the society in which we are living. It's a way of life that might be considered foolish by our friends and family, especially in societies like my own with low church attendance. It's a way of life that is about how we live each day, rather than about amassing and storing riches or treasure for a future we may never see.

While the parable of the rich person concerned only with how to preserve and store his wealth speaks about material possessions, it might as easily apply to the person who becomes focused on academic qualifications or travel or amassing social media contacts. It reminds us that that the abundance of possessions is not the true measure of who we are.

† May I live well and fully today and each day this week, concerned only to live in the light of the Jesus story.

Monday 3 February
Fools for Christ

Luke 18:15-30

A certain ruler asked him, 'Good teacher, what must I do to inherit eternal life?' ... [Jesus] said to him, 'You still lack one thing. Sell everything you have and give to the poor, and you will have treasure in heaven. Then come, follow me.' (verses 18 and 22)

I once knew someone who had lived a good life, had lots of friends, but had never partnered or had children. When faced with a terminal illness, my friend's sadness at having no successors was expressed in the words 'I do not want to be forgotten.' This friend was perhaps asking the same question as that asked of Jesus 'what do I have to do to inherit eternal life?' And Jesus' reply was to exhort the rich man to give away all his riches to the poor. My friend didn't quite do that but, in the months of life remaining, made generous gifts towards some conservation projects and provision for bequests to provide a range of educational scholarships. While future generations might know nothing of the person of their benefactor, my friend's name will indeed live on.

There's a well-known saying often associated with memorials: 'to live in the hearts of those we love is not to die'. Living in the light of the Jesus story takes it a step further. It's our commitment to justice, our willingness to give what we have to the poor, our courage to look and act beyond the comfortable circle of those we love that will ensure that our name lives on long after we have died, in other words, that we gain eternal life.

Not everyone has money to spare, let alone to give away .Your response might be to give some time each week or even each day to a literacy programme, or deliver meals to shut-in people, or some similar community activity.

† May I have the courage to let go of the abundance in my life so that others might live.

For further thought

• Make an inventory of your 'riches': money, time, skills, experience, friends and possessions. What do you have in abundance? Make a commitment to give something away each week.

Tuesday 4 February
A fool for Christ

1 Corinthians 1:18-31

But God chose the foolish things of the world to shame the wise; God chose the weak things of the world to shame the strong. (verse 27)

Recently I heard a radio interview with a wealthy businessman who had been knighted for his services to the community. Most recently, he has set aside $80 million for the purpose of addressing child poverty and abuse in New Zealand. This will enable substantial research into these causes and support actions to put an end to them.

When the interviewer asked him a question about being a philanthropist, he replied that it was not about philanthropy but about righting a wrong. The compunction to act in this way stemmed from his Christian upbringing and the resulting ethic of responsibility to do what one is able to put right the wrongs that one sees.

This same person is providing boots for thousands of children to play rugby league who could not otherwise play a sport because of the cost of the gear.

This man goes against much popular opinion in his conviction that, regardless of who might be responsible, if you see a wrong, such as hungry or abused children, you have a duty to put it right.

To some, his actions and generosity will be seen as sheer folly and a squandering of wealth. Others dispute that there is poverty in this country, citing the much worse conditions in other countries. Some might consider that the money would be better spent supporting the arts and the artistic community. As Paul suggests, going against the grain, or against the tide of popular opinion, is the kind of foolishness that comes from living in the light of the Jesus story.

† May justice, integrity and wholeness be evident in my life and my view of the world.

For further thought

• When have you gone against popular opinion for the sake of justice?

Wednesday 5 February
Be real!

1 Corinthians 4:8-13

Already you have all you want! Already you have become rich! (verse 8a)

Like many in my generation, I was brought up to not show off or boast of my successes but to be modest in how I described myself. Along the way, I also learned to be acutely aware of my own shortcomings, which meant that I didn't always appreciate the 'riches' I had.

Does this sound familiar to you? If you were growing up in a Christian environment in the 1950s and 1960s, you may well have been imbued with an overdose of modesty that had the effect of 'hiding your light under a bushel', of preventing you from appreciating and using well your gifts, abilities and riches.

We have a reminder in today's reading that living in the light of Christ is a contrary thing. Sometimes we will feel or appear weak and foolish; other times we will have wisdom and strength. Some people will find themselves growing in strength and honour, while others will find themselves despised and marginalised for standing for what is right.

We can put too much emphasis on receiving more gifts from the Spirit, without any assessment of the gifts or riches an individual may already possess. I remember someone saying in a study group that it seemed greedy to ask for more gifts from God when already she didn't use the many gifts she had been given.

What is required, it seems to me, is to have a realistic sense of one's riches – whether material wealth, personal qualities and ability, faith, friendship or whatever. Prayerful discernment will then show how these riches may be used for building up the body of Christ.

† May I grow in appreciation of the riches I have, and be thankful.

For further thought

- What might be the consequence for you of valuing what you have, and considering yourself rich?

Thursday 6 February
It's not OK

February

2 Corinthians 11:16-29

Besides everything else, I face daily the pressure of my concern for all the churches. Who is weak, and I do not feel weak? Who is led into sin, and I do not inwardly burn? (verses 28-29)

When I was about 11, my family moved and I changed schools mid-year. At the new school, some older girls teased and tormented me for a long time. I tried to avoid them as much as I could. I now know that was a mild form of bullying.

At various other times in my life I have been subjected to some moderate harassment. Such experiences have a diminishing effect that requires a long time and a lot of self-care to lose. It has given me some understanding of what it might be like for people who have to endure much more.

What I have experienced is nothing like Paul's hardship, nor does it in any way compare with the persecution many experience in our world today. Such persecution and torment is never right, and never what God intends for humankind. Nor does God send such suffering as a kind of endurance test or as a growth experience. What we most learn from humankind's inhumanity is that it is wrong. No person deserves to be tortured, persecuted, humiliated, disempowered for their religious or political beliefs, or simply because they are different.

The questions that emerge for me from reading this passage are: what can I do to support and sustain those who are being persecuted? What needs to happen in our world for people to grow in understanding of differing world views, without tolerating or condoning violence and injustice?

I wonder what Paul would write today, with the benefit of our knowledge of psychology and social order, in a global context where peace-making is of paramount importance?

† Pray today for those who are bullied, victimised and persecuted, and for those who perpetrate such crimes.

For further thought
• Rewrite this passage, putting Paul and the recipients of the letter into the twenty-first century.

Friday 7 February
Bewitched

Galatians 3:1-5

You foolish Galatians! Who has bewitched you? ... After beginning by means of the Spirit, are you now trying to finish by means of the flesh? (verses 1a and 3b)

It's an age-old argument – who's in and who's out? What do you have to do to belong to the community?

The Christians in Galatia were experiencing tension between Jewish and Gentile Christians, with principal concerns around observance of the law. Paul is reminding them that it is foolishness to be drawn back in to that view and to forget the story of Christ that has inspired them.

In today's church, there are similar tensions and arguments. Infant baptism or adult baptism? Women priests and bishops or only male clergy? Gay and lesbian people called and ordained to ministry or not, because they are viewed as sinful? The Bible as literally true or a collection of writings containing truths? These are just some of the theological differences that divide Christian communities the world over. It's easier to respond by making laws that control and restrict than it is to engage in dialogue with a view to growth in understanding and respect.

As I read the stories of Jesus, and the New Testament writings, I am reminded that Jesus drew attention to the folly of slavish and uncritical observance of the law. He encouraged people to look within themselves for signs of divine presence, and to have a wide focus on humanity.

The safety and security of tradition and law can be very attractive in times of personal or community upheaval. Living in the light of the Jesus story, or having faith, is less certain, sometimes scary, yet has the power to transform lives.

† May I be open to fresh understandings that the Spirit brings.

For further thought

• When have you found yourself allured by law and tradition, and why?

Saturday 8 February
Living wisely

Ephesians 5:15-20

Be very careful, then, how you live – not as unwise but as wise, making the most of every opportunity... (verses 15-16a)

It's summer in this part of the world. Schools have reopened after the summer holidays, and the world has resumed its relentless activity.

All summer we have been offered advice about all manner of things to do with living carefully – when driving on the roads, out boating, tramping or hiking in the mountains, using farm vehicles, out in the sun, when swimming in lakes, rivers or the sea. There has been advice about diet, budgeting, getting help with addictions, anger, or violent behaviour. To that is now added advice about keeping our children safe – teaching them how to cross roads safely, how to walk on footpaths, to be wary of strangers.

It's advice that is intended to keep people safe and healthy, and reduce the harm our careless actions may do to others and ourselves.

Some people, in the face of so much advice, become overcautious and spend their lives protecting themselves against every possible calamity.

Some go to the other extreme, with an 'it won't happen to me' attitude – driving recklessly, hiking with inadequate protective clothing and food supplies, not wearing lifejackets when boating.

It's all about living carefully, making wise decisions, and seizing what life offers.

† May I live wisely and well.

For further thought
• What would living wisely and carefully look like for you?

Readings in Matthew 5 – 7

1 'Blessed are you ... '

This week's notes are by **Malcolm Carroll**

Malcolm works for Greenpeace. Before that, he was at Aston Business School where he completed a PhD. He was ordained a Baptist minister in 1980 and served in Sheffield and Nottingham. He spent 10 years working for the Church of England in the Diocese of Lichfield and still accepts preaching engagements when he can. He divides his time between a boat in London and a cottage in mid-Wales, where he is into permaculture and other outdoor activities. His likes include classical music, Arsenal and real ale.

Sunday 9 February
Words for the powerless

Matthew 5:1-5

Now when Jesus saw the crowds, he went up on a mountainside and sat down. His disciples came to him, and he began to teach them. He said: 'Blessed ... ' (part of verses 1 to 3)

The Sermon on the Mount is the world's most famous sermon. But who is it for? Who can hear these words? Many people have built their lives upon these words: Martin Luther King and his public ministry, which helped lead to Black civil rights in the US; Mahatma Gandhi, himself one of the greatest religious figures of modern history. Who is it for? Everyone, surely?! Jesus thought not. The sermon finishes with a story about those who hear his words and those who do not. Those who hear build a lifetime on him; those who don't are washed away.

Matthew wrote for the early Jewish Church. His audience would spot in these verses a striking parallel with Moses. Moses went up a mountain and came down with God's law for the people of God; Jesus goes up and delivers the new law for the new people of God. All too soon, Jesus would make his way up another mountain, carrying a cross.

One theme that runs through this sermon, and through the notes for this week, is that the words of Jesus are for all who acknowledge their need – the poor, the powerless. Who is it for? All who acknowledge their need of God's mercy. It is irrelevant to those who don't.

† Lord, I am in constant need of your mercy and help. Give me the gift of humility to acknowledge that need.

Monday 10 February
Living the future now

Matthew 5:6-9

Blessed are those who hunger and thirst for righteousness, for they will be filled. (verse 6)

Jewish blessings were mainly detached and formal; these are direct and personal. Often blessings were accompanied by contrasting curses; here, by further blessing. Usually the blessing was future; with Jesus it is right now. Usually it was conditional; here it is for all who will hear.

Those who can hear are those who acknowledge their need: the poor, those who mourn, the humble, those who hunger and thirst. In the poetry of the four blessings in verses 3 to 6, these terms 'rhymed' with each other – those who acknowledge their need are blessed.

And what does it mean to be blessed? Again the terms rhyme: they get comfort and satisfaction, they inherit the earth, the kingdom of heaven is theirs. Yes, paradoxically, both earth and heaven are theirs. How come? Jewish thought held both options open: God's kingly rule over a transformed earth and being taken up bodily into heaven. They are one, both depicting God's kingly rule. And the final blessedness of God's kingly rule is both future and now. Those who hear Jesus' words are already citizens of the kingdom, already blessed, living the life of the future here and now.

The second set of four blessings (verses 7 to 10) is not just receiving but also giving blessing to others. And the blessing the disciple gives to the world is none other than the blessing of God himself. Here we are sent out into a sad and dangerous world, blessing amidst the blight. It is a world that needs mercy, purity (here, a quality of being set apart for God's purposes), peacemaking, and persecution (suffering wrong to make things right).

† Lord, turn me towards your blessed future.

For further thought

• So many people's lives are shaped by their past, but ours are also shaped by our future. We are citizens of the kingdom, living out the future here and now.

Tuesday 11 February
Blessing amidst blight

Matthew 5:10-12

Blessed are those who are persecuted because of righteousness, for theirs is the kingdom of heaven. (verse 10)

The Beatitudes – The Blessings. 'Blessing' was fundamental to Jewish religious life, how God would bless his people, the land, their children and so on. These blessings from Jesus would have been familiar. And very scary. In the expanded verse on persecution in verse 11, the focus isn't so much on 'this is going to hurt' but 'this is part of what it means – and it means that you're a part – of the new people of God'. These are blessings, to be sure, but they also send us out into a hurting world to be a blessing ourselves.

A ship in a harbour is safe. But that's not what ships are for. Safety isn't what discipleship is for. Not that we should make a virtue out of just having a hard time of it. But our discipleship has a certain character about it, and the qualities we bring to the blight around us are distinctive qualities: mercy, purity, peace-making, willingness to take the hurt. These qualities are the qualities of Jesus himself. Those who know they are in need of mercy are those who inevitably show mercy to others; those to whom God has granted his peace are therefore compulsive peacemakers.

† Lord, I want to be part of your new people of God. Give me courage and strength.

For further reflection
• We are stamped with the character of Jesus. We are the blessing of God in the places we walk.

Wednesday 12 February
Out in the open

Matthew 5:13-16

You are the light of the world. (verse 14a)

We are the citizens of the kingdom. Knowing our need, we hear those words that enable us to live the life of future blessedness in the everyday of now. The structure of the Sermon on the Mount echoes the structure of the Old Testament religion: built on the law and on worship. Over coming weeks we will see how Jesus fulfils and transforms both law and worship. But we haven't finished yet with how Jesus transforms us.

There's a famous painting, *The Light of the World*, painted by William Holman Hunt in 1853–4. Unsurprisingly, it's a picture of Jesus, in this case knocking at the door, waiting to get in. In these verses, Jesus paints a picture of us: we are the light of the world, the door is closed behind us and we've been sent out. We are to be visible. A mystery, then, that so much of our church life is behind closed doors.

Salt and light are in a way contrasts. Salt does its work when it isn't seen, light is all about visibility. In both cases it's about the disciple bringing God's blessing to wherever and whatever.

The Jews of Matthew's time were familiar with God, Israel, the Temple, and Jerusalem all being lights to the world. Neither they nor we are familiar with us, the disciples, as that same light of salvation.

The Christian life is great when it's God's mercy streaming to us; but us streaming God's salvation to others? Gulp. But God makes it so.

† Lord, help me not merely to live a Christian life but to live it so that it lights the way for others.

For further thought
• How can you light the way for others today?

Thursday 13 February
In trouble with the law

Matthew 5:17-20

Do not think that I have come to abolish the Law or the Prophets; I have not come to abolish them but to fulfil them. (verse 17)

From 5:17 onwards, Jesus transforms the law; not new rules for radicals so much as new radicals for his rules. The law as known to those of Matthew's day was deeply conservative and was focused on not doing wrong. Is a good person someone who doesn't do wrong? Jesus shows, by reinterpreting the Commandments, how, time and again, that notion of 'not doing wrong' is itself wrong. Even if the bad deed wasn't done, the bad thought was very much alive.

Jesus could have lived a perfect life and never done wrong. It would have been a wasted life, at odds with God's purposes of doing those things that make for peace. Take a look at the life of Jesus. He was in trouble with the law on numerous occasions – check through the Gospels to see how many. His life was not a sterile clean sheet but a life full of actions. Righteousness isn't the absence of negatives but the abundance of positives.

Does true righteousness belong now to those who get their hands dirty, who do and dare and make mistakes? Jesus delivered some of his harshest words to those who thought that 'perfect' was avoiding wrong.

† Lord, forgive me where my nerve has failed in doing what I know is right. Lead me again in your risky way of peace and life.

For further thought
• Not doing wrong is the righteousness of the coward. Far better to fail, and ask for forgiveness.

Friday 14 February
Practising the Beatitudes

Matthew 5:21-26

Therefore, if you are offering your gift at the altar and there remember that your brother or sister has something against you, leave your gift there in front of the altar. First go and be reconciled to them, then come and offer your gift. (verses 23-24)

Some of these verses seem troubling but, here, we are putting the Beatitudes into practice; here is an example of the law filled out with the life of Jesus. It is actually quite easy to avoid murder. But to avoid those thoughts and words that arise from frustration and misunderstanding? Words can kill, destroy someone's trust in another, kill off a reputation. Some kill with knives, Christians kill with gossip. Who can live a life avoiding such wrongdoing?

But there's more. Our lives are not about avoiding wrongdoing but a far higher challenge: doing right. It comes before all other considerations, including worship. Leave whatever it is you have for God, first be reconciled with the other. Christian worship is an offence to God while we offend others.

Until Jesus, the righteous would never commit murder, but now the right thing is to be a compulsive peacemaker. It's a priority far above trifles such as going to church.

† Lord, may I use my words to build others up, to help them be at peace with themselves, with others and with God.

For further thought
• Where do you need to be reconciled to your brother or sister?

Saturday 15 February
More than mores

Matthew 5:27-32

You have heard that it was said, 'You shall not commit adultery.' But I tell you that anyone who looks at a woman lustfully has already committed adultery with her in his heart. (verses 27-28)

Here's another commandment being transformed in Jesus. Like murder, adultery can be avoided, but is avoidance the kingdom life?

Sadly, there are those who take these words and apply them immediately to sexual morality. Oh boy, do we have trouble with sex! We're likely to meet Christians with cast-iron attitudes on sexual rights and wrongs, but blind to how their lifestyle keeps poorer people in poverty or does untold environmental damage: strong on personal morality, weak on every other sort of sin.

There's nothing wrong with sex. It's a gift – relax, enjoy! There's nothing wrong with sex, only with sin. We do want to apply Jesus' words to everyday life, but there is a danger of a becoming new Pharisees, judging others by their actions. Just as yesterday's passage wasn't Jesus' advice on criminal law, so this passage isn't his comment on sex in society. It's about salvation.

Take a deep breath of Beatitudes first, then come to this passage. I argue that the kingdom life, our peacemaker life, has been leading us towards a transformation where women, so often adjuncts in such passages, are full citizens of the kingdom; where Jesus' words can be equally liberating to various sexual orientations; where sexual morality is something that springs from the heart and not a code of behaviour; where sex is likely to belong to a covenanted relationship, neither a free-for-all nor a regime of dos and don'ts.

The kingdom life impacts on human sexuality but it does so through the positives of living a life stamped with the character of Jesus, not by merely avoiding putting a foot (or anything else) in the wrong place.

† Lord, show me how my life and my relationships can be a part of the transformation you seek.

For further thought

• Jesus is reinterpreting all these old commandments. What if he were to give us a new commandment – what would that look like?

Readings in Matthew 5 – 7
2 'But I tell you...'

This week's notes are by **James Pritchard**

James Pritchard is a university chaplain at Aston University, Birmingham, and a Methodist minister. James is interested in how faith and life connect and what it means to be a disciple today. Concern for issues of peace, justice and care for the environment come as a natural response to his Christian faith. James is married with two young children, and he enjoys walking, singing, photography, geocaching and playing with Lego! He is also interested in social media's ability to connect people across boundaries and as a tool for campaigning and mission.

Sunday 16 February
A life committed to Jesus

Matthew 5:33-37

But I tell you ... do not swear by your head, for you cannot make even one hair white or black. All you need to say is simply 'Yes,' or 'No'; anything beyond this comes from the evil one. (part of verses 34, 36-37)

This week's readings continue the teachings of Jesus from the Sermon on the Mount. These tough messages are about what discipleship means. Some days I wish I could take an easier path in life but, if we take scripture seriously, we discover that the path of Christ is not always easy. It is a tough path to follow.

Today's passage comes from a context where legal contracts would be focused on promises. What people promised was of great importance – unlike the promises that are often made in our world today, the promises of political manifestos or price matches!

Jesus urges us to be mindful of what we say with our mouths and for our promises to be ones we will keep, not just mere words. It's important that we live lives that are committed – committed to Christ and to following his ways; lives that respond to God with 'Yes'.

† Help me to listen to what you say – to listen and speak with conviction and commitment.

Monday 17 February
Living the way of humility

Matthew 5:38-42

You have heard that it was said, 'Eye for eye, and tooth for tooth.' But I tell you, do not resist an evil person. ... Give to the one who asks you, and do not turn away from the one who wants to borrow from you.
(verses 38-39a, 42)

Mahatma Gandhi, no doubt familiar with this passage, is reputed to have said 'an eye for an eye only makes the whole world blind'. How true that is! Jesus' way of peace is one where payback is not through violence or punishment but through humble submission: if someone insults you, *turn the other cheek*! To offer the other cheek may seem a weak thing to do – but there is great power in such a humble yet humiliating response. Violence can quickly escalate. Violence is the *easy* answer, but Jesus tells (and ultimately in his death shows) another way. Submitting to humiliation or seeming to accept violence can quickly defuse violence.

A warning, though: it's an easy leap from this position to becoming like doormats that others walk over. But that is not what I believe Jesus is encouraging us to be. Jesus encourages us to live differently, to give freely, with generous hearts.

† Christ, you suffered and took punishment, showing the power of love. Help me to follow in your way and return hate with love; rejection with acceptance and violence with peace.

For further thought

- When have you had to turn the other cheek? When have you acted out of violence of heart rather than with humility and love?

Tuesday 18 February
Living the way of love

Matthew 5:43-48

You have heard that it was said, 'Love your neighbour and hate your enemy.' But I tell you, love your enemies and pray for those who persecute you, that you may be children of your Father in heaven. (verses 43-45a)

When Jesus sums up the law, he says to love God and to love one another (Matthew 22:37-38). Today's passage gives substance to what it means to love one another – a simple thing to say but much harder to do. Jesus challenges us to live out that love, and the passage ends with an even harder command: 'Be perfect, therefore, as your heavenly Father is perfect' (verse 48). That is fairly clear – no ifs, buts or maybes. 'Be perfect.'

But none of us is perfect, so thank goodness for God's grace. The phrase reminds me of the sense of growth and change that we seek in our lives – the desire to live more as God's people, the desire to be better disciples. It goes back to the wholeheartedness that Jesus demands of those who really want to follow. Jesus doesn't say 'follow me when it suits', or 'listen to my words when they make sense': he says, live my life; live my way; live in God who is perfect and become more God's person.

† Help me this day and every day to change enemies to friends through your way of love. Hold me when it's hard and remind me I am loved, that your love might flow from me.

For further thought

• Think of someone you find it hard to love. How can you love them more?

Wednesday 19 February
Living generously

Matthew 6:1-4

When you give to the needy, do not announce it with trumpets, as the hypocrites do in the synagogues and on the streets, to be honoured by others. Truly I tell you, they have received their reward in full. But when you give to the needy, do not let your left hand know what your right hand is doing. (verses 2-3)

'Chuggers' – the paid workers who try to grab passers-by to sign them up to giving regularly to charity – have become an unpopular sight in the high street. Western society is such that people are often in things for themselves. To get people to think about others can be a particular challenge and many charities struggle as a result.

But giving to the needy is important and, hopefully, as people of faith we have hearts that are open to the needs of others. Jesus encourages us to live generously but he also warns against a 'look how great I am' mentality that can sometimes go hand in hand with giving. There are some celebrities who have favourite projects or causes they support or who even set up foundations in their name. Often the intention is clearly good, but it's also a helpful publicity stunt!

Jesus says give (as you are able); give with generosity of heart, but not for your own sake but for those to whom you are giving. Don't give because it makes you look good, but give quietly, because it is the right thing to do.

† Reflect on how you use your resources. Ask for God's guidance on decisions of how to respond to those in need.

For further thought

• How does your giving of yourself or your resources change you?

Thursday 20 February
Simply pray

Matthew 6:5-8

And when you pray, do not be like the hypocrites, for they love to pray standing in the synagogues and on the street corners to be seen by others. Truly I tell you, they have received their reward in full. But when you pray, go into your room, close the door and pray … (verses 5-6a)

In Jesus' commands, prayer and giving are linked. Today's passage begins 'and when', almost as though Jesus is just catching his breath before continuing where he left off. Biblical chapter and verse numbering sometimes breaks the meaning of passages; their purpose is as a reference to help us locate points in Scripture, not to define its meaning. Here, as with giving, Jesus is saying 'pray, but …' – pray without a great big show; don't waste words or make yourself look good. If you need to pray, find a quiet spot where you can talk to God, and speak plainly and simply.

Prayer and giving are not just linked by the ways Jesus encourages us to do them: giving should come from our praying, and vice versa. If we are praying for the needs of the world, then that prayer should speak into our heart to encourage us to respond. Likewise, if we are moved to give, why not also pray remembering the cause or the situation?

† Help me, God, to pray from my heart; to converse with you.

For further thought

• What do you really want to say to God today? Say it in just one sentence, with no extra words. (And don't forget to listen.)

Friday 21 February
Transformed by forgiveness

Matthew 6:9-13

Give us today our daily bread
And forgive us our debts,
as we also have forgiven our debtors.
And lead us not into temptation,
but deliver us from the evil one. (verses 11-13)

Good news: as people living in God's grace we can know ourselves forgiven! We can turn to God again and again to receive God's mercy and grace – that's great, isn't it? Some people think, though, that it means we can go on making the same mistakes, or living with our same failings; living without really changing. True forgiveness is a life-changing experience; it's not just an inner experience but something that should change how we live. To paraphrase the familiar words from the Lord's Prayer, Jesus says: 'as forgiven people, may we be people who forgive others'.

To know forgiveness is to experience something so powerful it should transform us. It should change us to become more forgiving, to become more like God. If each time we seek forgiveness we don't also learn a little more of what it means to forgive others, then maybe we have missed the point. After all, if we take Jesus' words seriously, can we really be receiving God's forgiveness fully if we are not also offering it to others?

† God of grace, help me know your forgiveness as a transforming power in my life so that I might learn more what it means to forgive.

For further thought

• What is it you find hard to forgive in others, or what might others find hard to forgive in you? What steps towards being more forgiving could you take today?

Saturday 22 February
God sees everything!

Matthew 6:14-18

But when you fast, put oil on your head and wash your face, so that it will not be obvious to others that you are fasting, but only to your Father, who is unseen; and your Father, who sees what is done in secret, will reward you. (verses 17-18)

Sportswomen and men need amazing discipline for hours of physical training. But to reach competition fitness a truly far-reaching regime is required! A top athlete's regime might include hours in the gym, track or pool; a strict sleep pattern; and a food diary with rules on what can and can't be eaten. This disciplined preparation happens without many people knowing about it.

This week Jesus has been talking about spiritual discipline: a commitment to God that should not be for the sake of others. Prayer or fasting are not to show how good you are: their purpose should be for God and you. Jesus reminds us that God understands our motives, and that is where true reward comes from. Our reward is not from putting on a show: rather, it lies in God's hands. It's easy to be drawn into thinking we have to act like others, or to seek to emulate others' practice in prayer or devotion, but Jesus reminds us to focus on God, for that is where true treasure is.

† Help me to care about what you think and not what others might do or say. May I recognise the reward that comes from a life in you.

For further thought

• When or how do you seek reward from others rather than from God?

Readings in Matthew 5 – 7
3 'Seek first his kingdom'

This week's notes are by **Eleanor Nesbitt**

Eleanor Nesbitt is a Quaker based in Coventry, UK. Brought up in the Church of England, she graduated in Classics and Theology, then taught and travelled in India. She has a Hindu family by marriage and her major research focus has been Sikhism. As a poet, Eleanor is especially interested in the imagery of the Bible's language. Her publications include *Interfaith Pilgrims: Living Truths and Truthful Living* (London, 2003).

Sunday 23 February
Single-minded commitment to God

Matthew 6:19-24

But store up for yourselves treasure in heaven, where moths and vermin do not destroy, and where thieves do not break in and steal. For where your treasure is, there your heart will be also ... No one can serve two masters ... You cannot serve both God and Money. **(part of verses 20-21, 24)**

This week's theme is Jesus' guidance for right living, expressed in cross-cultural images of treasure, lamps, birds and wild flowers, and of trees, carpentry, gifts, gates, roads, animals and fruit trees.

What does 'store up... treasures in heaven' mean? Jesus suggests that the best way to do so is by alleviating suffering (Matthew 26:31-46). Similarly, the Indian teacher Guru Nanak asked a rich man to carry a needle to heaven when he died. When he exclaimed, 'That's impossible!' Guru Nanak showed him all his wealth was valueless.

In this translation, verses 22-23 appear to be about good and bad eyesight. But the Greek word translated as 'good' means 'single' or 'simple' (literally 'without folds') and the word for 'bad' means 'evil'. The phrase 'casting the evil eye' still means envious ill-wishing. Did Jesus mean this too? Perhaps the 'good' eye here refers to integrity and goodwill.

Verse 24 unifies today's reading: we all have choices to make, between 'God' and 'money', for example. Each of these verses concerns our priorities. Jesus urges us to be single-minded in our commitment to God.

† Prayerfully call to mind one of your current dilemmas, especially if it involves choosing between different values. Hold your dilemma in the light and wait for discernment and for peace of mind.

Monday 24 February
Do not worry

Matthew 6:25-30

Therefore I tell you, do not worry about your life, what you will eat or drink; or about your body, what you will wear … And why do you worry about clothes? See how the flowers of the field grow. They do not labour or spin. (part of verses 25, 28)

Popular magazines, books and websites show us that our human priorities haven't changed much in the past two thousand years. We still worry about how long we'll live, about our physical appearance, what to wear, and what to eat. (Verse 27 may refer to either increasing one's lifespan or one's stature.) As consumers, we devote much of our lives to these matters, so providing livelihoods for farmers, chefs and food feature writers, for doctors, plastic surgeons and beauticians, as well as supporting the cosmetics and fashion industries.

Look at the *form* of Jesus' teaching, not just the content. Notice the rural images, the striking comparisons such as the one between wild flowers and King Solomon's finery, and his questions and commands. Imagine listening to him, with one picture flashing into your mind after another.

Each generation finds wisdom in the flight of birds: for the ancient Romans the direction of flight was the basis of predictions. Indian sages found an image for non-attachment to worldly things in birds' freedom to lift off in flight. In emphasising that his hearers must not 'worry', was Jesus, too, encouraging an attitude of non-attachment? Was he forbidding responsible forethought or simply discouraging his followers from needless anxiety and fretting?

† As you ponder Jesus' words, pray for an eye and an ear to find in nature images of divine truth and pointers to God's purpose.

For further thought
• Spend a few minutes reflecting on what spiritual truths we can discover from observing nature. Even in a city we're likely to encounter plants, birds and animals in parks and gardens.

Tuesday 25 February
Seek first

Matthew 6:31-34

So do not worry, saying, 'What shall we eat?' or 'What shall we drink?' or 'What shall we wear?'... But seek first his kingdom and his righteousness, and all these things will be given to you as well. Therefore do not worry about tomorrow ... Each day has enough trouble of its own. (part of verses 31, 33-34)

Today's reading continues yesterday's theme. Jesus reassures us that God knows our needs and so we should stop worrying about food, drink and clothes. Instead, Jesus tells us: 'seek first his kingdom and his righteousness'.

Are Jesus' words a call to social activism, to making heaven on earth, to helping to build a more godly and just future? Can his words also remind us that, if we observe and reflect, we will find the kingdom around us here and now? I read recently that social activism is like breathing out. Unless we breathe in first, our efforts will be weak and limited. Tuning in to the divine order that underlies our chaotic-seeming world is like breathing in deeply.

The poet Francis Thompson (1859–1907) wrote 'turn but a stone and start a wing' ('The kingdom of God', *Poems of Francis Thompson*, ed. Brigid Boardman, London and New York 2001). In other words, heaven is around us everywhere. All of us (not only poets) are already in the kingdom, if only we will pause and see.

Society needs both activists and contemplatives, just as our individual well-being depends on both these approaches to seeking God's kingdom. Even during illness, attentiveness to signs of God's grace may still be possible.

Verse 34 reminds us that we should focus on today, not on the uncertainties of tomorrow. When life is hard, the verse 'Each day has enough trouble of its own' rings very true.

† Let's be thankful for our many blessings, and pray 'your kingdom come, your will be done'.

For further thought

• In quiet contemplative openness, as we go about our daily duties, may we sense God at work.

Wednesday 26 February
Do not judge

Matthew 7:1-6

Do not judge, or you too will be judged. For in the same way as you judge others, you will be judged ... Why do you look at the speck of sawdust in your brother's eye and pay no attention to the plank in your own eye? (part of verses 1-2, 3)

Discernment is the word that sums up today's reading. But at first sight the sequence of thoughts seems disconnected, jumping from carpentry to pearls, dogs and pigs.

Verses 1-2 continue the idea of balance in our transactions that we found in the Lord's Prayer (Matthew 6:12). We will be judged (or forgiven) proportionately to how we judge (or forgive) others. But we need discernment in hearing his meaning, as Jesus had already dismissed the similarly reciprocal principle of 'an eye for an eye' (5:38).

Discernment also involves noting our own assumptions and hypocrisy. Jesus makes this point by referring to the plank and the sawdust (Matthew 7:3-5). The carpentry image in today's reading resonates particularly with me. In my home town of Christchurch, England, according to local tradition Jesus the carpenter of Nazareth miraculously lengthened a roof beam in the ancient church nearly a thousand years ago! It may, however, be helpful to substitute the contemporary metaphor of lenses. Each of us sees the world slightly differently, through different lenses. If we want to help others, it is useful to discern what affects – and even distorts – our view.

Like 'treasure', 'pearls' may be an oblique reference to 'the kingdom'. In any case, it is folly, not generosity, to offer something precious to those who cannot appreciate it. Dogs and pigs are still regarded as unclean by many communities, and Jesus' language here is particularly emotive.

† Lord, we pray for discernment. May we discern the message in your words; may we discern our own prejudices; may we discern signs of your kingdom and ways of sharing these with others.

For further thought

• If you feel yourself getting angry or irritated at someone today, reflect on what assumptions or issues you might be bringing to the situation.

Thursday 27 February
Do to others ...

Matthew 7:7-12

For everyone who asks receives; the one who seeks finds ... Which of you, if your son asks for bread, will give him a stone? ... So in everything, do to others what you would have them do to you, for this sums up the Law and the Prophets. (part of verses 8-9, 12)

Jesus urged his hearers not to hesitate, but to ask for what they wanted. Confidence and persistence often contribute to success in life generally, as well as in our prayers.

As you look at verse 9, other biblical references to bread, stones, fish and serpents may spring to mind. It is helpful to remember that flat stones in the Judaean desert and round Palestinian bread can look deceptively similar. (This visual similarity helps in understanding the Devil's temptation in Matthew 4:3, as well.)

The so-called 'golden rule' (verse 12) runs through world literature. Famously, Rabbi Hillel, a near contemporary of Jesus, summarised Jewish law as 'What you do not like yourself, you shall not do to your neighbour'. But while the principle is widely acknowledged, we need discernment in applying it. The adage 'One man's meat is another man's poison' usefully reminds us not to assume that our neighbour will appreciate what we appreciate. (Remember Jesus' caution about pearls and pigs.) Charities often discover that the donor community's priorities are different from those of the communities they are trying to help. We need to listen attentively to others' expressions of need, rather than rushing in with unwelcome solutions to other people's problems.

† May I be prompt in helping others. May I be open to asking God for assistance.

For further thought

• Reflect on the idea that, in the words of St Francis of Assisi, it is in pardoning that we are pardoned, it is in giving that we receive; and it is in losing that we find.

Friday 28 February
The narrow gate

Matthew 7:13-14

Enter through the narrow gate. For wide is the gate and broad is the road that leads to destruction, and many enter through it. But small is the gate and narrow the road that leads to life, and only a few find it. (verses 13-14)

Imagine that you are standing where two roads meet: one is broad and inviting and the other is narrow, less attractive, and full of potholes. Or imagine that you can easily see the wide, smooth road, but you cannot even find the way into the narrower path, which you have been told is the only way to your destination.

Into my mind's eye come two pictures: one of Christian, the pilgrim in John Bunyan's book *Pilgrim's Progress*, eventually finding his way through the 'wicket gate', despite being led astray by other people. The other is from the American poet Robert Frost's description of two paths diverging in a wood. He chose 'the one less travelled by' and 'that has made all the difference' (*Three Centuries of American Poetry*, eds A Mandelbaum and R D Richardson, New York 1999).

In Matthew 19:24, Jesus tells us that for a rich person to get through the 'narrow gate' is impossibly difficult, like a camel getting through the eye of a needle. If you have travelled by air, or if you've been a backpacker, or a refugee, you will be familiar with having to reduce your baggage to what you can carry, what you really need.

The two paths may be ways of living rather than courses of action – living kindly and forgivingly rather than being harsh, proud or selfish.

† Lord, we rely on you for direction, and trust your guidance along our way. We know that choices have consequences and pray that we will choose our path wisely.

For further thought

- Consider today how you can help others in their difficult decision-making and lovingly help them face challenges and obstacles.

Saturday 1 March
Tasting and testing

Matthew 7:15-20

Watch out for false prophets. They come to you in sheep's clothing, but inwardly they are ferocious wolves ... A good tree cannot bear bad fruit ... Every tree that does not bear good fruit is cut down and thrown into the fire. Thus, by their fruit you will recognise them. (verse 15, parts of verses 18-20)

Fables the world over feature one animal disguised as another. Thus, India's Panchatantra stories and the Greek fables told by Aesop, around 600 years before Jesus, tell of a donkey that briefly terrorised others after donning a panther's skin. In today's reading, Jesus alludes to the opposite scenario (also in Aesop): a wolf pretending to be a gentle sheep. The warning to 'watch out for false prophets' rings true today with stories of spiritual celebrities exploiting the gullible, or being discredited.

In between writing these notes, I picked blackberries and pruned back brambles. The metaphor of tree and fruit is as vivid and meaningful now as two thousand years ago. Marjorie Sykes, a Quaker living in India last century, wrote of the beautiful fruit that we can notice in other people's gardens. She meant that we must acknowledge the evidence of the Spirit's activity in others' lives, whether or not they belong to our country, our church, or our faith community. St Paul describes this fruit as 'love, joy, peace, forbearance, kindness, goodness, faithfulness, gentleness and self-control' (Galatians 5:22-23).

Remember that we know if fruit is good only by tasting it, by testing it. In our spiritual life we can become truly discerning only by taking the risk of living experimentally. Then we can understand with inner assurance the spiritual truths that Jesus shared with his first followers.

† Lord, help me to be vigilant, yet open-minded; receptive yet discerning.

For further thought

- Find a moment to be silent. Breathe in the Spirit's gifts of love, joy and peace, so that you may share the fruits of your Spirit with others.

Readings in Matthew 5 – 7
4 He taught as one who had authority

This week's notes are by **Gary Mason**

Gary is a Methodist minister at the East Belfast Mission, Northern Ireland, one of the largest missions in Europe. He helped set up the Skainos Project, a new worship and community centre on a former brownfield site aiming to aid the renewal of one of the most deprived areas of the country. In 2007, Gary was made a member of the Order of the British Empire for his work in Ireland's peace process and he holds a Doctorate of Philosophy in psychology from the University of Ulster. Gary enjoys going to the gym, playing squash, and travelling when he gets the chance.

Sunday 2 March
Obedient to whom?

Matthew 7:21-23

But only the one who does the will of my Father who is in heaven. (part of verse 21)

That slippery word 'obedience'!

It would be so easy for me to enter into a diatribe about Christians and their lack of obedience – to make a statement about this forgotten virtue among self-centred, narcissistic Christians in the West.

OK, I admit I was tempted to do that. Then I realised that in fact many of us are very good at obedience: the question is to whom and to what. I have ministered for over 25 years in a community in which people have shown blind obedience to political and nationalistic idolatry; where people have been more in love with the Union Jack and Irish Tricolour than with Jesus Christ; where people's Irish or British identity is more important than their 'citizenship in heaven', as St Paul describes it in Philippians 3:20.

To step outside of one's tribe takes courage, and it is risky. To really believe that God wants total obedience to his will is for most a big ask, yet I don't think Jesus was asking for any less in this passage. We can blur it all we want, but Jesus' words are clear, 'Only the one who does the will of my Father'.

† Lord, we want to be obedient to you but we are blind to our own tribal allegiances. Open our eyes to your way of peace and unity. Open our ears to your life-giving command.

Monday 3 March
Rising waters

Matthew 7:24-27

The rain came down, the streams rose, and the winds blew and beat against that house; yet it did not fall, because it had its foundation on the rock. (verse 25)

It is a temptation many in affluent societies engage in from time to time – browsing the internet and looking for that dream home. I confess up front that I have done it, maybe too often! Why? Because houses are important. We live in houses, bring up our families in houses and even express our architectural preferences in our houses. All of us in this parable are house builders; whether wise or foolish. Just as there is no escaping the building game, there is also no escaping the storm. Every house we build will face a storm. Jesus is not sharing a parable about how to build houses where there are no storms – this is a parable about foundations, not about finding a storm-free climate. Jesus is not telling us, 'if you just find the best area to live in, all will be well'.

Inner-city Belfast, scarred by 30 years of sectarian violence, knows a thing or two about storms. We have just opened a new £21-million faith-based inner city village called 'Skainos'. The Greek word *skaino*, used in John 1:14, literally means 'pitch a tent'. This word *skainos* (tent) is the word used in the New Testament to refer to the tabernacle of God used by Israel in its early worship of God. It symbolised God's presence. In the Greek New Testament, the word translated 'tabernacle' is *skainos*, 'the tent' (Acts 7:44, Hebrews 8:2, 5).

We built a building called Skainos, but the foundation was the Word among us. May that Word guide us in the storms, too.

† Shield us amidst the storms, God. Found us on your faith.

For further thought

• Where has the fragile tent of God been pitched in your community – perhaps in a community centre, or café, or church? Share it on our Facebook group: www.facebook.com/freshfromtheword

Tuesday 4 March
One with authority

Matthew 7:28-29

When Jesus finished saying these things, the crowds were amazed at his teaching, because he taught as one who had authority, and not as their teachers of the law. (verses 28-29)

This is the end of the Sermon on the Mount – the final parable. The true relevance and sustainability of this parable and the whole sermon depend upon the authority of the teacher. Jesus the master psychologist shows his instinctive insight into the human condition. We simply love to build and we continually build our houses by rivers with low banks. Jesus expects us to build – it is in our DNA – but when you do, follow that instinct: build on the rock!

Dr Ravi Zacharias, the Christian apologist, in a sermon entitled 'If the Foundations Be Destroyed', tells the story of being in a new building in Ohio State University that was designed in postmodernist style. The building was a confusing mix of random staircases and pillars that had no purpose. It was meant to reflect life – a kind of venture into meaninglessness architecturally. Zacharias asked if the foundations were as random and confusing as the rest of the building. The reply came: 'You can't do that with a foundation.' If you start tampering with the foundations of any building, postmodern or not, you will see serious structural problems in the rest of it.

Builders: build securely on the only thing that can shelter us from the storms of our world. Build upon the authority of the rock – the 'Teacher'.

† Lord, we worship you in a temple not made with human hands. Help us realise our unity in you beyond architectural differences.

For further thought

• A wise person once said, 'We shape a church building, and then it shapes us'. What does your worship space say about your worshipping community? How about your town or city centre?

God's hands and ours

1 Hands in the Old Testament (1)

This week's notes are by **Simon Goddard**

Simon Goddard is a Baptist minister in the village of Bottisham, near Cambridge, UK. He leads RE:NEW, which is an ecumenical expression of church, pioneering new ways of gathering and growing together. He is a mission consultant and co-author of *Big Hearted: The Gospel of Simple Words and a Large Heart*. He enjoys following the rise, and fall, of his beloved Reading FC, relaxes by watching *West Wing* DVDs, and occasionally acts in productions staged by his local amateur dramatics group.

Wednesday 5 March (Ash Wednesday)
Hand in hand with God

Genesis 27:5-23

Jacob went close to his father Isaac, who touched him and said, 'The voice is the voice of Jacob, but the hands are the hands of Esau.' He did not recognise him, for his hands were hairy like those of his brother Esau; so he proceeded to bless him. (verses 22-23)

On the ceiling of the Sistine Chapel are nine scenes from the book of Genesis, all painted by Michelangelo. The most famous of these is called 'The Creation of Adam' and depicts the hand of God reaching out and touching the hand of humanity, giving us life. Over the next week and a half we'll be looking at ten hand-related stories from the Old Testament and discovering how they might be able to help us in our own walk with God.

They say you can't choose your family, but God did! He hand-picked a man named Abraham, gave him a child in his old age and said that through this family he would bless the world. Within one generation, however, this special family was already surprisingly dysfunctional. Abraham's son, Isaac, got married to Rebekah, and she gave birth to twins, Esau and Jacob, who were fighting even before they left the womb (Genesis 25:22-26)! The feud continued and, as Isaac lay on his deathbed, Jacob's hands, that should have shown love and care for his dying father, were instead covered with goatskin and used to deceive and steal. Nevertheless, Jacob later has his own powerful encounters with God and is chosen to receive a legitimate blessing with which to fulfil his own divine calling.

† Lord God, this Ash Wednesday I remember that, however dysfunctional my past may have been, you still have a plan and a purpose for my life. Thank you. Amen

Thursday 6 March
The strong hand of God

Exodus 15:1-11

Pharaoh's chariots and his army he has hurled into the sea ... The deep waters have covered them; they sank to the depths like a stone. Your right hand, Lord, was majestic in power. Your right hand, Lord, shattered the enemy.' (part of verses 4-6)

I wonder if you were ever involved in, or witnessed, a playground argument between two children. One child has something that is bigger or better than the other, but quickly their opponent responds with their own boast, and so it goes on. A common conclusion to this squabble are the words 'my Dad is stronger than yours' – declaring the winner of a fight that they know will never take place.

Well, our heavenly Father *is* a great big God, a God who is strong and mighty, a God who steps in to save his children. We often talk of God's love (and think of those humble hands nailed to a cross) but sometimes that love is expressed through God's strong hands being used to rescue those who are suffering oppression or injustice. Today's passage is a defining moment in the history of God's people. Israel has been enslaved in Egypt for 430 years and God has given Pharaoh a number of chances to let his people go. Eventually, however, as Moses leads the people of Israel through the Red Sea to freedom, Pharaoh is defeated and his armies are destroyed.

Although God is slow to anger and abounding in love (Exodus 34:6) God will, in time and in his own way, act in power against those who exploit and abuse others. It's always better to walk in obedience to God, for God's strong hand is always victorious. Nothing and no one can stand against God, and in Christ even the power of sin and death are conquered on our behalf.

† Lord God, thank you that you don't abandon your children. I pray for all those in trouble today who need your strong hand to rescue them and lead them to freedom. Amen

For further thought
• Is there something practical you could do to make a small difference to the lives of those for whom you have just prayed?

Friday 7 March
Hands that bring a blessing

Leviticus 9:22-24

*Aaron lifted his hands towards the people and blessed them ... Moses
and Aaron then went into the tent of meeting. When they came out, they
blessed the people; and the glory of the LORD appeared to all the people.*
(part of verses 22-23)

When I was training as a Baptist pastor, the principal of my college
frequently said that the favourite aspect of ministry, for him, was
the opportunity to bless people. He inspired me to take time and
thought over the words I use at the end of church services and,
although it's not a very Baptist thing to do, I also often raise my
hands and make the sign of the cross as I conclude the blessing in
the name of the Father, the Son and the Holy Spirit.

Aaron was appointed as the priest (or worship leader) of Israel, and
God used both Moses and Aaron to guide and nurture the people
in their relationship with God. In this passage we see that Aaron's
priestly words and actions are not used as empty ritual, for the
glory of God visibly appears before the congregation. Indeed, as
Aaron lifts his own hands towards the people, it is as if the people
are receiving a blessing from the very hand of God himself.

In the New Testament we are told that all believers are 'a chosen
people, a royal priesthood, a holy nation, God's special possession'
(1 Peter 2:9). Each one of us can be used by God to bless others –
it's not only those who have been ordained who have this privilege.
Your words are powerful, particularly when they are spoken in
God's name, and they can have a very real impact on the lives of
those you meet day by day.

† Lord God, please use both the words of my mouth and the works of my hands to
bring blessings to others this day. Amen

For further thought

• Why not say 'God bless you' instead of 'goodbye' and, as you
do so, silently pray for something that person needs, such as
peace or joy.

Saturday 8 March
Handing on the baton

Numbers 27:15-23

So the L<small>ORD</small> said to Moses, 'Take Joshua son of Nun, a man in whom is the spirit of leadership, and lay your hand on him. Make him stand before Eleazar the priest and the entire assembly and commission him in their presence.' (verses 18-19)

For eleven days this summer, Glasgow will be hosting the Commonwealth Games, and athletes from 70 countries will be competing with one another. One of my favourite events, normally scheduled at the very end of the games, is the relay. Not only does every individual have to do his or her best for the team, each also has to ensure that the baton is passed on successfully.

That's sort of what we see going on in today's passage: Moses finishes his own race well by passing the baton of leadership to Joshua. This is a deliberately public event so that all the people can see authority being transferred from one person to the other by the laying on of hands, and the involvement of Eleazar the priest indicates the spiritual significance in this act of commissioning. Indeed, although Joshua had been equipped for the task of leadership through 40 years as an assistant to Moses, he had actually been chosen by God.

There are some important reminders here. First, when congregations select men and women to take a lead in the ministry and mission of the church, this should never be done solely on the basis of popularity or academic or professional qualifications. Rather, their task is to recognise those whom God has already chosen and prepared for the task. Second, those who feel called to lead shouldn't be focused on pushing themselves forward. Instead, they need to allow the Holy Spirit to work, refining their character and helping them grow. When they're handed the baton, they'll be ready to run the race well.

† Lord God, I pray for the leaders in my own church community. May they always depend on you and the power of your Spirit at work in their lives. Amen

For further thought
• We all lead others to some extent, for example, in our homes and among our friends. Why not pray again, this time for yourself.

God's hands and ours
2 Hands in the Old Testament (2)

This week's notes are by **Simon Goddard** (see page 66).

Sunday 9 March
The heavy hand of God

1 Samuel 5:6-12

So they called together all the rulers of the Philistines and said, 'Send the ark of the god of Israel away; let it go back to its own place, or it will kill us and our people.' For death had filled the city with panic; God's hand was very heavy on it. (verse 11)

Whenever I did something wrong as a child I usually confessed it straight away! Some children try to run and hide, but whether it was the sense of guilt, or the fear of punishment, it weighed so heavy upon me that I needed to unburden myself of those feelings as soon as I could. In today's passage it appears that the Philistines soon regretted capturing the ark of the covenant.

The ark, which contained the tablets of stone upon which the Ten Commandments were written, was more than just a symbol of the God of Israel. Indeed, it was upon the ark that the very glory of God dwelt when it was rightfully located among God's people. To those who walk *with* God, God's presence provides strength, comfort, direction and hope. To those who stand *against* God and his will, however, God's awesome presence can sometimes weigh so heavily that it is almost too much to bear.

As the ark is taken from one Philistine city to another, to each comes an outbreak of fear, panic, sickness and death. Soon the heavy hand of God causes them to cry out to heaven (verse 12) and eventually they return the ark to Israel (chapter 6). When we experience the conviction of the Holy Spirit, we too would be well advised to examine our lives and put ourselves right with God. We do this through Jesus, who upon the cross felt the heavy hand of God on our behalf.

† Lord God, thank you that in Jesus I can find forgiveness and can be cleansed of the guilt I carry. Guide me towards your will for my life. Amen

Monday 10 March
The big hands of God

1 Chronicles 29:10-19

In your hands are strength and power to exalt and give strength to all.
Now, our God, we give you thanks, and praise your glorious name …
Everything comes from you, and we have given you only what comes from
your hand. (part of verses 12-14)

There's a story of a teacher who asks her class 'If you've got five oranges in one hand, and six oranges in the other hand, what have you got?' One of the children, being smarter than the rest, calls out and says 'I know, Miss – big hands!' In this passage, David is rejoicing at the generosity of the people towards the building of the Temple. As he does so, he realises anew that God is the one who holds the entire universe in his hands. What the people have offered to God belonged to him anyway!

David is clear, however, that this realisation does not make the gift worthless or of no consequence. Rather, what it does is reveal the truth of what has been offered to God – the hearts of the people. While others may be impressed with the value of the gifts we bring, the Bible tells us that our motivations are what interest God (verse 17). He knows whether our donation is made reluctantly out of a sense of obligation, or whether it is willingly and joyfully given.

Our God is loving and generous – God has a big heart as well as big hands! When we begin to imitate God's loving generosity, we begin to realise, like David, that the storehouses of heaven are infinitely able to meet the needs of those who live according to God's will. Although it is not always exactly what we want when we want it, nonetheless, as individuals, families and churches seeking to fulfil God's purposes, we can be confident in God's provision.

† Lord God, thank you for your love and generosity towards me. May I in turn be generous in my giving to the work of your kingdom, and towards meeting the needs of others. Amen

For further thought
• Count your blessings one by one – you'll be surprised what God has done! List the good things in your life, and praise God for them.

Tuesday 11 March
Hands used in the service of God

Nehemiah 2:11-18

Then I said to them … 'Come, let us rebuild the wall of Jerusalem, and we will no longer be in disgrace.' I also told them about the gracious hand of my God on me and what the king had said to me … So they began this good work. (part of verses 17-18)

I love reading books on how to be a better leader and, if you look in your local bookshop, you'll find a wealth of them available. One of the best lessons on leadership, however, is found in the story of Nehemiah – a man who inspired the people of God to restore completely the broken walls of Jerusalem. Such was his passion and insight that despite opposition they managed to finish the task in less than two months!

When it comes to leadership within the church there is one thing that is more essential than any other. It is not personality or persuasion, but rather the presence of God powerfully visible in the one who seeks to lead. As Nehemiah spoke of what God had been saying and doing, it was clear to everyone that he was the one who had been divinely chosen to take on this important work.

The people of God were confident to follow his lead and pick up their trowels, but it was Nehemiah's employer, King Artaxerxes, who initially saw the hand of God upon him. First, God moved in Nehemiah's heart, causing him to grieve over the state of Jerusalem; then God gave the vision to do something about it; and finally God provided for Nehemiah through the king, who supplied him with all that he needed to complete the task (2:4-8).

Godly leadership is more than having a great idea and good people skills. Like a glove, shaped and moved by the hand of God, the one who leads, first and foremost, needs to be a servant.

† Lord God, thank you for the leaders who have inspired me in my Christian journey. Please reveal the good works you have prepared for me so I, like them, may also be your servant. Amen

For further thought

• As you pray for those who have guided you in the faith, why not contact them and let them know they are loved and appreciated?

Wednesday 12 March
Holding on to the hands of hope

Job 19:13-27

Have pity on me, my friends, have pity, for the hand of God has struck me … I know that my redeemer lives, and that in the end he will stand on the earth. And after my skin has been destroyed, yet in my flesh I will see God. (part of verses 21, 25-26)

Have you ever gone through a testing time – bereavement, serious illness, a loss of job or home? Such experiences of pain and sorrow are common to all humanity, but that doesn't stop us having all sorts of questions about them. Thankfully, the Bible isn't silent about suffering, and the story of Job provides us with some insights that can be useful in our own difficult situations.

We find out at the beginning of the book that Satan was permitted by God to test this righteous man. Almost everything he had – family, health and possessions – was taken from him, and even his wife told him to 'curse God and die!' (Job 2:9). To add insult to injury, Job's friends urged him to repent, incorrectly assuming that he must have done something wrong to cause all this loss and anguish.

Job's response, as seen in today's passage, is both honest and hopeful. It feels to him as if it is God who is the source of his suffering but, nonetheless, his faith stands firm. Job believes that God is ultimately in control; that even though he is in the midst of terrible circumstances, he is still, and will always be, in the hands of a good God. He doesn't understand why the trouble has come, and he can't see how everything will work out, but he knows God is with him and for Job that is enough. When those difficult times do come our way (and they will), let us, like Job, stay close to God, and in God's hands find hope.

† Lord God, I pray for all those who are struggling to hold on to you in the midst of their pain, sorrow and suffering. May they find strength and hope in your Word. Amen

For further thought

- 'In all things God works for the good of those who love him' (Romans 8:28). Have you ever seen something 'good' come out of suffering?

Thursday 13 March
Guiding hands

Psalm 16

I keep my eyes always on the LORD. With him at my right hand, I shall not be shaken … You make known to me the path of life; you will fill me with joy in your presence, with eternal pleasures at your right hand. (part of verses 8, 11)

As a young man I dreamt of being a rally driver: of racing around country lanes at breakneck speeds, before crossing the finishing line first and being adorned with the winner's garland. I neglected to consider, however, the need for that vital member of the rally team, the co-driver or navigator, without whom the driver finds himself driving through a hedge and ending up in a ditch!

Today's passage talks about the Lord being at our side, about him making known to us the paths of life. Like the navigator of our life, God can direct us through all the twists and turns, helping us to avoid unnecessary obstacles and diversions. As the one who knows the layout of the road ahead of us better than we can ever imagine, God is ideally placed to be our guide.

The psalm also talks about 'the LORD, who counsels me; even at night my heart instructs me' (verse 7). Here is the key to successful rally driving: the one at the wheel needs to listen to the one with the map! God is there for us, showing us which track to take but unfortunately many of us frequently decide to ignore those words of direction. We think we know better and we end up taking wrong turnings and finding ourselves down dead ends. Sometimes God speaks in a small still voice but, for those who do choose to listen, God guides them to places where they find life in all its fullness; in the here and now, and for all eternity.

† Lord God, thank you for being there to guide me through the journey of life. Help me to spend time considering your Word and listening for the promptings of your Spirit. Amen

For further thought
• Is there a crossroads ahead of you at the moment? Or a decision to make? Set some time aside to hear what God is saying.

Friday 14 March
Engraved hands

Isaiah 49:13-18

Shout for joy ... for the LORD comforts his people ... 'Can a mother forget the baby at her breast and have no compassion on the child she has borne? Though she may forget, I will not forget you! See, I have engraved you on the palms of my hands.' (part of verses 13, 15-16a)

A friend of mine has the names of his children tattooed up his arm, but it's not because he's likely to forget that he's a father, or that he needs to remind himself what each of them is called. These tattoos are a sign of his love for his children, and they symbolise the permanence of that affection.

In today's passage, God is speaking through the prophet Isaiah with words intended to comfort his people. They had been taken into exile in Babylon, and now they felt forgotten and abandoned by God – a feeling that, from time to time, many of us have experienced. God uses the strongest of human bonds, that between a mother and her child, and says that his love for them, and for us, is stronger even than this.

The idea of our names being engraved on the palms of God's hands is symbolic of the truth that he is our 'Everlasting Father' (Isaiah 9:6). Even though we may sometimes walk away from God, God never turns his back on us. Like the father in the parable of the prodigal son (Luke 15:11-32) God never forgets his children and is always longing for us to return.

Sadly, human parents do sometimes neglect, abuse or abandon their children but no one is unloved or insignificant to God. He has a plan for each of our lives, and his hands are always active in the world, working out his purposes in and through us. Remember today that God knows you, and loves you as the unique individual you were created to be.

† Father and Mother God, thank you that my name is engraved on the palms of your hands. Help me to live my life in the knowledge that I am a precious child of God. Amen

For further thought

- Is there someone you can encourage today by telling them about the extent of God's love for them? This love really does transform lives!

Saturday 15 March
Transforming hands

Jeremiah 18:1-12

But the pot he was shaping from the clay was marred in his hands; so the potter formed it into another pot, shaping it as seemed best to him. Then the word of the LORD came to me. 'Like clay in the hand of the potter, so are you in my hand.' (part of verses 4-6)

When I was a student I used to do a bit of ballroom dancing. For a couple to dance well together, I was told that two things are required: one person needs to know what they're doing, and the other needs to allow them to do it. If both partners decide they want to lead, that's when the problems start!

In today's reading of Jeremiah's vision of the potter and the clay we see a similar dynamic in action. In order for the final creation to be beautiful and useful, the clay needs to be malleable in the hands of the one making the pot. We are all like misshapen lumps of clay, warped and hardened by sin, and desperately in need of someone to reshape us and make us whole again. The trouble is that the process of being moulded is sometimes a painful one, particularly when we resist God, or have our own ideas about how he should be sculpting us.

The words of the prophet affirm that God's plans for his people are good (verse 10), but he warns them about the stubbornness of their hearts, and the disaster that will overcome them if they persist in saying 'we will continue with our own plans' (verse 12). Sometimes the crises we encounter are of our own making because we have chosen to resist the will of God. How much better it is to trust in the potter, placing ourselves in his hands, and allowing him to use our experiences to wonderfully shape and transform us?

† Lord God, thank you that you want the best for your children. Help me to allow myself, and my life, to be shaped by your hands, and transformed into something that gives you glory. Amen

For further thought

• Are there any aspects of your life in which you have been resisting the work of God? Confess them, and allow God to reshape you.

God's hands and ours
3 Jesus in his ministry

This week's notes are by **Julian Bond**

Julian Bond is Director of the Christian Muslim Forum for England (www.christianmuslimforum.org). He has a degree in Theology from the University of Aberystwyth and previously worked for HM Revenue & Customs. He has a passion for 'translating' the themes of scripture into a range of contexts. He meets regularly with imams, rabbis and other Christians to study scripture together. He is currently writing a book on the humanity of Jesus.

Sunday 16 March
Rule-breaker, or Lord of the Sabbath?

Luke 6:1-5

Jesus answered them, 'Have you never read what David did when he and his companions were hungry? He entered the house of God … he ate what is lawful only for priests to eat. And he also gave some to his companions.' … 'The Son of Man is Lord of the Sabbath.' **(part of verses 3-5)**

Jesus is challenged: 'Why aren't your disciples following the letter of the Law?' His followers walk innocently through fields on the Sabbath, plucking grain to eat. The religious 'police' come and lay down the law, telling Jesus his disciples' actions are forbidden. They confront Jesus and complain: change is a problem. Jesus accepts the challenge and trumps them; they have no comeback. He is a master of the old – reinterpreting what they already knew, re-imagining, recreating and renewing. The old is only old if you treat it as fossilised. If you are open, it is still new. Jesus encourages us to see things in a new way. For those who have power this is dangerous, especially if you are seen as a lawbreaker.

This passage is a challenge for us. Most of us no longer think about the Sabbath, though we may frown at those who shop after Sunday morning worship – until we run out of milk! But we may live by other iron-clad rules: Christians don't smoke, drink, or read particular newspapers, and we stay away from people of other religions. Are we open? Do we take Jesus seriously enough to be led into new places, new challenges, new risks?

† Lord, this Lent help us challenge our 'traditions' and rules. Keep us open and enable us to follow our Lord into new and risky situations. Amen

Monday 17 March
No need to wash!

Mark 7:1-8

So the Pharisees and teachers of the law asked Jesus, 'Why don't your disciples live according to the tradition of the elders instead of eating their food with defiled hands?' (verse 5)

Much the same issue presents itself in this passage as in yesterday's reading: again the religious leaders are watching the disciples and complain to Jesus. The passage says that they 'questioned' him, but their minds were already made up. The Gospel writer goes to some length to explain where they were coming from, suggesting that he was against their behaviour, rather than just seeking to inform the reader. Jesus' response to his accusers is to the point: 'you hypocrites' (verse 6).

When we read the Gospel today these practices are alien to us, unless we have Jewish friends or are familiar with the cleansing rituals of our Muslim neighbours. The temptation is for us to take sides and make the same accusations against 'Pharisees', perhaps looking down on Jewish believers (in fact, modern Jews trace their roots back to the Pharisaic tradition). Jesus would not want us to do this – he did not have a problem with religion or tradition, but with human intention. My Jewish and Muslim friends have never told me off for not washing before a meal. They are too polite. Jesus' opponents, according to the story, wanted only to accuse and undermine. So it is about more than hands – not about what we touch or whether they are clean but how we use them to relate to others. It doesn't matter where our hands are. Where are our hearts? Do we 'point the finger'? Jesus cautions us (quoting Isaiah 29:13) not to be like this: 'their hearts are far from me'.

† Lord, help us not to look down on others' traditions but look into our own hearts. Save us from judging others, seeing ourselves as superior. Help us lift our hands to you in humility.

For further thought

• Think about particular traditions in Christianity or other faiths. What do they mean? Are they valued by those following them, do they point towards God?

Tuesday 18 March
A steady hand

Luke 9:57-62

Another said, 'I will follow you, Lᴏʀᴅ; but first let me go back and say
goodbye to my family.' Jesus replied, 'No one who puts a hand to
the plough and looks back is fit for service in the kingdom of God.'
(verses 61-62)

Few people plough fields these days. We are a long way from hand-held ploughs, yet Jesus' meaning is all too clear: don't hesitate, don't delay, don't avoid your calling. The excuses are familiar. The first follower has not considered what he is signing up for, and the other two aren't ready.

We have a choice, but Jesus does not allow any conditions. Following Jesus is heading into the unknown, taking risks, being single-minded. Some people's descriptions of this can be off-putting: 'If you follow Jesus you must do this, not that.' Some want to add other conditions to Jesus' simple message 'follow me'. Jesus is warning us about distraction, asking us to keep focused, to keep hold of the plough and set our direction. Only then do we produce a straight furrow.

Life, of course, is not about straight furrows, but we go in the direction we are facing. Jesus asks us, 'Where are you heading?' Our hands still determine our course. Holding a small device we cross roads without looking, unaware that someone else's straight furrow has been diverted by our meandering, or we become the latest traffic casualty. With hands on steering wheel we let technology set our direction, realising too late that our digital furrow has led to a dead end.

Other religions talk about 'mindfulness', which may sound unusual to our Christian ears. But the concept is central to following Jesus: focus, direction, 'mission'. Are we distracted by what our hands are holding, like parents texting continuously while walking with children, or is the direction we have chosen expressed in our hands?

† Lord, thank you for extending your own hands to us. Help us to extend our hands to others and put them at your disposal. Amen

For further thought

• What can you put your hand to today? Do you see your hands in the service of God and neighbour?

Wednesday 19 March
Laying hands on the children

Mark 10:13-16

People were bringing little children to Jesus for him to place his hands on them, but the disciples rebuked them. When Jesus saw this, he was indignant. He said to them, 'Let the little children come to me, and do not hinder them, for the kingdom of God belongs to such as these.'
(verses 13-14)

Usually children make us think of innocence, but 2000 years ago things were more precarious. Children were shorthand for the marginalised and the vulnerable. They were often sidelined.

Children have particular religious significance. They are markers of how well we are living our religion. Thus, it is worth noting that in places of worship we have had to introduce safeguarding practices to prevent inappropriate contact between adults and children when their parents are not present.

We should be following Jesus and ensuring that we include children, young people and any who are marginalised, extending a hand to them. We all know the particular groups that are marginalised in various ways in our communities, and hopefully we realise how unwise and destructive this is, for everybody. Welcoming the 'little ones' may help us with this. In our society we can ask ourselves whether the 'little ones' may be people of different faiths and look up some of the news stories about churches giving Muslims a place to pray.

What is the disciples' first impulse? To drive them away! But Jesus is not too important for anyone. We need to recognise that the kingdom of God is not just for those who are like us. Jesus challenges us, saying 'anyone who will not receive the kingdom of God like a little child will never enter it' (verse 15). Jesus is not calling for innocence, but humility; there is no status in the kingdom of God. Too often we look up to status, forgetting that we are warned against status. The Hebrew scriptures show the prophets struggling with overbearing, unwise and 'childish' authority figures.

† Lord, take away my pride and attachment to status. Help me to be like a child – humble, open. Help me also to be adult in making room for others. Amen

For further thought

• Where are children in your church? Are they part of the worship? When do they leave and join the adults? Do they receive a blessing?

Thursday 20 March
Healing a withered hand

Luke 6:6-11

[They] were looking for a reason to accuse Jesus ... Jesus knew what they were thinking ... Then Jesus said to them, 'I ask you, which is lawful on the Sabbath: to do good or to do evil, to save life or to destroy it?' (part of verses 7, 8a and 9)

This is a story about a damaged hand. If it was us, I hope, we would be concerned about this man, especially if healing was a possibility. He is, however, of no interest to the 'religious police'. They are interested only in what Jesus would do, whether he would 'break the law'. Jesus draws attention to the man, and his hand, asking him to face the congregation. Jesus' would-be accusers say nothing, but he knows what they are thinking. What they kept to themselves Jesus makes obvious: here is someone who has needs; we should be concerned for him.

It's unlikely we will be in a position to do what Jesus did! However, do we take note of those in need or ignore them? Do we stretch out our hands? Have a look in your church for those who are disabled. One of my friends does have a 'withered hand'; he has lost most of the use of it since having a stroke. I notice that not too many people in the church take much notice of him, though whether that is because of his physical disability I do not know.

Can we see other people's disabilities, or differences, as an invitation to respond? A little while ago I met a woman who had previously converted to Islam, but she was not welcomed warmly in the Muslim community. Now you might think, 'Well that wouldn't happen with Christians,' but it did. She decided to convert back to Christianity and attended church still wearing a hijab. No one spoke to her because they thought she was a Muslim.

† Father, help us to notice those you notice, and not to stumble over the 'little ones'. We praise you for the diversity of human beings with all their challenges, opportunities and rewards. Amen

For further thought

• What opportunities has God given you to notice others?
  Are you more concerned about what you do than what you don't do?

Friday 21 March
Jesus' tenderness

Luke 8:40-56

They laughed at him, knowing that she was dead. But he took her by the hand and said, 'My child, get up!' Her spirit returned, and at once she stood up. Then Jesus told them to give her something to eat.
(verses 53-55)

As Jesus goes to heal Jairus' daughter we meet a woman suffering for a long time. No one can help her and she has heard about Jesus. She follows him and touches his cloak and her words to herself set the scene for her healing. End of story? It seems that no one was interested in this woman. Jesus could have moved on, but he is aware that someone's life has been transformed and seeks her out. Knowing this, she comes to him trembling in fear, as if she would be accused of being unclean and touching a man. He makes time for her and speaks kindly to her, celebrating her wholeness and relief.

Spending time with this woman means that Jesus is too late for Jairus' daughter, who has now died. On arriving, Jesus meets those who are mourning the girl's death. Unlike her father, or the woman he has just encountered, they mock him, so he sends them away. Without ceremony, he holds her hand and in his mother tongue gently asks her to get up. His caring attitude – one that singles out the neglected and those for whom it seems to be too late – is wasted on the masses.

We notice tenderness because it is rare; perhaps it seems like an optional extra. But it is vital. Those who care for us – friends, family, ministers, chaplains – have the opportunity, even the calling, to be tender; at least we hope they do. But we need to do it ourselves: be tender and kind to the stranger, the person of another religion or ethnicity.

† Lord, help us to be tender, too. May Jesus' love be ours and may our hands be used for gentle touch, rather than conflict. Amen

For further thought

• How important is tenderness to you, for yourself and for others? Do you see Jesus as a role model of tenderness?

Saturday 22 March
Hostile hands

Mark 9:30-32

They left that place and passed through Galilee. Jesus did not want anyone to know where they were, because he was teaching his disciples. He said to them, 'The Son of Man is going to be delivered into the hands of men. They will kill him, and after three days he will rise.' (verses 30-31)

These are the first hostile hands that we have read about this week. Previously this week Jesus has advised wise use of our hands and used his own hands kindly and well; now we are in a place of contrast. Jesus offered much with his hands, but the hands of men (it is rarely women!) offer only death. We read elsewhere in the Gospels that Jesus avoided being grabbed by the crowds; earlier in his ministry some had sought to kill him. But we need to be wary of pointing at others. Too often in the past, the hands of 'Christians' have been raised against others to kill them, as in attacks on Jews, and the death penalty for those who broke 'biblical' laws.

Where are our hands when Jesus commissions us and completes his message? Are we seeking to be his hands? Have we renounced violence and war? Do we see peace as the answer? Have we extended the hand of friendship to 'strangers and foreigners'? As I write this there are protests in an English city against the turning of a disused and abandoned building into a mosque. The hands of a community are turned against those who seek to pray and worship God. Some invoke Jesus' name, saying that Christianity needs to be preserved in this country by opposing such developments. Jesus expects better: the 'hands of men' (and women) should be doing God's work. Let's all take a hand in living a life of love for God and neighbour.

† Lord, give us peace, make us peace, let us share peace. Forgive our anger and give us your love. Let us love difference and welcome strangers, and give us hands for others, not against them.

For further thought

• Is peace and bridge-building a key part of your faith? Have you been involved in peace initiatives? How can we follow 'the Prince of Peace'? Share an experience at www.facebook.com/freshfromtheword.

God's hands and ours
4 God so loved the world

This week's notes are by **Nicola Slee**

Nicola Slee is a theologian and poet based at the Queen's Foundation, Birmingham, where she teaches contextual and feminist theology, and supervises research students. A respected author, she was formerly editor of *Words for Today*. She is currently working on two collaborative writing projects – one on poetry and faith, and the other on research into the faith lives of women and girls.

Sunday 23 March
All things given into his hands

John 13:1-11

Jesus knew that the Father had put all things under his power, and that he had come from God and was returning to God; so he got up from the meal … and wrapped a towel round his waist … He poured water into a basin and began to wash his disciples' feet, drying them with the towel. (verses 3-5)

The foot-washings enacted in most English churches on Maundy Thursday are rather staid affairs. They are a world away from the dust and dirt of a hot, Middle Eastern climate in which feet would have been filthy at day's end. Servants washed the feet of those entering a house to maintain basic health and hygiene, and it would hardly have been a pleasant job. Jesus adopts this role, and invites his followers to do likewise.

Jesus is shown throughout John's Gospel as one who is utterly clear about his own identity. He knows who he is and whose he is – God's. Secure in that knowledge, he sits lightly to his own status and authority. He chooses to divest himself of them in order to serve those who might have been expected to serve him. He demonstrates the freedom of one who is rooted and grounded in God; knowing that he stands tall before God, he can choose to kneel and serve. No one coerces this gift: it is a free offering from a self generously poured out.

This week, by paying careful attention to the interaction between Jesus' hands and the hands of others, we may enter more deeply into the costly love of God that is freely poured out to us, this Lent.

† Hands that washed filthy feet, tend my weary, work-worn places. As you renew my aching limbs, may I stand tall and know who I am again.

March

84

Monday 24 March
No one to be snatched from his hand

John 10:22-30

My sheep listen to my voice; I know them, and they follow me. I give them eternal life, and they shall never perish; no one will snatch them out of my hand. My Father, who has given them to me, is greater than all; no one can snatch them out of my Father's hand. (verses 27-29)

In yesterday's reading, we considered the deep security of Jesus that enabled him to pour his selfhood out freely, knowing that he could never lose his identity (what theologians speak of as 'kenosis'). In today's passage, Jesus talks about how this same deep security is a reality for his disciples.

The analogy that Jesus draws between the relationship of a shepherd and the sheep and his own relationship to his disciples is a familiar one. There are plenty of parables in the scriptures that portray sheep that wander and get lost, as well as feckless shepherds who do not protect the flock. In John 10, Jesus issues warnings about thieves and robbers who come to steal and kill the sheep. He contrasts himself with the hired hand who runs off when danger approaches, leaving the sheep to the wolf's attack.

One of the earliest depictions of Jesus in Christian art is as the Good Shepherd. In the catacombs, he is shown as a fit, good-looking youth, carrying a lamb across his shoulders. One hand grasps the sheep firmly so that it will not wriggle free. The shepherd–sheep metaphor has been criticised for portraying disciples as passive and helpless, even stupid. Any image has its limitations and this one is no exception. What we can take positively from John's parable is the intimate knowledge the shepherd has of the flock, and the security of the sheep in that knowledge. The metaphor may break down at this point: we need other images to express the creative freedom of the disciple responding to the depth of the saviour's care.

† Hands that grasp the wanderer, protect all who are in danger, that none may be snatched out of the divine embrace.

For further thought
• How do you respond to the image of Jesus as the Good Shepherd? Which other metaphors need to supplement it?

85

Tuesday 25 March
They took Jesus

Mark 14.53-59

They took Jesus to the high priest, and all the chief priests, elders and teachers of the law came together …[They] were looking for evidence against Jesus so that they could put him to death… **(part of verses 53, 55)**

In Mark's passion narrative, Jesus is 'handed over' to those who seek his downfall and death. Mark highlights in a stark way the contrast between the earlier, active time of Jesus' ministry of healing, teaching and miracles and the time when all this had to be laid down and Jesus is given into the hands of wicked men. The one who had been intensely, urgently active – a powerful, wonder-working saviour – becomes passive, done to, acted upon. The hands that had healed and released others are bound. The mouth that had uttered God's wisdom and truth is mute. The body that had stridden around Galilee is condemned to be flogged and crucified.

Although it may not be so stark, we also know the contrast in our own lives between phases of activity, engagement and living at full stretch, and times when we are compelled – by ill health, ageing or external pressures – to stop, and wait, and be in passive/receptive mode. There are times when our hands are busily occupied, full of life poured into and through them, and times when our hands must lie still and empty.

Should we say that God is more present in one of these states than the other? Surely not. The life and passion of Jesus demonstrate how God may be present both in activity and passivity, in doing and being done to. The wisdom is in knowing how to respond to both realities and to integrate them into a whole.

† Hands that were bound, minister to all who are compelled to lay down their lives. Teach us to grasp the moment for acting and to know the time for being acted upon.

For further thought

• As you go about your day, notice people who are able to act meaningfully and those who are largely acted upon. What do you learn?

Wednesday 26 March
Seated at the right hand of power

Mark 14:60-65

'You will see the Son of Man sitting at the right hand of the Mighty One and coming on the clouds of heaven.' ... Then some began to spit at him; they blindfolded him, struck him with their fists, and said, 'Prophesy!' And the guards took him and beat him. (part of verses 62, 65)

The inventiveness of human intelligence and imagination can be both awesome and chilling. Human hands that shape objects of beauty and practical usefulness may also be used to design weapons of mass destruction, techniques of torture or, simply, utilitarian objects of great ugliness – think of sprawling outer estates where cheap functionality seems to have been the main criterion of design.

In today's passage, we witness the hands of Jesus' accusers being employed in a variety of ways to inflict pain, humiliation and abuse. Some strike him, others blindfold him, others beat him, while others again spit at him. It is not difficult to think of instances in our own time when human creativity is misemployed to inflict similar indignity, torture and cruelty: from human trafficking and child abuse to warfare in Syria and Gaza.

In the face of accusations and torture, Jesus demonstrates extraordinary dignity and spiritual freedom. While he remains silent at first, at the high priest's insistent questioning he retorts with ringing authority and confidence, declaring himself to be God's Christ and announcing the coming victory and judgement of God.

Jesus is not alone in demonstrating such dignity, presence and authority in the face of torture and injustice. His sisters and brothers in every age have stood tall in the confidence of the love and victory of God. In their company, as well as in the faith of Jesus, we too may hope to withstand injustice and untruth with steadfast confidence.

† Hands that chose only to do good, restrain the ingenuity of human creativity from working evil against others and the earth. Teach us to use our hands for beauty and justice.

For further thought

• Try to be aware, throughout the day, of how you are using your hands, your skills and creativity, whether for good or for evil.

Thursday 27 March
Into your hands

Luke 23:44-49

Jesus called out with a loud voice, 'Father, into your hands I commit my spirit.' When he had said this, he breathed his last ... When all the people who had gathered to witness this sight saw what took place, they beat their breasts and went away. (part of verses 46 and 48)

Now we turn to Luke's account of the death of Jesus. Unlike Mark, whose passion narrative climaxes in Jesus' terrible cry of dereliction from the cross ('My God, my God, why have you forsaken me?' Mark 15:34), Luke gives us a Jesus who is serene and confident in his Father to the very end. Having promised the penitent thief that he will be with him in paradise, he then cries out triumphantly, as darkness covers the land, offering himself back into the hands of the one from whom he had come.

Where else has Jesus to go in death except back into his Father/Mother's hands? He places himself, in confidence and trust, into the hands of the one who moulded the life of the world and of human beings from the clay; into the hands of the one who brings forth life from the womb, who nurtures and holds and plays with the infant; who then lets that child go free to find his or her own way in the world; who welcomes the returning child back into wide-open arms.

The hands of the Mother/Father God remain open to welcome and receive all God's beloved children. At various times, God's hands create life, cherish and nourish and heal life; at other times they let go and let free. But in a fundamental sense, they never cease to hold all that is, and all that shall be. Into just these hands, Jesus entrusted his life and soul; and so may we.

† Hands that create and hold all life, even in death: hold all who die today and all who will care for them and mourn their passing. Teach us to entrust all that we are into your hands.

For further thought
• As you go about your day, pay attention to human hands that hold, comfort, support and release. Let them be an image of God's hands.

Friday 28 March
The mark of the nails in his hands

John 20:24-29

Jesus came and stood among them and said, 'Peace be with you!' Then he said to Thomas, 'Put your finger here; see my hands. Reach out your hand and put it into my side. Stop doubting and believe.' (verses 26b-27)

John's Gospel is full of maternal imagery (though, until recently, this has hardly been noticed), and this passage forms part of that imagery. The side of Jesus into which Thomas must enter is, in fact, the womb – the same womb that Jesus speaks about in the third chapter of John, when he tells Nicodemus that he must be 'born again' (John 3:7). Jesus is the mother who has given birth to every believer, through the birth canal that is his body (John 16:21). Jesus' death is a birthing – of the church, which John shows starting under the cross (John 19:26-7) when Jesus' mother and the beloved disciple are given into each other's care. So the nail-marked hands of Jesus that Thomas is instructed to touch are the compassionate hands of the midwife who assists at the birth and delivers the life of the newborn. It is his wounded hands, now transfigured and glorified, that bring forth life.

I have a vivid memory of my grandfather at his death, lying in a hospital bed with his two great lumps of hands, misshapen from years of farm labour, at rest on the white linen. Though they might have appeared ugly to anyone else, to me they were full of beauty. I realised only then how, throughout his life, he had been holding and loving not only me, but my entire extended family. Touching his hands as he lay there unconscious, was for me a moment of revelation. During the past year, my own hands have started to become misshapen at the joints due to arthritis. I am trying to learn to regard them in the same light as I saw my grandfather's hands.

† Wounded hands that assist at the birth of every believer, bring forth the new life that is waiting to be born in me. Teach me how to enter again into the womb of your side, that I may be reborn.

For further thought

• In what part of your life might Jesus' transfigured hands be bringing something new to birth?

Saturday 29 March
Lifting up his hands

Luke 24:50-53

When he had led them out to the vicinity of Bethany, he lifted up his hands and blessed them. While he was blessing them, he left them and was taken up into heaven. (verses 50-51)

Today's text forms the closing verses of Luke's Gospel, in which Jesus takes his leave of the disciples, blessing them with upraised hands before being taken up into heaven. His final gesture is one of triumph, blessing and exaltation. This posture of standing with outstretched arms to pray and bless – what is technically called the 'orans posture' – is, in fact, the classic posture of Jewish and early Christian prayer. Although we tend nowadays to associate it with the posture of a priest presiding at the altar or blessing a congregation, the catacombs are full of frescoes showing many characters adopting this posture, and it is the way Jesus himself and the early disciples would have prayed in the synagogue. It is, then, a posture for all Christians.

It is not, however, a posture for lazy Christians! Standing requires us to be alert, expectant, ready to move. Lifting our hands up requires the chest to be open and the head erect; it takes stamina (remember how Moses got weary of lifting his arms up over Israel, and had to have help from Aaron and Hur in Exodus 17:11-12). Try praying in this posture and see how adopting this bodily prayer changes the nature of your prayer.

Jesus lifted up his hands to bless the disciples. Our hands, too, are called to the work of blessing. As we take up the tools of our daily work, we are to bless them and the work we do. As we touch others, in gestures of greeting and meeting, or comfort and consoling, we are to bless them. As we lift up our hands to pray and to praise, we are to bless God – who delights in the offering of our hands and our lives.

† Hands that were raised to bless, bless the work of our hands and the offering of our lives. Teach us to bless God and each other in all that we do.

For further thought
• How can your work or activity today be a blessing to others?

God's hands and ours

5 Hands in the life of young churches

This week's notes are by Liz Clutterbuck

Liz Clutterbuck is a Church of England ordinand in her final year at St Mellitus College. As part of her training, she is on the leadership team of a church in central London where she leads student ministry. Prior to ordination training, she was a researcher for the Methodist Church in Britain, researching the 'missing generation' (those aged 25–40) within the church. She is passionate about blogging, Twitter, mission, baking, travel and handbags – and loves it when she manages to combine as many of her passions as possible!

Sunday 30 March
Handing on the Spirit

Acts 8:9-24

Then Peter and John placed their hands on them, and they received the Holy Spirit. (verse 17)

It sounds so simple. The disciples placed their hands upon those who believed in the gospel, and the Holy Spirit was received. But the Spirit cannot be received without faith and an understanding of the purpose of the kingdom of God. This is why Simon the Sorcerer was rebuked for believing that money could buy the gift of passing on the Holy Spirit – it cannot be bought, it is a gift from God. This is why the laying-on of hands is so significant in scripture and the history of the church.

Hands are amazing – a complex design that enables human beings to do anything from playing a Mozart piano concerto, tying shoelaces or holding a newborn baby. It's easy to take them for granted; but injure one, and you soon realise just how important they are. Our hands are to be used by God – to bless, commission, heal, ordain, work, help and communicate. We may all have hands that function in the same way physically, but we use them in different ways according to the unique gifts he has given us.

† Bless the hands that you have given us, so that they may do the work you have set out for us to further your kingdom.

Monday 31 March
Many hands make light work

Acts 6:1-6

They presented these men to the apostles, who prayed and laid their hands on them. (verse 6)

One of the pressures of leadership – whatever it is you're leading – is having competing demands upon your time. When every task appears to be as important as the next, how do you begin to prioritise?

It's especially true of church leaders. How on earth do you choose between preaching the gospel, visiting the sick and discipling your community? It's a no-win situation as, whichever way you decide, someone is likely to criticise you for your decision.

This isn't a recent phenomenon. The earliest church leaders faced exactly the same pressures (minus working out how to lead a church while also maintaining its website and Twitter stream) and were criticised when their followers thought they'd got it wrong. They realised that they needed to look at their community's gifts and empower people to take up roles that would free up the leadership for other work. The disciples wanted to be evangelists, not waiters, and therefore commissioned – through the laying on of hands – seven individuals to take responsibility for the daily distribution of food amongst the widows. Our role as leaders is to look for opportunities to relieve the pressure of leadership by looking to delegate to and empower others within our communities.

It's a bit of a cliché, but it's true – many hands do make light work of a big job. Especially when you choose the right people for the right jobs.

† Lord, forgive us when we get our priorities wrong. We ask that you would bring people alongside us who can share the burden of leadership.

For further thought

• What are the conflicting pressures in your life at the moment? Whom could you empower by delegating work to them? Take the time to affirm the gifts of someone in your community.

Tuesday 1 April
Reaching out to enemies

Acts 9:10-19

Placing his hands on Saul, he said, 'Brother Saul, the Lord – Jesus, who appeared to you on the road as you were coming here – has sent me so that you may see again and be filled with the Holy Spirit.' (part of verse 17)

I have an unfortunate desire to be proved right whenever I get into an argument. Thanks to Google, Wikipedia and my iPhone, I can access evidence that supports me virtually anywhere, so that I can prove my point when such situations arise. However, every so often I have to swallow my pride and admit that I'm mistaken.

Ananias had a moment of trying to correct Jesus. He simply could not believe that the Lord was asking him to go to Saul – the very same Saul (as he points out to Jesus) who has been persecuting Christians in Jerusalem. But the Lord knows exactly what he is asking Ananias to do and insists that he goes. Ananias has to swallow his pride – and probably his fear as well – and not just meet with Saul, but lay his hands on him so that he might receive the Holy Spirit.

Sometimes we need to swallow our pride, but sometimes there is no 'right' or 'wrong' and we need to be able to enter into a discussion with grace and openness. We might not have to touch our enemy as Ananias did, but as 21st-century Christians, this could mean engaging in debate with atheists, or reading Richard Dawkins even when we're convinced he's wrong. We need to be open to the Lord's call to the unexpected.

† Lord, remove the scales from our eyes this Lenten season and enable us to swallow our human pride so that we can respond to your call in our lives – especially when it challenges us.

For further thought

• Whom do you find challenging in your life? Is there someone to whom you need to show the Lord's compassion and grace?

Commissioned by hand

1 Timothy 4:7-16

Do not neglect your gift, which was given you through prophecy when the body of elders laid their hands on you. (verse 14)

This year, God willing, a bishop will lay his hands on my head and ordain me a deacon of the Church of England. It won't be the first (or the last) time a major moment of my spiritual life has been marked in this way: when I was 13, I became a member of the church through the laying-on of hands and, next summer, all being well, I will be made a priest in the same way. It may seem like yet another church quirk, but I find it incredibly powerful that I will be commissioned in ministry in exactly the same way as the first apostles of the church.

Paul was writing to Timothy, an apostle whom he had commissioned by laying his hands upon his head. In his letter, he is trying to encourage Timothy in his ministry and one of the ways in which Paul does this is by reminding him of how it began, of the way in which he was filled with the Holy Spirit and prophesied over.

Sometimes, when I have moments of doubt and question my calling, I think back to the first indications of what God was calling me into and of the words that have been spoken over me. I pray that, as I continue into ministry, the moment when hands were laid upon me at ordination will continue to inspire and motivate me day by day.

† Empowering God, we ask that today you would commission us afresh by your hands and the power of the Holy Spirit. We thank you that you have given each of us unique gifts and a unique calling.

For further thought

• What words or prophecies have been spoken over you? Spend some time meditating and reflecting upon them. Who could you inspire today?

Thursday 3 April
Not just handy – indispensable

1 Corinthians 12:12-27

The eye cannot say to the hand, 'I don't need you!' And the head cannot say to the feet, 'I don't need you!' … Now you are the body of Christ, and each one of you is a part of it. (verses 21, 27)

Human beings can't seem to help wanting to be someone other than themselves – many of us spend huge amounts of money 'improving' our appearance, learning new skills, getting fitter and generally trying to please people. No matter how many singing lessons I have, I'm never going to turn into Adele and there's probably little point in trying. Do I have gifts that Adele doesn't have? Almost certainly – in fact I'm pretty sure she's not going to become a vicar any day soon! Does the world need another Adele? Probably not – she's unique. We all are.

Every single human is a unique piece of God's creation, with different God-given gifts, talents and eccentricities, and together we make up a pretty awesome body. Every single one of us is useful in our own way – our different skills enable us to further the work of the kingdom in countless ways. Just as the parts of a body are indispensable to the whole body's work, so are the individuals that make up the church. God has put us together, like the body, 'so that there should be no division … but that its parts should have equal concern for each other. If one part suffers, every part suffers with it; if one part is honoured, every part rejoices with it' (verses 25-26).

† Thank you that we are all one, and valued in Christ. Help us to acknowledge the awesome creation of God that we are and teach us not to wish that we could be someone else.

For further thought
• Take the time to affirm someone today in their uniqueness and their contribution to the body of Christ.

Friday 4 April
Singing with the choir

Ephesians 4:25-28

Anyone who has been stealing must steal no longer, but must work, doing something useful with their own hands, that they may have something to share with those in need. (verse 28)

Have you ever been part of a team where some individuals didn't quite pull their weight? Who didn't do their fair share of the work? When you're meant to be functioning as one unit, having people who are not doing their fair share of the work can let everybody down. Imagine singing in a choir where a few people couldn't be bothered to go to all the rehearsals – when it gets to the concert, they might not know all the music properly and their mistakes would prevent the whole choir's performance from being as good as it could be. When performing as one body, every part of that body has a responsibility to the rest to do their fair share of the work.

Yesterday's passage from 1 Corinthians showed how we all have a unique role within the body of Christ. In Ephesians 4, the importance of sharing and contributing to that body is emphasised alongside maintaining its healthiness. We have all experienced situations where anger, crime and lies have worked against a community and destroyed relationships. Here, the Ephesians are urged not to let this happen to them. Instead, their responsibility was to use their hands to make a contribution to the life of the community and those it served. It's an incredibly practical suggestion to a church, especially one so young. Think about your own church. Would it be better to invest your energies in practically helping those in need, rather than wasting energy in petty arguments and debates?

† Protect our communities from human failings that can destroy. Equip us with grace and a vision of how we can provide practical help for those in need.

For further thought

• What contribution could you as an individual make to your community, however you define it? What practical skills do your hands have to offer? Post a reflection on Facebook: www.facebook.com/freshfromtheword.

Handwritten

Colossians 4:10-18

I, Paul, write this greeting in my own hand. Remember my chains. Grace be with you. (verse 18)

When was the last time you handwrote a letter to someone? In fact, when did you last receive one? If you're anything like me, it's a rare occasion. But once upon a time, that wasn't the case. As a teenager, my family moved to another city and the friends I left behind would correspond regularly. I knew each friend's handwriting intimately and the sight of it on an envelope on the doormat would cause great excitement. Today, I could probably recognise the handwriting of only a very small group of people. A name in an inbox or a photo next to a tweet or Facebook post isn't quite the same.

We know Paul thought letter writing was important. It was the only way he had of passing on his teaching, guiding the new churches and passing on greetings to and from other Christians. But this letter to the Colossians was written while Paul was imprisoned – he could not visit these people in person because of his chains, so this letter had to suffice. Paul wanted to emphasise that, even though he couldn't travel and speak to them face to face, the words in his letter were his own and meant just as much as if he were speaking to them in their presence.

Our handwriting is a little bit of ourselves. For Paul, it was his way of reaching a place he could not visit. Today, we have countless ways of communicating, but is there anything as special as a handwritten letter?

† Lord, help us to communicate with those we cannot be with today. Give us wisdom to use the right words at the right time, and to touch the heart of someone far away.

For further thought

• Write a handwritten letter to someone you do not see every day, and invite that person to reply in the same way.

Readings in Matthew 26 – 27
1 The last week

This week's notes are by **Tom Arthur**

In 1988, Tom Arthur was recruited to serve the United Reformed Church in the UK, primarily in Wales, where he still lives with his Dutch wife Marieke after retirement. Before moving to Wales, Tom served as a Presbyterian minister in Chicago and taught literature at Chicago's Loyola University. He has also taught at the University of Birmingham's Westhill College and currently teaches New Testament Greek and other New Testament subjects in the Cardiff Adult Christian Education Centre. He is the author of *The Year of the Lord's Favor: Proclaiming Grace in the Year of Luke*.

Sunday 6 April
Up against church and state

Matthew 26:1-5

... and they schemed to arrest Jesus secretly and kill him. (verse 4)

Jesus has just finished explaining that, whenever we feed the hungry, satisfy the thirsty and so on, we do these things to him. So, here, the 'Son of Man' who is handed over to be crucified is anyone who falls foul of the powers of state and religion.

The most compelling and visible story of someone falling foul of the authorities today is the saga of the Moscow-based punk band Pussy Riot's confrontation with the Russian Orthodox Church and the Russian state, which attracted worldwide attention in recent years. The choice of Moscow's Cathedral of Christ the Saviour to perform its 'punk prayer' song 'Mother of God, chase Putin away' reminds me of Jesus' own bit of guerrilla theatre, enacting the Last Days' triumphal entry of the king of Israel into the city of David as described in Zechariah 9:9. The Pussy Riot women, like Jesus, were questioning the legitimacy of the one on the throne, and the religious and state authorities charged them with blasphemy and hooliganism (political dissidence). Such is the common fate of 'the Son of Man', or 'the Human Being', to speak more correctly – our identity as those who stand faithfully in the presence of God and in solidarity with all humanity, regardless of the consequences. The story of the Passion becomes our story, the trial and conviction our destiny.

† Let us not be so quick to condemn those who challenge the church, but learn to listen.

Monday 7 April
Charity or solidarity

Matthew 26:6-16

'Why this waste?' they asked. 'This perfume could have been sold at a high price and the money given to the poor.' (verses 8b-9)

Dining with lepers is a preview of the kind of society we expect the kingdom to be, and anointing Jesus is a gesture proclaiming the one who will be betrayed and crucified as the real Messiah, the one who brings in that kingdom. But the disciples don't get it. They still see the Messiah according to the public myth, as the muscular arm of an us-against-them God.

One would think that giving to the poor the money that is wasted on this expensive ointment would be a good thing to do. Isn't this what the churches do in their charitable giving? By throwing money at 'the poor' the bourgeois church practises a virtue of sympathy that keeps the poor distant and enables us to avoid the more threatening virtue of solidarity, like the wealthy politician who gives millions to charitable causes but opposes any change to the economic status quo. Money is the symbol of what binds bourgeois society, what defines its relationships and motivates its betrayals.

What the Gospel wants is the social equivalent of dining with lepers, the kind of solidarity with the down-and-out and the excluded we see in the one crucified in the company of thieves. Johann Baptist Metz, in *The Emergent Church: The Future of Christianity in a Postbourgeois World* (London 1980), speaks of the important priority of 'a holiness that proves itself in ... that militant love which draws upon itself the suffering of others'. The church's prevailing priorities, sadly, focus on its own survival, its own flourishing. And so we continue to demonstrate our preference for keeping company with Judas.

† Spend prayer time thinking how to get your priorities straight.

For further thought:

• How is a church or group you know making efforts to order its priorities after Jesus' rather than Judas' vision? How can you be a part of this?

Tuesday 8 April
A gracious gathering

Matthew 26:17-25

And while they were eating, he said, 'Truly I tell you, one of you will betray me.' (verse 21)

Ayn Rand, the godmother of greed-driven, libertarian capitalism, once caricatured Christianity as 'a kindergarten for Communism' (quoted in J Burns, *Goddess of the Market: Ayn Rand and the American Right*, Oxford 2009). Maybe that is what the church looks like from the outside, from the perspective of Rand's ruthless individualism. From the inside, it looks much like what Matthew describes here, a table fellowship at which all are fed, even those who will betray it.

This gracious gathering is what the church is like. Some communions attempt to live as the disciples did in the early hours after the crucifixion, behind locked doors and drawn curtains, as a tidy but frightened enclave apart from the world, venturing out only to expand their exclusive company by ensnaring others. But even these churches include the betrayer, despite their best efforts.

The church as the body of Christ moves in a contrary direction, not grabbing after security but emptying itself, making a gracious space for others. The church is defined by the gesture of breaking and sharing bread, by a meal shared in common with good and bad alike. Such extravagant generosity is what we call 'the means of grace'.

But such a generous spirit is not always recognised. The traditional words just before the sharing of bread and cup, 'Lord, I am not worthy to receive you, but only say the word and I shall be healed' are variously translated as the 'prayer of humble access'. My father-in-law, a Dutch Calvinist, remembers a communion service when no one felt sufficiently healed to come forward. The minister then covered up the elements with the communion cloths and said, 'Nor am I worthy.' The bread remained unbroken.

† Lord, none of us is worthy to receive you. Yet we are bold to entreat you: let you yourself be our worthiness, and break the bread among us yourself.

For further thought
- We've all betrayed Christ. Ask for forgiveness for those times in your life, in assurance of welcome at Christ's table. How does your church make real this extravagant welcome?

Wednesday 9 April
The way we live

Matthew 26:26-35

Then Jesus told them, 'This very night you will all fall away on account of me, for it is written: "I will strike the shepherd, and the sheep of the flock will be scattered."' (verse 31)

A young Christopher Marlowe wrote, in *The Passionate Shepherd to His Love*:

Come live with me and be my love,
And we will all the pleasures prove.

The more experienced Sir Walter Raleigh wrote a reply, *The Nymph's Reply to the Shepherd*:

Thy gowns, thy shoes, thy beds of roses,
Thy cap, thy kirtle, and thy posies
Soon break, soon wither, soon forgotten –
In folly ripe, in reason rotten.

Raleigh corrects Marlowe's youthful enthusiasm. All things fade, he says, including the promises of love and devotion. There is something like betrayal at the heart of human nature, and even at the heart of nature itself. In science, they call it the Second Law of Thermodynamics. All things fade, irreversibly.

In our story the disciples are like the youthful Marlowe, protesting their undying loyalty. Jesus knows better. The story of sheep scattering in the absence of the shepherd is an old biblical story. But Jesus will do something that science, observing the inevitable degradation of energy in a system towards a state of inert uniformity, says can't be done. The undying loyalty he shows on the cross to humanity's most wretched puts energy and structure back into the system. His act of solidarity on the cross sums up a way of life that denies death's dominion. Christ crucified leads the sheep to a new way of life. The cross becomes an invitation:

Come live with me and be my love,
And we will all the pleasures prove.

† Discover the loyalty at the heart of our human nature as the image of God that overcomes cynicism.

For further thought

• In a time of prayer, imagine Jesus speaking Marlowe's couplet to you. What other words of invitation might Jesus use?

Thursday 10 April
Yes, yes, yes, yes

Matthew 26:36-46

My Father, if it is possible, may this cup be taken from me. Yet not as I will, but as you will. (part of verse 39)

During the Montgomery bus boycott, and three days before his home was bombed, Martin Luther King Jr came home one night after a long strategy meeting. The phone rang. A snarling voice told him that, if he wanted to live, he had to leave Montgomery. King was devastated. He went into the kitchen to make a cup of coffee and there he had what he later described as the most profound spiritual experience of his life. Bowing over the kitchen table, he prayed, aloud, the now famous words: 'I am here taking a stand for what I believe is right. But now I am afraid. The people are looking to me for leadership, and if I stand before them without strength and courage, they too will falter. I've come to the end of my powers. I have nothing left. I can't face it alone.'

As he prayed he had a profound sense of God's presence, and he heard an inner voice saying, 'Stand up for justice, stand up for truth; and God will be at your side for ever.' King was ready now, he would later say, to face anything.

The moment when Jesus kneels in prayer in Gethsemane is the true moment of incarnation, when the will of God takes on flesh in his life. King's story illustrates – and your own prayer life confirms – that this kind of experience belongs to true discipleship. But saying 'yes' to God's presence in us is never easy. It comes with great tension, with all the fear and trembling Jesus knew in Gethsemane. But it defines what it means to be Christian in critical times.

† Let us make God present in the world through what we do.

For further thought

• Who are the best 'yea'-sayers you know personally? Where do they get their resolve from? Say 'yes' to God today in moments when you face tempting alternatives.

Friday 11 April
Being true

Matthew 26:47-56

Going at once to Jesus, Judas said, 'Greetings, Rabbi!' and kissed him.
(verse 49)

The Kiss, painted by Austrian artist Gustav Klimt over a century ago, depicts a couple's embrace in shimmering gold – symbolic of the heady optimism that came just before the carnage of the First World War. Fifty years earlier Matthew Arnold also described an embrace as a refuge from a meaningless world in his poem 'Dover Beach' (1867):

Ah, love, let us be true
To one another! for the world, which seems
To lie before us like a land of dreams…
Hath really neither…
… certitude, nor peace, nor help for pain;
And we are here as on a darkling plain
Swept with confused alarms of struggle and flight,
Where ignorant armies clash by night.

(The Poems of Matthew Arnold, ed. Allott, London 1965)

The kiss is a gesture not only of desire but, particularly among males, of bonding. But for Judas, the kiss masks betrayal. It becomes part of a world of uncertainty where ignorant armies clash by night. The kiss of Judas is like going to war against Iraq promising to bring democracy, with a hidden agenda of grasping oil resources. Enmity takes hold, spreads, becomes large-scale infection.

We need more than an interpersonal clinging together in a meaningless world. We need the integrity of a people willing to live honestly and loyally beyond narrow personal, ethnic, national or credal allegiances. In his willingness to stand in (and so fulfil) the biblical prophetic tradition of those who stand up for what it means to be true, regardless of consequences, Jesus gives us our vocation.

† Don't let the Church say 'I love you' and not mean it.

For further thought
• Let your embraces, handshakes, greetings and goodbyes have goodwill and integrity today.

Saturday 12 April
God with us

Matthew 26:57-68

The high priest said to him, 'I charge you under oath by the living God: Tell us if you are the Messiah, the Son of God.' 'You have said so,' Jesus replied. (verses 63b-64a)

In classical Greek drama, when plots got stuck, a god would be lowered by a mechanical pulley device on to the stage to sort things out. The Latin poet Horace used the term *deus ex machina* (god from a machine) to describe such a contrived intervention. Whether a literal god lowered by machine or a contrived intervention by any sort of event or character, the device doesn't make for good drama. Horace condemned it.

The Messiah story, which had its roots in the broad mythology of the Middle East, became a feature of Jewish–Christian thought at a time when people were feeling particularly powerless, and needed something like the *deus ex machina*, which the Messiah story so closely resembles, to sort things out. The historical situation was so overwhelming no ordinary mortal could fix it.

The high priest in our story is offended that Jesus seems to be claiming actually to *be* the Messiah. The offence they take, Matthew's Gospel implies, is a lack of trust that God can be present in ordinary, faithful human discipleship. They accuse Jesus of blasphemy. Jesus acknowledges their understanding ('You have said so'), but goes on in the high poetic language of Daniel to say that the 'son of man' – the true humanity emerging from the faithful practice of the human community – redefines that Messiah.

Matthew's Gospel begins with the promise of Emmanuel – God-with-us – and ends with the promise that, as the Christian community remains faithful, Christ will be present among us. This is not just good news but good drama.

† Gracious God, let the story of our lives unfold in your steadfast faith rather than through our own cynical contrivances or desperate plot devices.

For further thought

• On the eve of Holy Week, consider where you might find God in your discipleship.

Readings in Matthew 26 – 27
2 The last hours

This week's readings are by **Jessica Dalton-Cheetham**

Jessica works for the Oxford-based peacekeeping charity The Fellowship of Reconciliation, where she coordinates the Young Peacemaker Programme and serves as a contact for schools, universities and youth and student campaign groups. She is a Methodist local preacher, lives with her husband Tom in Birmingham, and is studying for a PhD at Bristol University. Her first degrees are in theology and her research centres around the relationship between Christianity and the justice system. She is a writer and activist, and is also Convenor of the Student Christian Movement, an organisation inspiring students to live out a radically inclusive faith (online at www.movement.org.uk/).

Sunday 13 April
Being present in Christ's last hours

Matthew 26:69-73

But he denied it before them all. 'I don't know what you are talking about,' he said. (verse 70)

Holy Week is a time to reflect on how the story of Christ's Crucifixion and Resurrection relates to our own struggles, sorrows and questions. In a way, we act out the despair and pain that the disciples felt all those centuries ago in Jerusalem so that we can similarly act out the elation they must have felt upon seeing the empty tomb on Easter Sunday. Living that experience can help reignite our faith and our joy at knowing Jesus Christ.

This reading speaks of a betrayal: Peter's refusal to acknowledge his experience of Jesus. One of the reasons he denies Christ is to avoid discomfort, challenge and confrontation. We might not deny Jesus by refusing to admit we're Christians but we might still be guilty of betrayal when we refuse to choose the just, godly way because it is easier to exploit our neighbour. It is often easier to grab the brand of coffee at hand rather than walk a little further for the ethical alternative, for example. And it takes courage to challenge an unfair decision at work. This week we will see both that courage, in Jesus' witness, and the lack of it, too – and have a chance to reflect on both in our own lives.

† God of forgiveness, this week graciously show us the ways we have betrayed Jesus and his values of love, justice and compassion.

Monday 14 April
Promises of a second chance

Matthew 27:1-10

'I have sinned,' he said, 'for I have betrayed innocent blood.' 'What is that to us?' they replied. 'That's your responsibility.' So Judas threw the money into the temple and left. Then he went away and hanged himself. (verses 4-5)

This is one of the saddest passages in scripture. Judas' choices have been so disastrous and miserable that he enters a despair from which he cannot release himself, and so he kills himself. We too can feel that life is not worth living, that our decisions and choices have been so awful and destructive that it's not worth carrying on. We've all made mistakes: they might not be as drastic as Judas', but we've all acted in ways that hurt others or ourselves, even when we thought we were doing the right thing. We might well have been in Judas' shoes, paralysed by disappointment and fear.

At Easter, Jesus always promises us a second chance. He is a God who always seeks to restore and to reconcile; he is never tired of us. Even when others desert us or reject us and claim they want no more to do with us, God's love is eternal. Judas thought he deserved retribution but God has promised us something else. Judas felt the burden of responsibility so keenly that it killed him; we also need to accept responsibility but we are set free from carrying such a heavy load alone. When we feel tired of life we are invited to rest in God and to share our burden, rather than to struggle on alone. Our lives are always worth living. Where Judas did not see hope or the chance for another go at life, we can.

† Sometimes bad decisions can weigh on us and grind us down until we become inconsolable. Pray for the courage to forgive yourself your wrongs and to move forward this Holy Week, to receive the new life of Easter.

For further thought

• Think of your friends and family. Are you available to talk to and to pray with, as those you love make peace with themselves?

Tuesday 15 April
Difficult choices

Matthew 27:11-26

'What shall I do, then, with Jesus who is called the Messiah?' Pilate asked.
(verse 22a)

Holy Week is full of decisions: Jesus' choice to be loving and compassionate and follow the road to crucifixion; Judas' decision to sell Christ; Peter's decision to deny Jesus; and Pilate's decision to ignore his better judgement and crucify Jesus.

Pilate is under a lot of pressure. He has imperial powers breathing down his neck and the expectations of an angry crowd to deal with. He is trying to do the right thing and attempting to persuade others of the right course of action. It will take a lot of courage to remain true to his conviction but ultimately he caves in to pressure and makes the wrong decision.

This is a day to reflect on our own decisions because, more often than not, our lives are also full of choices. Do we allow ourselves to be easily swayed by popular opinion, ignoring what we know to be right because to pursue it would be difficult and uncomfortable? Perhaps we aren't quite in situations like Pilate, but at work or at home we may face choices where to choose the right action is extremely difficult in the face of pressure to do otherwise. How can we strive to find the strength to choose the right course of action – to be more like Jesus and less like Pilate? How do we react to these challenges? Are we prepared to deal with the consequences of the right decisions? How tempting is it simply to sell out?

† Pray for the strength and courage to pursue the right course of action in the face of opposition.

For further thought
• Around the world there are many people in prison for speaking out the truth. Find out how you can campaign for their release or support them.

Wednesday 16 April
Christ suffers with us

Matthew 27:27-31

Then they knelt in front of him and mocked him. 'Hail, king of the Jews!'
they said. They spat on him, and took the staff and struck him on the head
again and again. (verses 29b-30)

Jesus' experience is humiliating in the extreme. He is physically abused and verbally assaulted in the most horrific manner, in the knowledge that all that awaits him is a violent death. It is not easy to imagine this scene. We imagine Jesus as king, sitting with God the Father in heaven, or we picture him as a wise teacher, attended to by huge crowds. We think he never knew what it felt like to be mocked and treated like dirt. We forget that he experienced humiliation, degradation and shame – it was very much part of Jesus' experiences on earth, and to an extreme degree.

We live in a world where people and institutions shame us and make us feel unworthy. We also live in a world where whole groups of people are abused, physically and emotionally, by individuals, corporate structures and regimes. Jesus has suffered with us, and with them. Easter reminds us that Jesus is a powerful victor over the death-bringing forces of this world and that he has proclaimed freedom from sin and pain, but the physical abuse of Christ also reminds us that he has been treated as the least and the last among us. He has experienced our suffering and weeps with us as we live through it.

Eli Wiesel, the political activist, writer and Holocaust survivor, was once asked where God had been during the Holocaust. He replied that he believed Christ had being hanging on the gallows alongside those Jewish children murdered by the Nazis. There is terrible suffering in this world, in our hearts and all around us, but Jesus suffers with us.

† In a time of prayer, allow yourself to be comforted by Christ as you share with him the pains and injustices that have hurt you.

For further thought

• Who are you aware of who is being humiliated or shamed either by another person or by society? How can you extend friendship and compassion, inspired by Christ's example?

Thursday 17 April
Meditating on the cross

Matthew 27:32-44

When they had crucified him, they divided up his clothes by casting lots. And sitting down, they kept watch over him there. Above his head they placed the written charge against him: THIS IS JESUS, THE KING OF THE JEWS. (verses 35-37)

In the Middle Ages, many holy women would meditate on the image of Christ's Crucifixion in their cells or local church. These periods of extended contemplation led to visionary experiences and revelations of knowledge. The image of the Crucifixion was particularly poignant for women in this era, as the depiction of Christ's body in physical torment resonated with them as the main care-givers in a society and culture where pregnancy was dangerous and deadly disease was an everyday occurrence. It was an image that spoke about their reality, their lives, the way they spent their days. Maundy Thursday is a wonderful opportunity to imitate the great medieval mystics and meditate on an image of Christ on the cross.

Set aside some quiet time. If you find silence difficult you could play some restful music in the background. Sit comfortably with an image of the Crucifixion that you find inspiring or beautiful. As you consider the image, remember that on Maundy Thursday Jesus washed the feet of his disciples; not only was this an indication of Christ's servanthood but it was also a gift to his followers. Just like the visions and revelations of medieval Europe, God still seeks to give us the gifts of knowledge and comfort as we grow closer to God through meditation and prayer.

† As you pray and spend some time in stillness, ask God to help prepare you for the mourning and celebrations of the weekend to come. Consider how you can let the story of Easter change you.

For further thought

• Does the image of the crucified Christ move you? How does it make you feel? In what ways is it relevant to your experience?

Friday 18 April (Good Friday)
The beginnings of new life

Matthew 27:45-56

At that moment the curtain of the temple was torn in two from top to bottom. (verse 51a)

One of the pivots on which the Christian journey turns is the death of Christ on Good Friday. It is traditionally a day of mourning, of grief and of repentance for sins. In our path towards Easter, it is a good opportunity indeed to reflect on where we are making mistakes, where we have hurt ourselves and others and the things we have done that crucify the God within us, as we have been made in his image.

But already in this reading from Matthew we see the second half of the story beginning, the story of new life. The curtain of the Temple is torn in two, symbolising Christ destroying the walls we have built between ourselves and God by choosing self-destructive action and selfish deeds. It's a wall that God never wanted between us, a wall that we have built, and Jesus rips it apart. Tradition holds that the bodies of the saints rise from the dead as Christ dies. The message of Resurrection and restoration is beginning to be told even as Jesus breathes his last on the cross. It is a wonderful symbol of the uncontainable love of God, desperate to rescue us from ourselves.

† Pray a traditional Good Friday prayer; use the day to meditate on the areas of your life you seek to change or leave behind.

For further thought
• Today allow the reassurance this passage gives of new life and new beginnings to settle in your heart, and in your mind.

Saturday 19 April
A day of waiting

Matthew 27:57-66

So give the order for the tomb to be made secure until the third day.
(verse 64a)

Traditionally, the Saturday between Good Friday and Easter Sunday is a day of waiting with the followers of Jesus. We remember the pain and desolation the disciples must have felt on that day, thinking their dreams of a triumphant ruler of Jerusalem had been destroyed. We, too, can often find ourselves waiting for grace after a period of pain, thinking our hopes for the future have come to nothing. Perhaps a job interview was unsuccessful, a relationship has ended, or we simply find ourselves stuck in a situation that is draining.

We re-enact the disciples' period of waiting as we consider our own sorrows and losses on this day. While the world resembled a calm after the storm, the disciples' hearts must have remained in turmoil. It can be the same for us, especially if we're grieving: everyone seems to move on but our hearts are still broken, still waiting. But, as we saw in yesterday's reading, God is already present and full of signs of new life in our waiting as well, even though it can seem hopeless. Not only does he mourn with us in our grief, but he is like the flowers springing up in the cracks between cobblestones, constantly injecting possibilities for new life and growth into our waiting.

† Pray for signs of new life in your periods of waiting and for the opportunity to be that sign of grace in the lives of people you know who suffer.

For further thought

- Try to consider times when you have seen the beginnings of new life in times of waiting. Did recognising those signs mark a time of change?

Easter appearances

This week's notes are by **David Bartlett**

David Bartlett is ordained in the American Baptist Churches and is an emeritus professor of New Testament and preaching at Columbia Theological Seminary (Georgia, USA) and Yale Divinity School (Connecticut, USA), respectively. He is passionate about preaching and the life of the church and is co-editor of the major lectionary commentary *Feasting on the Word* (Westminster/John Knox). His wife, Carol, is a retired social worker and early childhood educator, and they have two grown sons.

Sunday 20 April (Easter Day)
Fear and joy

Matthew 28:1-10

Then Jesus said to them, 'Do not be afraid. Go and tell my brothers to go on to Galilee; there they will see me.' (**verse 10**)

We were taking a favourite 3-year-old boy from his home in the city to a cottage near the shore for a weekend. As we got into the car, he confessed: 'I'm a little bit afraid.' We soon discovered the extent of that fear. He was scared sick. When we had cleaned him up, we asked if he was ready to take on this new adventure or needed to go home and he assured us that he wanted to continue on our way. When we got to the island, we took the boy's hand and walked out onto the sand. When he saw the sea before him – larger and more majestic than any sight he had ever experienced – he ran as fast as he could and splashed into the water at the ocean's edge. Terror had turned to joy.

When Matthew tells the story of Jesus' appearance to the women after his Resurrection, he speaks both of terror and of joy. The Resurrection of Jesus is not an ordinary event. It is a huge intervention by God.

In the face of Resurrection we are bound to be afraid. But when we begin to trust in the reality of the Resurrection, Matthew promises us that we can know the living Lord in our own lives. And then we move from fear to joy.

† Kind and triumphant God, we confess how often we are afraid of your majesty. Grant us the grace to receive you with joy.

Monday 21 April
The convenient lie

Matthew 28:11-15

While the women were on their way, some of the guards went into the city and reported to the chief priests everything that had happened.
(verse 11)

We all know the old adage that 'truth is the best policy'. However, truth is often not the most useful policy. Indeed it is not clear that we should think of telling the truth as a policy at all. We usually adopt a 'policy' in order to get something we very much want. We tell the truth because that is what God wants of us.

In this story from Matthew the leaders of the people get what they want: people have reason to doubt the claim that Jesus is risen. The soldiers get what they want: a large sum of money.

In the end God gets what God wants. God's truth outdoes and outshines the lies that deny that Christ lives. While the religious authorities and the soldiers are spreading the big lie through Jerusalem, Christ is proclaiming the big truth in Galilee. Try to define God by what the official leaders say and God will call a whole new band of disciples to spread the word.

We can spend a good deal of time debating whether there are occasions where a little lie saves a lot of trouble and a big lie may save even more. In the kingdom where God reigns, however, we are told that all authority – all power and all wisdom – are given to the risen Jesus. And he is absolutely true, absolute truth.

† Lord Jesus, we know that you are truth. Strengthen in us the gift of honesty and trust that we may live in truth, too.

For further thought

• How can we hold on to the truth when so much of consumer society depends on stretching the truth or ignoring it altogether?

Tuesday 22 April
Too good to be true

Luke 24:36-44

'Why are you troubled, and why do doubts rise in your minds? Look at my hands and my feet. It is I myself! Touch me and see ...' (part of verses 38-39)

Many years ago, in my first year as a university student, I was unable to join my family for the Easter holidays. Along with several other stranded students, I went on a retreat with the student fellowship from a local church. The theme of the retreat, appropriately, was Easter and we read through the Easter stories and, under the leadership of a local pastor, sought to understand what the stories might mean.

After we had engaged in about an hour of conversation, one young woman who was in our group simply slammed shut her Bible and with considerable exasperation declared: 'That can't be true.'

'Why not?' the pastor asked.

'Because if that is true then everything is changed.'

When the risen Jesus shows the disciples his hands and feet, they realise that death, even death on the cross, could not conquer him. When he ate the piece of fish, they realised that they were not seeing ghosts but were socialising with an old friend. When he started to read the Bible (our Old Testament) to them, the old words came alive in a remarkable new way. Texts that seemed obscure in themselves shone with light when Jesus interpreted them – as texts about himself.

For them, as for us, everything was changed. For them, as for us, the time had come for us to accept that good news. And rejoice.

† We are ready to be changed, kind God. Change us according to your mercy, to live by your will. Through Christ, Amen

For further thought

• When you take seriously the claim that God is stronger than death, what changes in your life?

Wednesday 23 April
Witnessing forgiveness

Luke 24:45-53

[Jesus] told them, 'This is what is written: the Messiah will suffer and rise from the dead on the third day, and repentance for the forgiveness of sins will be preached in his name to all nations, beginning at Jerusalem.'
(verses 46-47)

More than any other book in the New Testament, Luke's Gospel is about forgiveness. In this Gospel Jesus tells the story we call 'The Prodigal Son', though it is really the story of the forgiving father. In the story a son acts as if he wishes his father were dead, by asking for his inheritance while the father lives. He wastes the fortune he receives. He discovers that he is both hungry and alone. He turns for home, practising a little speech that will ask his father for forgiveness. But before he gets home, as he rounds the last bend, his father sees him and runs down the road to forgive him.

After his Resurrection, Jesus tells us that that story of forgiveness is the good news he tells. It is also the good news he acts out. His death on the cross (which we did not deserve) and his Resurrection (which we did not expect) are the ways in which God is always running down the road to greet us, to forgive us, to welcome us home.

And now Jesus says that all those who have known God's forgiveness are 'witnesses of these things'. It is not only that we have known *about* forgiveness, we have *known* forgiveness. In that way, even though we were not in Judaea on that first Easter, we are true witnesses of the Resurrection.

† Kind God, strengthen us to accept the gift of your forgiveness, and let us turn to others in forgiveness, too. Through Christ our Lord.

For further thought

• It is very difficult to forgive; sometimes it is even harder to accept forgiveness. Where in your life can you grow in trust in God's forgiving goodness?

Thursday 24 April
Breakfast with Jesus

John 21:4-14

Jesus said to them, 'Come and have breakfast' ... Jesus came, took the bread and gave it to them, and did the same with the fish. (part of verses 12-13)

A study in the US sought to find any correlation between the flourishing of children and the practices of their families. The researchers distinguished between children who had been in trouble with the legal authorities and those who had not. They discovered one astonishing correlation between family practice and children's well-being. The families with positive outcomes were overwhelmingly families who shared at least one meal together every day.

When Jesus appears to the disciples at the Sea of Tiberias, he comes to strengthen the family. His first words to them are family words. In verse 5 he calls out, 'Friends, haven't you any fish?' A more accurate translation of 'friends' would be 'children'. We know only one of his 'children' stood with Jesus' mother at the foot of the cross. When Jesus sets out to strengthen this wobbly family, he does an exceedingly familial thing: he shares a meal.

The reason Christians share meals with one another is not simply that we get hungry, it is that we get lonely. We need, all of us, to be family, fellowship, friends.

Wise theologians give us many good reasons why we celebrate Eucharist or the Lord's Supper together. One of the best reasons is that the shared meal brings us together as Christ's children, and therefore as brothers and sisters one of another. Jesus' word to the disciples is still a word to us: 'Come and have breakfast (or lunch, or the Supper).' Come to communion. Come to become communion.

† What prayer might you share over a common meal that stresses the way in which meals bring us to each other and to God?

For further thought

• How often do you take time to eat – and talk – with the people you love best?

Friday 25 April
Jesus talks with Peter

John 21:15-23

Again Jesus said, 'Simon son of John, do you love me?' (verse 16a)

The word 'gospel' means 'good news'. It is easy enough to see why this passage is good news for Peter, and then good news for us as well. The passage provides a word of forgiveness to somebody who has messed up. Peter has denied Jesus three times (John 18:15-18, 25-27).

Deliberately, then, Jesus asks Peter three times if Peter loves him. Three times Peter says yes. The fact that Jesus will even speak to Peter is a kind of forgiveness. The fact that Jesus asks Peter to love suggests the kind of hopefulness that forgiveness requires.

More than that, Jesus trusts Peter's answer, trusts Peter's love enough to give him responsibility along with his forgiveness. He trusts that Peter does love him and confirms that trust by entrusting Peter with work to do.

Yale University Professor William Muehl used to say that the prodigal son wouldn't know that he was really forgiven just because his father threw a huge party. He would know that he was forgiven when his father told him it was time to get out of bed and get out in the fields and take his full place as a member of the family. So Peter knows he is forgiven because he is not allowed to bask in the warm glow of feeling forgiven. He needs to act out the mercy he has received. 'Follow me!' says Jesus (21:19).

† We ask not only that you will forgive us, O God, but that you will use us to work your will and to serve your goodly reign. Through Christ our Lord.

For further thought

• In your own life, where can you trust God's love enough that you can take on more responsibility for others?

Saturday 26 April
Jesus' appearance to Peter

1 Corinthians 15:1-8

For what I received I passed on to you as of first importance: that Christ died for our sins according to the Scriptures, that he was buried, that he was raised on the third day according to the Scriptures, and that he appeared to Cephas and then to the Twelve. (**verses 3-5**)

The apostle Paul wrote the earliest books in the New Testament. Jesus preached before Paul wrote his letters, but the four Gospel writers wrote later. And before Paul had written a single word of his letters, he had heard a report that was older still – the report of Jesus rising from the dead and appearing to a number of people. Some, like Peter, were already Jesus' followers and some, like James, Jesus' brother, and Paul himself were not.

In this Easter Week we are invited to remember that the Christian faith really began with the confidence that Jesus had been raised from the dead. His ministry did not end on the cross. His words did not die on the cross. He did die on the cross, but God was stronger and smarter even than death.

Matthew tells us that Peter was the 'rock' on whom Jesus built the Church, built the community of his followers. 'Peter' itself is really a nickname. (His mother had named him 'Simon'.) And the word means 'the rock'.

We know from reading in all four Gospels, and from reading Paul's letter to the Galatians, that Peter was not always rock solid. What was rock solid was what he saw and what he told: Christ is not dead; he is risen. Christ lived for Peter and Christians believe that he lives still. We do not simply remember Christ fondly. We follow him gladly.

† Make yourself known to us, too, living Christ, in whatever way and at whatever time you choose.

For further thought

- Even if we do not see the risen Lord as clearly as Peter did, where can we find assurances that God in Christ is with us?

Readings in Joshua
1 Preparations for invasion

This week's notes are by **Rachel Montagu**

Rachel Montagu teaches Judaism and Biblical Hebrew. She believes teaching people to understand the Bible in Hebrew, without translators' interpretations, empowers them as readers. She has been involved in interfaith dialogue for many years. She trained to be a rabbi at the Leo Baeck College, London. She lives in London with her husband, Francis Treuherz (a homeopath), their two sons and the family's combined library of more than 15,000 books.

Sunday 27 April
Be strong and courageous!

Joshua 1:1-18

Be strong and courageous, because you will lead these people to inherit the land I swore to their ancestors to give them ... Be careful to obey all the law my servant Moses gave you. (part of verses 6 and 7)

The book of Joshua is about the difficulties of adapting to change. In the wilderness, the children of Israel have been fed, shod and clothed by God (Deuteronomy 29:4-5), like children whose parents supply all their needs. Now they must inhabit the land that is their promised inheritance, and live independently. Because Moses could not cross into the land, they must move on from mourning him and accustom themselves to the leadership of Joshua, until now known to them as Moses' assistant. No wonder this first chapter includes three times the words 'Be strong and courageous'; Joshua must quickly grow into a leader great enough to facilitate this change. To help him succeed, he has Moses' teachings, which must be looked at constantly to be vivid enough to help him.

As I write this commentary, I am very aware how hard it can be to cope with or contemplate even positive changes. One son has just gone to university, leaving us to grow into a new pattern of family life and the other is mourning the sudden loss of his treble voice, part of his sense of who he is, and which gave him the role he loves in the synagogue choir.

† Blessed are you, Eternal God, who provides for all my needs.

Monday 28 April
Your God is the only God

Joshua 2:1-14

Now then, please swear to me by the LORD that you will show kindness to my family, because I have shown kindness to you. Give me a sure sign that you will spare the lives of my father and mother, my brothers and sisters, and all who belong to them – and that you will save us from death. (verses 12-13)

Traditional Jewish commentators wanted Rahab to be respected by readers, and creatively interpreted the word *zonah* (prostitute) to mean that she ran a café (*miznon* in Hebrew); either role would explain why strangers could enter her house. There may be a connection in biblical thought between spying and overstepping sexual boundaries: the Hebrew words of Genesis 42:9 link spying and being a voyeur.

Rahab recognised that the Eternal is God of heaven and earth; she was willing to risk her life to hide the spies, so that she and her family would be saved later. The men promise that they will treat her with kindness and keep faith with their assurances.

The phrase used here for kindness and faithfulness is quoted several times in the prayers Jews say while washing and shrouding a corpse before burial. Preparing the dead is a kindness to the dead and the bereaved and helps those who do it realise the true reality of life and death. The first time I took part in this process I had never seen or touched a dead body before, and I found it hard. The words of the prayers and the kindness of the other women doing it were what enabled me to continue.

Rahab realised that, even if her fellow citizens would consider her behaviour disloyal, the reality is that the Eternal is God and had given the Israelites the land. Jewish tradition esteems her like other non-Israelites, for example Jethro (Exodus 18:10-11), who acknowledge God's existence.

† Blessed are you, Eternal God, who show us an example of loving-kindness.

For further thought

• Think whether you have stereotyped someone because of the work they do and, if so, how to avoid doing this again.

Tuesday 29 April
Help us help you

Joshua 2:15-24

They said to Joshua, 'The Lord has surely given the whole land into our hands; all the people are melting in fear because of us.' (verse 24)

In verse 17 the spies are not going back on their promise, but are setting realistic conditions to enable them to keep it; when they return to the city they can protect defined premises, especially ones conveniently recognisable from outside like Rahab's house, built into the thickness of the city wall. But they cannot promise to protect her entire clan unless her family has the sense to shelter in her house and keep quiet about what will happen – an equivalent of the Second World War slogan 'careless talk costs lives'.

Verse 24 echoes the language of Moses' song of gratitude after crossing the sea (Exodus 15). The song says the nations they will meet melt in fear. There and here, however fearful the other peoples felt, it is the children of Israel who we understand are melting in fear of the nations ahead of them; they are desperate for reassurance that they will succeed in conquering the land and not be either overthrown by the strong nations dwelling there, or corrupted by their idolatry, as Moses warned. There are places in the Bible that teach a strongly universalistic message: God is God of all nations, God forgives all humanity and all humanity will know God (Jonah, Isaiah 2:2-4, 56:7). That message may be what we need to learn today but, at that time, at the point of transition into the land that flowed with milk and honey but was also full of unknown and potentially hostile tribes, the Israelites needed confidence and assurances that God would protect them.

† Blessed are you, Eternal God ,who directs the way we go.

For further thought

• Read a book or visit a gallery to appreciate the art or literature of a culture very different from your own.

The living God is among you

Joshua 3:1-17

The priests who carried the ark of the covenant of the LORD stopped in the middle of the Jordan and stood on dry ground, while all Israel passed by until the whole nation had completed the crossing on dry ground.
(verse 17)

There are a number of parallels between the Exodus from Egypt and the entrance into the land. Just as the Israelites walked dry-shod across the Sea of Reeds, they walk dry-shod across the Jordan. There are also contrasts: Joshua tells the people (1:11) to use the three days before the crossing to prepare provisions, unlike the Exodus when their hasty departure left them no time to do anything except carry out unleavened dough to be baked (Exodus 12:39). Now they must learn to be self-reliant and cater for themselves.

A Jewish legend says the waters of the Reed Sea parted only when one man had the faith to walk into the water. A certain Nachshon ben Amminadav walked into the sea until the water reached his nostrils; only then did the flow of waters stop, enabling the people to walk on dry land. Here it is the ark whose arrival tells the water to part. When they left Egypt, the people had only their faith in God to rely on, which Nachshon demonstrated, and Moses with his miracle-working staff. Now God has given them the Torah/teaching, which leads them as they march and here signals the waters to stop. God promises Joshua that the events of the day will give him status in the eyes of Israel. At the end of the chapter, Joshua tells the Israelites that they will realise that the living God is in their midst. So God wants Joshua to be respected and Joshua wants the people to acknowledge God: this is a model to us of mutual respect and co-operation.

† Blessed are you, Eternal God, who gives wisdom to human beings.

For further thought

• Think how you can show gratitude to our religious leaders and teachers.

Thursday 1 May
What endures and what does not

Joshua 4:1-14

In the future, when your children ask you, 'What do these stones mean?'
tell them that the flow of the Jordan was cut off before the ark of the
covenant of the LORD. (verses 6b-7a)

Verse 6 echoes Exodus 12:26: today children still begin the Passover *seder* that Jewish families celebrate each year by asking the meaning of the night's service and of the Exodus. The redemption from Egyptian slavery is a key Jewish belief. Parents explain its importance to children during this home ritual and this is how Jewish tradition has been passed down through the ages.

Many versions of the *Haggadah*, the service book for the Passover *seder*, have been produced over the centuries everywhere Jews have lived. Illustrations and commentaries vary but the fundamental message, that all Jews must think they personally were rescued from Egypt by God and praise God in thanksgiving, is always the same. Since the destruction of the first and second Temples, the majority of Jews have lived scattered among the nations, although there have always been some Jews living in Israel. This ritual with the stones, prescribed in Joshua but limited to one place, unlike the Passover celebration of redemption, which is remembered in every Jewish home wherever that is, has not continued until today. But the link to the land of the covenant promise is still very important to Jews – when Theodore Herzl put the British government's suggestion that Jews should make themselves a homeland in Uganda to the International Zionist Congress in 1903 and 1905, the Congress refused any alternative to Israel. The development of a modern Jewish culture as a nation and revival of Hebrew as a living, rather than liturgical, language seem to many Jews to be something wonderful to set against the many Jewish tragedies of the twentieth century.

† Blessed are you, Eternal God, who redeems and rescues Israel.

For further thought

- I was recently with a group of people, none of whom knew anything their great-grandparents had said. I do know some sayings from mine, passed on by my grandparents. What memories would you like continued? Write them down or ensure younger family members hear them.

May

Friday 2 May
Time to be independent

Joshua 5:1-15

The commander of the LORD's army replied, 'Take off your sandals, for the place where you are standing is holy.' And Joshua did so. (verse 15)

In Numbers 13 to 14 the people listened to the ten spies scared by the land's inhabitants and refused to enter it, thus undermining the purpose of the Exodus (Exodus 3:16-17). Therefore God refused to let them enter the land. Only their children, here defined as under 20, survived. Nowadays Jewish parents may circumcise their sons only on the eighth day, according to the command given to Abraham (Genesis 17:12) if the baby is healthy, a reasonable size and has regained his birthweight. The Bible assumes that circumcision causes intense weakness immediately afterwards (Genesis 34:24). Because they never knew when they would move on during their 40 years' journey (Exodus 40:36-8), you can understand why they postponed circumcision. But once they arrived in the land and were preparing to celebrate Passover, circumcision was essential (Exodus 12:48). God brought them from Egypt to bring them to the land, nurturing them en route. On arrival they thanked God for redeeming them by the Passover. The manna they ate in the wilderness then ceased; it was time for them to become self-supporting, even if initially the land's riches could sustain them (Deuteronomy 8).

Verses 13-15 add to the parallels between Exodus and arrival – Moses was told at the burning bush and Joshua is told now to take off his shoes as they stand on holy ground. Joshua asks on whose side is the 'man', not immediately recognised as God's messenger (as often in the Bible). Joshua then asks the angel the question we should all ask about what God is saying to us. Unlike Moses at the burning bush, the answer Joshua received was not recorded.

† May God who makes peace in the highest realm, make peace for us, for all Israel and for all the peoples of the earth.

For further thought
• God provided food for the people until they could produce their own. Think what you, as God's agent in the world, can do to provide food for people who are unable to provide for themselves.

Saturday 3 May
Not by power, but by my spirit

Joshua 6:1-14

Then the Lord said to Joshua, 'See, I have delivered Jericho into your hands, along with its king and its fighting men … When you hear them sound a long blast on the trumpets, make the whole army give a loud shout; then the wall of the city will collapse…' (verses 2 and 5a)

The children of Israel were still uncertain about their powers against the skilled fighting men and walled cities of Canaan. The collapse of Jericho's walls shows them that they are not dependent on their own abilities. After the many miracles *en route* in the wilderness, it seems they should hardly need more proof of God's power, yet another miracle happens here. A ram's horn trumpet, *shofar*, is blown in synagogues on the Jewish New Year as a wake-up call to break open the community's hearts to repentance in the ten days until the Day of Atonement. It is a harsh and powerful sound. But we need not believe that six days of seven shofars blasting, seven circuits of blasts, and a shout from the whole people would have collapsed the walls had God not wanted to prove both to the children of Israel and the Canaanites that the land was theirs to conquer.

Therefore, the daily processions round the town were more to scare the inhabitants of Jericho. The ark's position heading the daily march was the visible sign to both the children of Israel and the inhabitants of Jericho that they followed God's Torah.

As 21st-century people who know about the United Nations, peace treaties and multiculturalism, we might wonder whether peaceful co-existence could have been possible. But this is not our world. The fears about the Canaanites' military strength and capacity to corrupt the people into sharing their idol worship, which Moses mentioned so frequently in Deuteronomy, prevent the neighbourly relations Abraham and his family sometimes managed with those round them.

† May the All-Merciful God grant peace between us and send blessing and success to all the work of our hands.

For further thought

- Note that the Israelites do not rest on the Sabbath, having learned about Sabbath rest while in the wilderness. Think what you can do to bring more Sabbath rest, relaxation, serenity and joy into your life.

Readings in Joshua
2 Into the promised land

This week's notes are by **Monica Jyotsna Melanchthon**

Church worker and theological educator, Dr Monica Jyotsna
Melanchthon belongs to the Andhra Evangelical Lutheran
Church, India. She currently teaches Old Testament/Hebrew Bible
at the Uniting Church Theological College, Melbourne, Australia.
She has strong commitments to marginalised and poor people,
women, and Dalits. She interprets biblical texts drawing on
insights from the social biographies of these communities and
their lived experiences.

Sunday 4 May
Honour the land as God's gift!

Joshua 6:15-25

At the sound of the trumpet, when the men gave a loud shout, the wall collapsed; so everyone charged straight in, and they took the city. (part of verse 20)

The book of Joshua is a disturbing book, particularly for colonised peoples. It seems to provide a blueprint for invasion, conquest and destruction of another's land. Is the book's objective to provide licence for invasion, or is it a critique of this manner of take-over? Is it an example of how God punishes those who oppress (namely the Canaanites), and a warning to the Israelites? How may we read accounts of displacement and dispossession? How are we to live with the indigenous or original inhabitants of the land? I believe that amidst the violence and the colonising allure of the book are values and virtues that serve as guidelines for life in the promised land.

Land provides one with a sense of home, identity and belonging, and is a primary capital resource. The land sworn to Abraham is a fulcrum in the relationship between God and Israel, testifying to both. In it, the Israelites were to live in obedience to Yahweh their God. 'The Lord has given you this city!' But the promise that the land holds will be realised only when Israel lives a life of obedience to God's covenant, to justice and equity. What is your relationship to the land in which you live? How do you care for it?

† Gracious God, we hold up to you for healing our relationships with the land and its peoples, mindful that this earth is a gift from you and that we are but tenants.

May

Monday 5 May
Honour justice for all!

Joshua 7:1-6, 10-26

Israel has sinned; they have violated my covenant, which I commanded them to keep. (verse 11a)

Israel was put into the world for the sake of justice and hence obliged to do justice. Doing justice is a 'nota', an identity marker, of Israel and is of special importance. It was theologically intentional and a required practice to attend to the needs of those who are poor and weak – a covenantal obligation. The riches and social assets of the land are understood as common resources that are to be managed and deployed for the enhancement of the community by the empowerment of its weakest and most disadvantaged members. This specific and radical command to do justice is to characterise the whole life of Israel. The story of Achan shows the public quality of this demand, for Achan withheld for private purposes the goods of the community, and so did enormous damage to the community. The public good requires that active social power must be mobilised to augment the entire community and to resist personal enhancement of some at the expense of the others.

In today's India, for example, we have unprecedented economic growth but also increasing inequality, rural discontent and increased malnutrition and violence against women. Justice is denied to many. Individualism and communalism are on the rise and are contradictory to the biblical expectation of common good. What can we do to ensure justice for the weak?

† Dear God, just and loving, may we work towards enabling policy and practice for the common good of the land and its peoples.

For further thought

• Who are the weak in your community? What does your church do to fulfil God's command in relation to them?

Honour the covenant!

Joshua 9:3-21

'Let them live, but let them be woodcutters and water-carriers in the service of the whole assembly.' **(part of verse 21)**

From the perspective of caste, this story is not helpful for the Dalits, the group traditionally regarded as 'untouchable' in India. The text provides reason and justifies the relegation of a community to servitude for life, which bears similarity to the plight of countless Dalits in India. Fear and the desire for self preservation lead to the Gibeonite ruse, condemning them to a life of servitude. Fearing for their lives, they seek to enter into a peace treaty with the Israelites. They deceive Joshua by presenting themselves as a people from a faraway land that have heard of the saving deeds of Yahweh and are now prepared to become the servants of the Israelites. Joshua believes them and makes a treaty with them. The Israelites soon discover that the Gibeonites are in fact neighbours, living near them. But they are hindered from attacking them on account of the treaty. As a result of this ruse, the Gibeonites are rendered to serve as 'wood-cutters' and 'water-carriers' for the house of Yahweh and for the community of Israel, which, the text notes, 'they are to this day'.

Joshua is often critiqued for not having consulted Yahweh before making the treaty. But here is one example of a relationship made without violence and bloodshed. Even the Israelites benefited from not having to wage war. It is my hope that the Gibeonites eventually were able to do other things outside the tasks assigned to them – but for the time being they had life! Not a small matter. Would this not be the will of God?

† God of grace and mercy, please give me the grace and the strength to honour you by doing your will, to respect and value relationships and partnerships.

For further thought

- Read more about the situation of Dalits by visiting the National Campaign on Dalit Human Rights (www.ncdhr.org.in/). If you feel strongly about their plight, what do you make of Joshua's decision regarding the Gibeonites?

Wednesday 7 May
Honour creation!

Joshua 10:1-14

The sun stopped in the middle of the sky and delayed going down about a full day. There has never been a day like it before or since ... (verses 13b-14a)

In keeping with the covenant between Israel and Gibeon, Israel comes to the rescue of Gibeon when five kings attack them for being an ally of Israel. Yahweh was an active participant, for he rained huge hailstones upon them and killed many, more than those killed by the sword. Yahweh is said to have responded to Joshua, who commanded that the sun stand still and the moon to stop rising until the nation was avenged. Was Joshua really able to lengthen the battle day? Remarkable as this is, what the story highlights is two things: the response of creation/nature to Joshua's request, and Joshua's faith – a faith that can stop the earth from moving until the battle was won. Joshua seemed to know that creation can also contribute to and assist in God's salvific work; for creation too awaits its liberation from pollution and decay. God is and becomes present through creation.

The story emphasises the role played by nature in the securing of and the settlement in the land of promise. Many of us today pay little attention to creation and nature and its continued involvement in our affairs and, in so doing, ignore God who is revealed through creation.

† Creator God, help me be mindful of the relationship between human beings and nature and to remember that we are interdependent. Help me to live audaciously but to care for and respect nature and life, in the many paths where you lead me.

For further thought
• What part of growing, changing creation immediately around you can you recognise and honour today?

Thursday 8 May
Honour faith and duty!

Joshua 14:1-15

Then Joshua blessed Caleb son of Jephunneh and gave him Hebron as his inheritance. So Hebron has belonged to Caleb son of Jephunneh the Kenizzite ever since, because he followed the Lord, the God of Israel, wholeheartedly. (verses 13-14)

Joshua and Caleb were the minority in the group of twelve spies who brought back a report to Moses (Numbers 13 and 14). Their report pleased God, and for this they were spared and allowed to enter the promised land. Caleb held nothing back and surrendered completely to God. He did his duty and reported honestly and out of faith; he was patient, generous, courageous and trusting upon God's power and word.

Caleb approaches Joshua on his own initiative and requests the land. He is rewarded for his faithfulness and Hebron becomes his inheritance. But Hebron was not an easy place: it was the hill country, a rugged area, that was home to the *anakim*, the giants, the strongest of the Canaanite soldiers! But he was not deterred by this and was confident in his own capabilities and in God's promise and help to claim the land for the Israelites. The text calls upon each one of us to remember God's promises, and act on those promises with faith in God and in oneself as well. The promised land is one in which faith in God and commitment to duty is rewarded. Have there been times when you have disregarded an opportunity for growth and development? Why?

† God of promise, God of faith, help me use the guidance, the wisdom and the knowledge that you have given me for effective service in the church and to the world. Fulfil your promise in me for the sake of all human beings.

For further thought

• When have you disregarded an opportunity for growth and development?

Friday 9 May
Honour your inheritance!

Joshua 18:1-20

Joshua said to the Israelites, 'How long will you wait before you begin to take possession of the land that the LORD, the God of your ancestors, has given you?' (verse 3)

While boundaries and borders provide security, identity, and belonging, they also have the potential to create conflict because of the emotion evoked by such membership. In the promised land, tribal boundaries had to be established to avoid future boundary disputes. This had to be done soon. Besides, being allotted a portion of Yahweh's land and being able to live on it was proof of one's membership among God's people. The land therefore was the focus of one's practical response to the grace and goodness of God, theologically and ethically. Despite the long lapse of time from the entry into the land, seven tribes had not yet taken possession of the land assigned to them, meaning that they had not driven out the enemy. Joshua was concerned. Were the indigenous people too strong to be overpowered? If this was their inheritance, why were they hesitant? We often take our inheritance and blessings and directions for granted and ignore the value of appropriating them. Reasons could be many, ranging from fear to sheer laziness and indifference. How have you appropriated your inheritance in God's saving grace in your life? Reflect on this. It wasn't a theoretical question for Joshua and Israel, and neither is it for us.

† Patient and gentle God, I seek your help in acknowledging the inheritance I have in you. Help me stay motivated and to seize on opportunities for service and mission.

For further thought
• How have you appropriated your inheritance in God's saving grace in your life?

Honour life!

Joshua 20:1-9

Then the elders are to admit the fugitive into their city and provide a place to live among them. (verse 4b)

At a time when so-called places of safety and refuge have become potential death traps and abuse, Joshua 20 comes across as a strange text. The narratives about land distribution conclude with a section on the establishment of the cities of refuge. The tribes had been apportioned the land, much of the Canaanite territory had been occupied, and now it was time to implement the command given by Moses in Numbers 35:1-34. Six cities were to be appointed as cities of refuge for those who had killed accidentally, as a safe haven until a public trial decided on the issue. This was a divine mandate that recognised that offenders deserve to be punished but those who killed accidentally deserve mercy and a fair trial. These cities were strategically located on both sides of the Jordan; they provided asylum, safety and security. The manslayer stayed in the city of refuge – until the death of the residing High Priest, for his death cleared the guilt and restored fellowship in Israel. The cities were therefore a visible and tangible expression of God's commitment to the created order and to the preservation and maintenance of life.

What and where are our cities of refuge today, whether for the victim of abuse or the accidental manslayer? How can our lives be sources of refuge to another?

† God of mercy, God of life, grant us strength that we may give deeply of ourselves for the maintenance and perpetuation of life, yet never grow weak.

For further thought
• How can your city be a city of refuge? Visit http://www. cityofsanctuary.org/ to find many stories from the UK.

Readings in Joshua
3 Getting organised

This week's notes are by **Oral Thomas**

 Oral A W Thomas is a minister in the Methodist Church in the Caribbean and the Americas and a lecturer at the United Theological College of the West Indies. He is an Antiguan by birth and a Jamaican by marriage. He enjoys playing cricket, studying Caribbean political economy, and swimming off some of Antigua's three hundred and sixty-five beaches. He is the author of *Biblical Resistance Hermeneutics in a Caribbean Context* (Vermont 2010).

Sunday 11 May
God's word amidst violence

May

Joshua 21:1-19

The LORD commanded through Moses that you give us towns to live in, with pasture-lands for our livestock. (**verse 2**)

Joshua deals frankly with uprootedness, genocide, domination and imposition. For Caribbean people, Joshua recounts the experiences of uprootedness, dispossession, murder and exploitation by Europeans of the Caribbean from the 1400s to the 1800s. What, then, do these texts from the book of Joshua say to a people with a history of dispossession and domination? Is there a word from the Lord in the midst of blood and violence?

In Joshua 21 the Israelites are given towns and pasturelands, that is, a place or seat of governance and means of survival. This seeming willingness to hand over governance and means of survival does not seem to expose the hardships that would come to those whose lives and livelihoods are thrown into confusion. Peoples and their culture are involved, not just vegetation, bush and animals. This conquest is no mere clearing of land for beautification, like building lawns to enhance the beauty of the surroundings. All action to impose one's will on another, no matter the justification, involves the other's dignity and humanity and rejects God's purposes for well-being and empowerment.

† God of all people in all places, may love for the dignity of all human beings reign in our hearts.

Monday 12 May
Everywhere is war

Joshua 22:1-20

When they came to Geliloth near the Jordan in the land of Canaan, the Reubenites, the Gadites and the half-tribe of Manasseh built an imposing altar there by the Jordan. (verse 10)

This passage is not a simple quarrel about the placement of a building for worship. Neither is it a simple misunderstanding concerning the preference of the tribes of Gad, Reuben and Manasseh for the good grazing land of Gilead. Nor is it simply the desire to return to their waiting families, having participated in the conquest of the land.

Rather, this readiness 'to go to war against them' (verse 12) is also about the superiority and power of the majority to impose its will on the native inhabitants of the land. In other words, it is the conquerors imposing their will on the conquered.

Wherever there is domination and imposition of will of one people over another, it is never just a war or a just war. Where there is no justice, there is war.

In 1976, reggae artist Bob Marley famously recorded this perspective in the song 'War', using words from a speech made by Ethiopian Emperor Haile Selassie I before the United Nations General Assembly in 1963:

Until the philosophy which holds one race superior
And another inferior
Is finally and permanently
Discredited and abandoned
Everywhere is war … me say war

† God of justice, may your love for right relations and relationships between all people reign among people everywhere.

For further thought

• Where is there conflict in the world at the moment? Does it seem clear which party is in the right, or is it more ambiguous, as this conflict was?

Tuesday 13 May
Witnesses to a just God

Joshua 22:21-34

And the Reubenites and the Gadites gave the altar this name: A Witness Between Us – that the Lord is God. (**verse 34**)

May

As it turned out, the Reubenites, Gadites and the half-tribe of Manasseh have honourable intentions. Neither abandonment of belief in Yahweh (apostasy) nor attributing obligation and devotion to another God besides Yahweh (idolatry) is their objective.

The real issue is the fear and self-interest of the majority of Israelite tribes. Having the benefit of remembering the punishment at the hands of Yahweh for their immoral relations with the daughters of Moab that led to the worshipping of the local God Ba'al (Numbers 25) and Achan stealing forbidden goods (Joshua 7), the Israelites do not want to suffer for the 'sins of others'. Fear and self-interest at home almost led to the wiping out of the tribes of the Reubenites, Gadites and the half-tribe of Manasseh, and not for the last time. Dominant powers are known more for subjugating, exploiting and alienating than for mutuality and respect.

In the native and Black experience of Caribbean people, the historical colonial economy and, often, the current global economy have been (and are) cruel, dominating powers. By the right hand of God, the dominated peoples of the world will not continue to suffer at the hands of dominant powers for ever. Reuben, Gad, and the half-tribe of Manasseh were listened to and injustice was averted. Surely a God who listens to and acts for the poor was active here. Surely this God must be active today!

† God of suffering people everywhere, may love for one another guide the daily life of all people.

For further thought

• Where might a God of justice be active in a conflict today, listening and building peace?

Wednesday 14 May
What God requires

Joshua 23:1-16

The Lord your God himself will push them out for your sake. He will drive them out before you and you will take possession of their land, as the Lord your God promised you. **(verse 5)**

While God fulfilled the promise of conquest to the Israelites without conditions, God still required the Israelites to practise justice and live in righteousness – their pathway to blessings and prosperity from then on. God entered into a covenant with Israel freely and graciously, purely out of love for God's chosen people. But Israel had to hold up its end of the agreement, too. The covenant didn't mean that Israel was guaranteed the blessing of security no matter what.

It is not always the case that the most faithful person is the most healthy, prosperous and blessed. To link faithfulness with blessings is to entertain the belief that God can be manipulated. God can choose to be distant and hidden, as the prophet Jeremiah argues against other prophets who peddle false hopes of security (Jeremiah 23:23). Job challenges God to defend his actions, and discovers that God stands not so much in the halls of justice but rather shrouded in mystery and approached only in faith (Job 38:1-2).

Many conquerors down the centuries have found that their regime fails when they do not practise justice. Would this be true for Israel? This is the question Joshua leaves the Israelites with. Joshua reminds us, too, and reminds all would-be conquerors: God cannot be manipulated! Practise justice and thereby uphold your end of the covenant.

† God of the conquered, may your love for freedom set captives free.

For further thought
• Where is the God of the conquered to be found in your society?

God of liberation

Joshua 24:1-13

So I gave you a land on which you did not toil and cities you did not build, and you live in them and eat from vineyards and olive groves that you did not plant. (verse 13)

The history recorded and told here by Joshua in his speech at Shechem is not simply facts about events. Here the record of experiences is told from the perspective of the actors, not those acted upon. We hear the Israelite version of the story, not the Canaanite one.

For the actors, God's intention for the liberation of the Israelites unfolded right from the start, beginning with God's call and guidance of Abraham and the patriarchs (verses 2-4), God's triumph over Egyptian might (verses 5-7) and God's fulfilment of the promise of the gift of land (verses 8-13). In other words, Israelite history did not happen by chance. God has been the initiator and actor.

Covered over by this history are the lives and livelihoods destroyed by the conquest – the experiences of the people who planted the vineyards and olive groves enjoyed by the Israelites. Their voices have been silenced. But perhaps we can hear their voices now, when we read this story with the experience of colonised people fresh in our minds. What are the voices saying? Is the God of liberation – the same God who led the Israelites to freedom from slavery – helping us hear them?

† God of tears, may you continue to hear the prayers of tears.

For further thought
• Listen for the voices of the silenced in your community today.

May

Choose and live

Joshua 24:14-28

But if serving the LORD seems undesirable to you, then choose for yourselves this day whom you will serve … as for me and my household, we will serve the LORD. (part of verse 15)

As he continues his speech, Joshua sets a decision before the Israelites. Joshua and his family are completely on the side of God (verse 15). By Joshua's example, the Israelites are now aware that they cannot profess loyalty to God *and* follow a god of their own making. They must choose. Here is no narrow nationalism and glory in conquest but a challenge to marry words and action. The idolatry of nationalism is an ever-present temptation and danger for Israel.

The Jamaican national hero and leader of an 1831 slave rebellion, Sam Sharpe, also put a choice to his followers. He was guided in part by Matthew 6:24 ('no one can serve two masters … you cannot serve God and money'), John 8:36 ('so if the Son sets you free, you will be free indeed'). After the rebellion was crushed, Sharpe's last words are recorded as, 'I would rather die among yonder gallows than live in slavery.'

Whether for the enslaved or free, the practice of justice and living in righteousness cannot be limited by those who hold the reins of power. It must be a way of life that all can enjoy. The saying 'Ah fo' we time now' means that the exercise of power will always lead to injustice.

We, too, have a decision: to follow the God of liberation, whatever the cost. Joshua and Sam Sharpe made their choice. What will yours be?

† God of well-being, may those who control the reins of power be guided by the power of love, not the love of power.

For further thought
• Where is the power of love, rather than the love of power, visible in your activities today?

Saturday 17 May
Open-ended

Joshua 24:29-33

After these things, Joshua son of Nun, the servant of the LORD, died at the age of a hundred and ten. (verse 29)

The choice that Joshua put to the assembly at Shechem resonated down Israelite history.

With the deaths of Joshua, Joseph and Eleazar, a new chapter begins in the life of Israel. The boundaries have now been set, and it is now up to the new leaders to lead the covenanted community in changing, rather than being changed by, their new home in the promised land.

But that was not the way things turned out. Israelite history shows that the Israelite community in Canaan was adopted by its new home more than they changed it. The prophetic ministry of Elijah and Hosea, for example, was a protest against Israel worshipping Canaanite gods (1 Kings 17 – 19). During the reign of Jehoash (2 Kings 12 ff), Ba'alism was a corrupt influence, and God sent Hosea as messenger to announce judgement (Hosea 2:6-7).

The Caribbean has a history of several hundred years' worth of Euro-American cultural imposition. But the history here is not finished yet. Matthew's Jesus has a sobering word for all involved in the process of adaptation: 'Woe to you, teachers of the law and Pharisees, you hypocrites! You travel over land and sea to win a single convert, and when you have succeeded, you make them twice as much a child of hell as you are' (Matthew 23:15). God in Christ will have the last word, not the nations of the world.

Israel's history was still open in the promised land as we conclude the book of Joshua. The history of the Caribbean and its peoples, too, is not yet finished. Where is God still seeking liberation in your community?

† God of truth and love, may we always seek your perfect way.

For further thought
• Is the world becoming more or less just and equitable?

The greening Spirit

1 At work in the whole creation

This week's notes are by **Robert Parkinson**

Robert Parkinson is a Baptist minister. Ordained in 1982, he has served congregations in the United States of America and the UK. He and his wife Dawn have three grown-up children. A student of the Hebrew Bible, Robert is passionate about biblical studies. In his spare time, he is an avid reader, a keen walker and a lover of the outdoors. He is minister of Didsbury Baptist Church in Manchester and an associate tutor with the Northern Baptist Learning Community.

May

Sunday 18 May
Wind over the waters

Genesis 1:1-2

Now the earth was formless and empty, darkness was over the surface of the deep, and the Spirit of God was hovering over the waters. (verse 2)

At creation, the Spirit of God was hovering over the face of the waters. Or was it? The New Revised Standard Version reads, 'a wind from God' rather than 'the Spirit of God'. The Hebrew *ruach* can be rendered either as 'wind' or 'spirit'. Both translations are valid but each paints a significantly different picture. For the NRSV, the wind seems to be an aspect of the chaos out of which God makes the world. In the NIV, the Spirit's presence seems to signal the beginning of God's creative work. A decision about the best translation involves other issues too. If we prefer 'spirit' to 'wind', should the first letter be capitalised, as in the NIV, or does this force us to think in terms of the Holy Trinity?

I prefer the translation offered by the NRSV. Even so, the wind sweeping over the face of the primordial waters is associated in some way with God. It is a 'divine wind' (New Jerusalem Bible), 'a wind from God'. Thus, even in the chaos, God is present. This is a common feature in the Bible readings for the coming week. In most of them we will find the Spirit of God at work creating, sustaining and affirming life all over God's world.

† Life-giving God, may your Spirit, as gentle breeze and mighty wind, inspire us to life, love and action in and for your world. Amen

Monday 19 May
God's wisdom and ours

Proverbs 3:13-20

[Wisdom's] ways are pleasant ways, and all her paths are peace. She is a tree of life to those who take hold of her; those who hold her fast will be blessed. By wisdom the LORD laid the earth's foundations, by understanding he set the heavens in place. (verses 17-19)

If the Spirit of God is thought to be present at the dawn of creation, so too is divine wisdom. For, according to verse 19, 'By Wisdom the Lord laid the earth's foundations'. Thus wisdom and the Spirit have become inextricably linked in our thinking. Joshua, we are told, 'was filled with the spirit of wisdom' (Deuteronomy 34:9). In the New Testament, the seven chosen to serve the church in Jerusalem were to be 'full of the Spirit and wisdom' (Acts 6:3) and Paul thought of wisdom as one of the gifts of the Spirit (1 Corinthians 12:8).

In Jewish thought, wisdom is identified with Torah. Thus, when the Torah scroll (containing the first five books of the Bible) is returned to the ark during the synagogue service, the words of this passage (verses 17-18) are recited. Christian theology associates divine wisdom not only with the Holy Spirit but also the eternal Word made flesh in Jesus Christ (John 1:14).

Our passage makes an audacious claim. The wisdom by which the world was made is now available to human beings! Whether we think of it as contained in Torah, imparted by the Spirit or made known in Jesus (and for me, it is all of the above), wisdom can be found by the person who searches for it as the most precious of all possessions.

In a world besotted by money and power, we do well to remember that wisdom is more precious than rubies and yields better returns than silver or gold.

† God who made the world by wisdom, save us from the folly of godless ways and grant us the wisdom to make the world of human affairs according to the ways of peace. Amen

For further thought

- What do the levels of violence in our world suggest about the priority we give to the pursuit of wisdom?

Tuesday 20 May
Theatres of God's glory

Psalm 19:1-10

The heavens declare the glory of God; the skies proclaim the work of his hands. Day after day they pour forth speech; night after night they reveal knowledge ... The commands of the LORD are radiant, giving light to the eyes. (verses 1-2, 8b)

Sometimes people say to me, 'I don't have to go to church or read the Bible to hear the word of God; I would rather take a walk in the countryside and commune with nature.' Of course, they have a point. Today's psalm agrees with them in part. God can indeed be 'heard' through what we see. The world is, as Calvin expressed it, 'the theatre of God's glory'. Our psalm focuses particularly on the sky and especially the sun. Without speech these wonders of creation speak of God's glory and show forth God's radiance.

Conversely, however, we can also 'see' through what we hear. For the word of God in scripture gives insight and illumination. 'The commands of the Lord are radiant, giving light to the eyes'.

It is thought that, in the construction of Psalm 19, two (or perhaps three) psalms have been joined together. Where once one psalm extolled the glory of nature and another the radiance of God's instruction, now both poles are brought together. Those who find God in nature are affirmed and invited to see God's radiance also in scripture and those who hear God in scripture are invited to hear him too in the natural world. It ought not to be one or the other. We are invited to see and hear the work and word of God and pay attention to it.

† Glorious God, open my eyes to the wonders of your world and my ears to the music of your word. In Jesus' name. Amen

For further thought

• Are you more a reader of the word or a reader of the world? Why not major in the other approach this week?

Wednesday 21 May
Never again!

Genesis 8:15-22

The LORD smelled the pleasing aroma and said in his heart: 'Never again will I curse the ground because of humans, even though every inclination of the human heart is evil from childhood. And never again will I destroy all living creatures… As long as the earth endures, seedtime and harvest, cold and heat, summer and winter, day and night will never cease.'
(verses 21-22)

In this section of Genesis, God is given human characteristics. God 'smells' the aroma of Noah's offering and is pleased with it. God 'speaks in his heart'. Having learned that the flood has solved nothing, God resolves never again to punish the earth or its creatures on account of human wrongdoing. Other parts of the Bible resist such anthropomorphic language but here it is allowed to stand as a way of telling us something about God.

God's great creative project was threatened by human evil but, after the flood, God determines that human evil will not triumph. God is for the world and its creatures. God is for humanity, the very pinnacle of God's creative work. Even so, it is human beings who turn out to be the greatest threat to the creation. They incline towards evil and this inclination affects everyone and everything around them. What is more, the attempt to rid the world of this evil is seen in these verses to have been unsuccessful. Even after the flood, when only righteous Noah and family remain, 'every inclination of the human heart is evil'. God knows that, while human beings remain on the earth, evil will be an ever-present possibility. The dark side of human freedom is human evil. What is new, however, is the determination that this will not be allowed to derail God's purpose for the world and for humanity. Christians sometimes give up on the world but God never will. This is God's promise, God's covenant, with the earth.

† Creator God, whose faithfulness is demonstrated with each new day, we thank you for your commitment to the earth and we ask you to strengthen in us the resolve to act for its good. Amen

For further thought

• Find the words of the hymn 'Great is thy faithfulness' (T O Chisholm). In what ways does the hymn reflect or not reflect Genesis 8?

Generativity

Matthew 13:31-33

The kingdom of heaven is like a mustard seed … Though it is the smallest of all seeds, yet when it grows, it is the largest of garden plants and becomes a tree, so that the birds come and perch in its branches. (part of verses 31-32)

I am writing this on a cold day in January having just returned from a walk round the park. The days are still short and dark but are just beginning to lengthen very slightly. This is enough for a few birds to begin collecting nesting materials and for some of the earlier budding trees to begin to green. The changes are almost imperceptible. One must look carefully to detect any change but it is certainly happening. Spring is on its way and new life will soon be everywhere. People of faith, of course, detect the power of God in the ability of the natural world to keep growing, changing, reproducing and evolving.

Jesus tells two parables, about mustard seed and leaven, to suggest something about the presence and growth of the kingdom of God. They offer encouragement to those who wonder if or when the reign of God will ever really come. It is already here, says the Gospel of Matthew, in the person and work of Jesus, in the existence of the church and in a thousand almost imperceptible signs. God is at work if only you would open your eyes to see it.

There is perhaps also a word of challenge for every disciple. If creation is imbued with hidden but creative energy and if God's kingdom is being unleashed with comparable dynamic power, what about the people of God? Are we not called to a similar generativity? I wonder, are we living and working, however quietly and unobtrusively, so as to make a difference in the world of tomorrow?

† Generative God, forgive us our dull resignation to the way things are and grant us the power to live so as to make the world a better place for future generations. Amen

For further thought

- What values do you hope to pass on to the next generation? What are you doing to make the world a better place?

Creation groans – and so do we!

Romans 8:22-27

We know that the whole creation has been groaning as in the pains of childbirth right up to the present time. Not only so, but we ourselves, who have the firstfruits of the Spirit, groan inwardly as we wait eagerly for our adoption to sonship, the redemption of our bodies. (verses 22-23)

The earth is suffering. 'The whole creation', says Paul, 'has been groaning as in the pains of childbirth right up until the present time.' Perhaps Paul is thinking of natural disasters, of earthquakes and volcanic eruptions, or perhaps he has in mind the perpetual cycle of life and death within the created order. He clearly could have no comprehension of the suffering of the planet at human hands today. Still, Paul imagines the natural world writhing in pain as it awaits a new day of ecological harmony and peace.

For Paul, a transformation is taking place. In Christ, a process has begun that affects not only believers but the whole universe. Those who have come to faith in Christ are in on the early stages of this transformation or recreation. The Spirit brings the benefits of the age to come to the believers in Jesus living in this new but yet-to-be-completed age. The same Spirit fills our hearts with hope and with the strength to intercede and thereby work with God in the unfolding of God's purpose.

God has not given up on the world in favour of an ethereal heavenly kingdom. Rather, God is at work in and for the whole universe. All creation seems to anticipate its own liberation from pain and death as it is caught up in the longing of God's people for final redemption. This longing is not so much to be liberated from the world but to be redeemed along with the world.

† God of Creation, may your Spirit so fill our hearts that we live and long not only for our good but for the good of all the world. Amen

For further thought

• Do you think that Christians are sometimes too heavenly minded to be any earthly good?

Saturday 24 May
Creation care

Genesis 1:26 – 2:1

God blessed them and said to them, 'Be fruitful and increase in number;
fill the earth and subdue it. Rule over the fish of the sea and the birds
in the sky and over every living creature that moves on the ground.'
(verse 28)

In this passage, God blesses human beings and commands them to
'fill', 'subdue' and 'rule' the earth and its creatures. This is sometimes
read as a mandate to exploit the earth and its resources without
regard for the damage that may be caused. Read in this way, the
text promotes a humans-against-nature model for human life and
endeavour. Is this the best way to read the passage? I think not.

In Genesis 1, human beings are distinct from the animals they
are to 'rule'. The fish, birds and other animals, like the plants,
are brought forth from the earth or the waters. Only of human
beings is it said that they are made directly by God and in God's
image. Humans are set apart from the rest of creation and are
given a governing role but they are in no way seen to be against
the natural world. The commission to rule over creation is not a
licence to exploit the earth irresponsibly. Rather, as those made in
God's image, humans are to function as stewards of God's good
earth. They are to care for the world as God's representatives. They
are to become partners with God in the task of tending the earth
and caring for its creatures. This mandate confers on humankind
immense responsibility, for human beings are to treasure and tend
the world as God would.

† Life-giving God, thank you for the good earth on which we depend for our
survival. Forgive us our misuse of the world's resources and help us to live
sustainably for the sake of all. Amen

For further thought

• Check out the work of A Rocha at www.arocha.org and consider
becoming involved with one of its projects.

The greening Spirit

2 The Spirit as the source of life and fruitfulness

This week's notes are by **Paul Nicholson**

Paul Nicholson SJ is a Roman Catholic priest, a member of the Society of Jesus, popularly known as the Jesuits. Since 2006 he has been based in Birmingham, UK, responsible for the first two years of training (the novitiate) for candidates for the order from Britain, Ireland, Flanders and Holland. He joined the Jesuits in 1978, after completing a zoology degree at Durham University, and was ordained in 1988. He has since worked principally in the fields of spirituality and social justice. He is editor of the British Jesuit spirituality journal *The Way,* and author of *Growing Into Silence*.

Sunday 25 May
Meeting God's Spirit at home

Psalm 87

Glorious things are said of you, city of God … As they make music they will sing, 'All my fountains are in you.' (verses 3, 7)

In the northern hemisphere, where I live, it is now late spring. Within nature, signs of life and growth are everywhere. Trees have new leaves, animals are nursing their newborn young, the hours of daylight continue to lengthen. The Bible teaches that the ultimate source of all life and growth is God's Spirit. In our prayer over the next few days, we'll trace the work of the Spirit, bringing life and fruitfulness to human beings and the whole of creation.

Psalm 87 sings the praises of Zion, God's holy city. Happy indeed those who live there! They are proud to think that their names will be recorded in the list of her inhabitants. In the last line, they proclaim 'all my fountains are in you'. The Spirit has given them all good things through this city in which they live.

Yet the Spirit is alive in all cities, and indeed everywhere on earth, for those who can see. The Spirit gives me good gifts every day through my city of Birmingham, its people and its institutions. My neighbours are mostly friendly. Public transport lets me travel round easily. I can rely on gas, electricity and water. Not everyone is so fortunate. But most can think of gifts they receive simply from the place they live in.

† Lord, your Spirit works in city and town, village and countryside. Help me recognise the new life your Spirit offers daily here, where I live.

Filled with the Spirit of Christ

Isaiah 11:1-5

The Spirit of the L<small>ORD</small> will rest on him – the Spirit of wisdom and of understanding, the Spirit of counsel and of might, the Spirit of knowledge and of the fear of the L<small>ORD</small>. (verse 2)

Ignatius of Loyola, a sixteenth-century Basque nobleman who founded the religious order I belong to, practised a form of prayer he called the 'discernment of spirits'. This involves carefully reviewing, with God's help, the various influences underlying your actions. Did you criticise colleagues in a genuine effort to help them improve, or because you were jealous of their success? Did you go out of your way to help someone prompted by real charity, or were you just hoping to be noticed? This kind of discernment recognises that we can be influenced by good and bad motives, and we can grow in Christian discipleship by being more aware of these influences. Ultimately, the good influences come from God's Spirit, the bad from everything in the world that opposes God.

Isaiah's words here, applied in the Gospels to Jesus, speak of the nature of the Spirit who will motivate him throughout his life and ministry. If I open myself to God's Spirit breathing life into me, I too will grow to be wise and understanding, knowledgeable and God-fearing, drawing on God's power and able to offer others wise counsel. And as I grow in this way, I will find myself more ready to share Christ's mission, as it is described in the second part of this passage: to 'give decisions for the poor of the earth'. Because one way of judging the motives of any Christian is to look at how far their actions benefit those most in need.

† Father, your Spirit is in work at me, as it was in your Son Jesus. Help me to be open to the Spirit prompting my actions, so that I grow more like Christ each day.

For further thought

• What decisions, large or small, will you be making today? How might they help the most needy around you?

Tuesday 27 May
Fresh green shoots of the Spirit

Isaiah 55:10-13

As the rain and the snow come down from heaven, and do not return to it without watering the earth and making it bud and flourish, so that it yields seed for the sower and bread for the eater, so is my word that goes out from my mouth. (verses 10-11a)

Three houseplants stand on a cupboard in front of my office window. I'm not the greatest of gardeners, and don't always tend them as often as I should. But when I do finally notice them looking parched and wilting, I'm always amazed by how quickly they respond to a little water. Almost as I look, stems become firmer and leaves grow green and healthy again.

Isaiah tells us that God's word is at least as effective as that. When God's word is spoken, when God's Spirit is sent out into the world, expect things to change! Nor do they change simply at random. God has a purpose in sending out the Spirit and, in the end, we are assured God's purposes will be carried out.

Sometimes God's purposes will be large scale and clear, if not to everybody, at least to many. When the Berlin Wall fell, and with it seemingly impregnable Communist oppression in Eastern Europe – or when in South Africa apartheid was abolished without the level of violence that many had feared – Christians of many denominations felt that they had cause to rejoice and thank God, as Isaiah believes the people will do in seeing God's work. Perhaps more often, the Spirit operates on a level noticeable only by those who stay alert. That's when I'll usually become aware first of the new life around me, in myself, those close by, in a situation or a problem. Once I notice the new life – like the green shoots of a watered plant – I can trace it back to God's Spirit active in my world.

† Send forth your Spirit, O Lord, and we shall be created. And you will renew the face of the earth.

For further thought
• Can you be on the lookout today for those signs of life and light, and energy that point to God's Spirit at work?

Is love all you need?

Song of Songs 2:1-3, 11-13; 4:12-15

Like a lily among thorns is my darling among the young women. Like an apple tree among the trees of the forest is my beloved among the young men... Arise, my darling; my beautiful one, come with me. (verses 2-3 and 10a)

The Song of Songs is often read as an extended allegory, a book describing at length through its images the love between God and God's people. Maybe, though, it can also be approached more at face value, as a love-song, delighting in the passion that exists between two people. The version of the Bible used here (the New International Version), unlike others, actually supports this reading, by assigning alternate sections of the poem to a lover and his beloved.

Where, after all, do you learn what the love of God is like, that love which is one of the greatest gifts of God's Spirit? Usually through the experience of being loved by other people. Family first, if you're fortunate, through the love of parents and siblings. Perhaps then from the loving acceptance of friends. But for many people the chief experience of loving and being loved will come from their relationship with the one they fall in love with, someone who perhaps in time becomes a husband or a wife. It is this kind of love that the Song of Songs revels in.

In that first flush of love, it's not difficult to have the beloved at the centre of your world. No self-sacrifice is too great, no price too high to pay. No doubt this fire dies down. But if you're fortunate you'll have found it replaced by something even deeper, and stronger, and longer-lasting. Our Song sings of this love, and assures me that God loves me every bit as passionately.

† For a few minutes, pray the phrase 'God is love' in tune with your breathing; speak the word 'God' as you breathe in and the words 'is love' as you breathe out. Let this mantra fill your consciousness.

For further thought

• Take time today thinking of someone you love, or someone who loves you. What might this tell you of the way God feels about you?

Thursday 29 May (Ascension Day)
Source of all fruitfulness

John 15:1-8

I am the vine, you are the branches. If you remain in me and I in you, you will bear much fruit; apart from me you can do nothing … This is to my Father's glory, that you bear much fruit, showing yourselves to be my disciples. (verse 5 and 8)

Today much of the Christian Church remembers that day when Christ, after his Resurrection, finally returned to his Father in heaven. It would be easy to interpret this as an abandonment. After three decades with us, Jesus, God-made-man, leaves, not to return again until the end of time. But the Gospel is clear that we are not being abandoned. More than that, only when Jesus goes can God's Spirit be sent in full strength, working through each of us and indeed throughout the world.

Not far from where I grew up, in the royal palace at Hampton Court, there is a huge grapevine, nearly 250 years old and said to be the largest in the world. There are grapes growing 120 feet from the main stem. But they can do so only by drawing water and nutrients from that stem. Make a single cut anywhere along that length and the grapes would die. This is the image that Jesus evokes in today's Gospel. He is the main stem, and God's Spirit flows from him into us, no matter how distant we may feel from him at times. If the Spirit flows into us, it is certain that we will live fruitfully in the world.

Grapes, the 'fruit of the vine', and the wine that comes from them, are rich biblical images for the joy the Spirit can stir up in the hearts of men and women. Our call is to be channels of that joy, through our close connection with Jesus as he is close to his Father.

† Lord Jesus, never permit me to separate myself from you. Grant that I may love you always; and then do with me whatever you will.

For further thought
• 'No man is an island', said the preacher-poet John Donne. Notice today how many people you are connected to in different ways.

Friday 30 May
Scattered by the handful

Matthew 13:1-9

Then he told them many things in parables saying: 'A farmer went out to sow his seed … Still other seed fell on good soil, where it produced a crop – a hundred, sixty or thirty times what was sown. Whoever has ears, let them hear.' (verses 3 and 8-9)

Packets of the larger kind of seed, intended for gardeners more than farmers, will often tell you now how many seeds they contain: twenty-five lupins, a dozen sweet peas. In sowing them you hope to get, with luck, very nearly one healthy plant for each seed sown. It's a completely different kind of sowing that is being done in this parable. The farmer of Jesus' time throws out handfuls of seeds, and they fall all over the place. Some will grow, many will not. The farmer makes little attempt to ensure that each seed finds its own patch of fertile ground. What matters is the overall harvest, not so much the individual plant.

So it is, Jesus assures us, with the work of the Spirit. God's Spirit gives me all sorts of gifts and talents, leads me into all kinds of opportunities and situations. Some will prove productive, drawing myself or others closer to God, building up corners of God's kingdom. Others, which might in other circumstances have been equally fruitful, here and now lead nowhere. It's important that I don't spend so much time grieving over lost opportunities or roads not taken that I miss the continual newness of what the Spirit is leading me into. Only in that way will I, or rather the Spirit in me, be able to produce the rich harvest that God intends.

† Spirit of God, day by day you scatter across my life people and opportunities, gifts and challenges. Help me to recognise and nurture these, for the growth of your kingdom here on earth.

For further thought
• In any local or global news you encounter today, try to notice signs of God's Spirit building up justice, peace, and the integrity of creation.

Saturday 31 May
The hidden work of God's Spirit

Luke 12:22-28

I tell you, do not worry about your life, what you will eat; or about your body, what you will wear … Consider how the wild flowers grow. They do not labour or spin. Yet I tell you, not even Solomon in all his splendour was dressed like one of these. (verses 22 and 27)

All this week, our prayer has been tracing the work of God's Spirit, in my own life, in the people around me, and in the world in general. Perhaps surprisingly, only one of the scripture passages has explicitly mentioned the Spirit. Yet that seems to be the way that God chooses to operate in our world. The work of the Spirit is largely hidden, and recognised only by those who take the time to trace the results of this work back to its source.

This situation can lead to the kind of worry that Jesus is at pains here to dispel. I become anxious for myself. Do I have all that I need, and can I be sure that I will continue to have it in the future? Or I grow concerned about aspects of my faith. Is God's Spirit really at work in the world, in my life? Even when so much seems humdrum, or unimportant, or at times even heading away from God and God's dream for the world and for me?

It is to this kind of situation that Jesus speaks when he says 'Don't worry!' If you look around you confidently, as our prayer has tried to do in the last few days, you will see that God's Spirit is indeed alive and active. You have your part to play in carrying out God's plans. But it is God alone who assures the eventual outcome.

† Grant me, Lord, an optimistic outlook, full of hope; confident not in my own powers, but in the power of your Spirit always at work in our world.

For further thought

• Choose something currently worrying you, in your own life or beyond. Simply sit quietly with it for a few minutes, aware of God with you.

The greening Spirit

3 The Spirit restores life to decaying creation

This week's notes are by **Annie Heppenstall**

 Annie Heppenstall is the author of *Reclaiming the Sealskin*, *Wild Goose Chase* and *The Healer's Tree*, published by Wild Goose Publications, and *Hiding in God*, published by Kevin Mayhew. She is qualified as a teacher and has also trained in counselling skills and spiritual direction. Annie has a degree in Theology and Religious Studies and has held various roles serving church communities in different ways, through lay ministry. She is a professed member of the Third Order of the Society of St Francis and lives with her husband and son in a culturally diverse area of Birmingham.

Sunday 1 June
Outer journey, inner journey

Isaiah 35

The desert and the parched land will be glad; the wilderness will rejoice and blossom. (verse 1)

The text today sets the scene for the week ahead, with its images of fresh water and greenery in the desert, human healing and a clear path allowing return to Zion. While the picture is full of hope, 'Zion' presents a challenge. We are painfully aware of the turmoil in the lands of the Bible today, and the daily risk-making, partially informed judgements that affect our actions, words and prayers. The significance and the violence of the place awakens strong feelings – sorrow perhaps, anger and hatred, or fervent hope, but how often the Christ-like love of the true peacemaker? This week especially, notice thoughts and feelings arising from the passages, and invite the Holy Spirit to transform your own inner desert into life-giving and creative love.

Whatever our opinion and perspective on 'Zion', the unique experience of the Jewish people – crushed, exiled and then brought back to their homeland – and the extraordinary visions arising from that time, can help us to contemplate our own walk with God and our desire to come 'home' in peace, wholeness and joy. The vision of restoration is also integral to the Christian calling, for we are emissaries in the world of God's City of Peace. The gifts God gives us are leaves for the healing of the nations.

† God, rain down love! Let the Holy Spirit's fruits grow abundantly in me, that I may serve you and your creation well. Amen

Monday 2 June
In love and compassion

Hosea 2:14-23

I will betroth you to me for ever; I will betroth you in righteousness and justice, in love and compassion. (verse 19)

The theme of marriage takes up a great deal of the book of Hosea, who enters into a difficult relationship with a former sex-worker struggling to settle down into monogamous life. God uses this as an illustration of the troubled relationship between the chosen people – the bride – and God. In today's passage, however, all the love of God for the Jewish people wells up in a promise of renewed relationship; despite everything, the divine impulse is still towards peace and harmony, represented by the abundance of nature.

Although we may begin by looking critically at a people long ago, their situation holds up a mirror for us to look at ourselves. We call the church the bride of Christ and, mystically, the soul has often been described as God's beloved. What does it mean then, to be so loved by God? What is expected of us? What is forgiven us? How well and how eagerly do we return the love God bestows on us day by day? And how often are we seduced away from the values of the kingdom, by our hunger for attention, self-promotion, material comfort and status?

Commitment to God is commitment to a relationship that requires a fidelity we struggle to maintain. Our hope lies in God's grace: divine love forgives, and time and again sweeps clean and offers a new beginning. Restoration is ongoing, and needs to be, because of our human weakness.

† In the words of Charles Wesley (1707–1788): 'Jesu lover of my soul/let me to thy bosom fly/…Safe into the haven guide;/Oh, receive my soul at last.'

For further thought
• When have you noticed the tug of the Holy Spirit in your life, leading you back into the 'wilderness' to rediscover your love of God?

June

Return and repentance

> ### Joel 2:21b-27
>
> *You will have plenty to eat, until you are full, and you will praise the name of the LORD your God, who has worked wonders for you; never again will my people be shamed.* (verse 26)

Today's passage is the second half of a text (2:15-27) often used in the Jewish Shabbat Shuvah, the Sabbath of Return and Repentance, which falls between the solemn holy days Rosh Hashana and Yom Kippur. This special sabbath emphasises the process of repentance, lamentation, forgiveness by God and restoration to relationship. The promise of natural abundance follows a collective expression of sorrow for rebellion against God. The divine reassurance to these Jewish worshippers in verse 26, repeated in the next verse for emphasis – 'never again will my people be shamed' – haunts us. We know that many shameful acts have been perpetrated against the Jewish people over the centuries, escalating to (but sadly not ending with) the atrocity of the Holocaust.

The book of Joel invites us to look with humility at ourselves and our relationship with our brothers and sisters the Jews. We include ourselves into the Jewish hope 'by adoption' through Christ, but should beware selective reading, the sifting out of words of hope and joy, while overlooking the essential call for self-reflection and repentance. Similarly, although we believe the words of promise apply to us, we need to avoid the implication that they no longer apply to the people to whom they were spoken.

It is the same Holy Spirit who drove Jesus into the wilderness to face temptation that stirs our conscience and calls us to wrestle with the question of how to live on God's earth and how to relate to other peoples, other creatures – *all* God's children. Jesus' first instruction is 'repent'. Second comes the call to 'believe the good news' (Mark 1:15).

† Give me a spirit of humility, O God, that I may be so emptied of my self-centredness and so filled with your love that I may know your indwelling presence in me and in all your children. Amen

For further thought

• When and where have you noticed the process of repentance, lamentation, forgiveness by God and reconciliation in your own spiritual journeying?

Wednesday 4 June
God's agents of mercy

Isaiah 61:1-6, 11

They will rebuild the ancient ruins and restore the places long devastated;
they will renew the ruined cities that have been devastated for
generations. (verse 4)

Today's passage is very down-to-earth, a picture of God's justice
and mercy at work in the world. In Isaiah 44:28 we discover how
this vision was actualised: God's agent of mercy was the Emperor
of the Persians, Cyrus, who decided to let the Jewish people go
home from exile.

We know so much more about global affairs than people did in the
time of Cyrus. We see, and sometimes experience, the bloodshed of
nations rising and falling, walls erected and demolished, orchards
and crops destroyed and replanted, peoples oppressed and peoples
liberated. Watching all this unfold day by day can sometimes be
too much for us to take in: there is so much suffering, so much
anger and confusion, even in our own hearts. Yet there is also
hope, sometimes in unexpected places. God, it seems, does not
always work through those we might expect. How often do our
own leaders – even our church leaders – disappoint us? Yet where
are the strong voices of compassion, of mercy, justice, wisdom and
the will not just to talk about doing good but to bring it about in
the world? Here are God's agents, touched whether they know it
or not by the Spirit of God's love. When John's disciples ask Jesus if
he is 'the one' (Matthew 11:2-6), Jesus refers to empirical evidence.
'The blind receive sight … good news is proclaimed to the poor… '.
Even now, the Spirit is at work in the world, through many agents
of mercy.

† Holy One, let me see you at work in the world and rejoice; and let me stand
among your blessed, the peacemakers and mercy-bringers. Amen

For further thought
• When have you been challenged by the good deeds of
  somebody outside the Christian faith?

157

The source of living water

Ezekiel 47:1-12

Swarms of living creatures will live wherever the river flows. There will be large numbers of fish, because this water flows there and makes the salt water fresh; so where the river flows everything will live. (verse 9)

The river in Ezekiel's vision follows the route of the primal river of the garden of Eden. It continues to gush forth, but now it emerges from the foundations of the Temple, which is mystically equated with Eden. Paul tells us our own bodies are the Holy Spirit's temple (1 Corinthians 3:16) and Jesus describes living water – the Spirit – welling up within our hearts (John 7:38). A Christian reading of this vision, then, can help us look into our own inner being, and the presence of God's Holy Spirit within us. But, like flowing water, the Spirit is not static; it does not pool up in us for our own benefit. The Holy Spirit flows out into the world, for the good of all.

Ezekiel's vision shows us the nature of the Spirit's work: to bring life to what was dead. This is not a human work. No labourer has planned a course and dug out the channel down which the river runs; it has a freedom and power of its own, to refresh and to spread joy. We cannot predict what blessings will come, once the Spirit starts to flow, and we cannot choose what works it will do or not do. In the vision, this grace-filled blessing is shown by the trees that grow along the water's edge, bearing nourishing fruit and leaves for healing. How, then, do we become sources of this miraculous Spirit, so that the living water can flow from us, and the fruits of the Holy Spirit ripen in us as gifts to the world?

† Empty me, O God, that I may be filled to overflowing with your living love, for the good of all. Amen

For further thought

• When have you felt stirred by the Spirit of God's love, to let love flow freely through you?

Friday 6 June
The fullness of God: around and within

Colossians 1:15-20

For God was pleased to have all his fullness dwell in him. (verse 19)

This remarkable passage about the 'cosmic Christ' takes a theme already existent in Hebrew scripture – that of God's wisdom as described in Proverbs 8 and some inter-testamental scriptures such as the Wisdom of Solomon. Wisdom is pre-existent and through her all things come into being. She is a reflection, emanation or feminine personification of God. Paul, in 1 Corinthians 1 – 2 makes it clear that, to us, Christ is God's wisdom. (The opening of John's Gospel uses the term '*logos*' or 'word', but the concept is similar.) The risen Jesus is more than his human companions ever imagined: uncontainable, unfathomable, limitless, undying, pre-existent; he is the meaning, purpose and agent of all that is. What a claim!

Later, in Colossians 3:11, Paul adds that 'Christ is all and in all.' Christ is everywhere. The thought echoes a verse from Jeremiah 23:24, where God asks, 'Do not I fill heaven and earth?' And in today's passage, we read that God is pleased for all that divine fullness to dwell in Christ. What does that mean for us, as we look around us at other people and living things, except that the whole of creation is infused with the divine wisdom of Christ, as are we? This is surely a demand to look at all creation as holy and to search for Christ within ourselves and in all we meet: it is not just we who are temples of the Holy Spirit.

† 'Christ be with me, Christ within me, Christ behind me, Christ before me …
Christ in hearts of all that love me, Christ in mouth of friend and stranger.' Amen
(from 'St Patrick's Breastplate', trans. Cecil Frances Alexander, 1818–1895)

For further thought

• In whom do you find it most difficult to find Christ's presence? Is that your failing or theirs?

The community of God's love

Revelation 21:1-4; 22:1-5

He will wipe every tear from their eyes. There will be no more death or mourning or crying or pain, for the old order of things has passed away. (verse 4)

There is a connection between this vision and that of Ezekiel, which we read on Thursday. Ezekiel saw the Temple at the source of Eden's river, and now John sees a whole new city around the Temple. The water flows down the high street and the healing trees are now within the holy city. This is still Eden; paradise now has a thriving community of love at its centre. The vision brings us back to God's ideal, a time when there is no more death or suffering. (In Eden, there was no killing; the creatures all ate vegetation.)

'How can this be?' we might ask. There would indeed need to be a fundamental change if there were no more decay – would there still be birth? What would worms eat? Would the world not become full up? Is this a different *kind* of world? We do not and cannot know or understand in any literal sense. But the vision that God gives us is that the transformation we await is one of healing and peace, and in this we can trust. Yet is this simply a vision of the future? In some sense, just as Eden has always existed in the longing of our hearts, so too does this reality. We live in the community of God's love – God's presence our light, God's Spirit within us our inspiration and impulse to do good. How do we get to this place, if not by the work of the Holy Spirit, which gradually washes away the violence within us, to make us into emissaries of that city of peace?

† Bring me into your city of peace, O God; be my light and my joy, and live in me so all the world may know your love. Amen

For further thought

• What does it mean, what does it involve, to belong to the city of God?

2 Corinthians

1 Treasure in jars of clay

This week's notes are by **Andrew Boakye**

 Andrew Boakye is a Graduate Teaching Assistant in New Testament at the University of Manchester, with degrees in Theology and Biblical Studies. For his PhD he is studying the significance of resurrection and restoration in Galatians, and the implications for the way we think about identity in the church. When not reading the Greek New Testament, he is watching sci-fi thrillers, listening to obscure underground rap music, teaching his kids to box or cheering on Tottenham Hotspur.

Sunday 8 June (Pentecost)
Comforted – and comforting

2 Corinthians 1:1-11

Praise be to ... the Father of compassion and the God of all comfort, who comforts us in all our troubles, so that we can comfort those in any trouble with the comfort we ourselves receive from God. (part of verses 3-4)

June

The letter of 2 Corinthians is decidedly 'cross-shaped'. Paul and his entourage were preaching throughout the Mediterranean that the apparent catastrophe of Jesus' execution mysteriously contained the fulfilment of God's ancient promises. This narrative of victory from suffering had now been cast on a powerful canvas: the Resurrection of Jesus, life coming from death (1:9).

Easter was for Paul a template for how God was repairing a sin-ravaged world. Paul wanted the Corinthians to know how he and his companions had suffered in Asia and been delivered. Readers are privy in this emotionally fraught letter to how Paul suffered at the hands of his Corinthian opponents and was delivered. Jesus' example, mirrored in Paul, was being mirrored in Corinth.

On 17 January 2010, my third child (a son – we called him Noah hoping he might be saved through the waters) was stillborn at 36 weeks, after months of complications. Once we had asked all the 'Why us?'-type questions, my wife and I reflected on the text above and found peace and clarity: 'We suffered so God could comfort other sufferers through us.' Pain is not avoidable but it can either be gnawing ache, or healing tool. Is your suffering helping other sufferers today?

† God of all comfort, please take my pain in your hands today, and use it to take someone else's away.

Monday 9 June
Whom can we trust?

2 Corinthians 1:12-22

For no matter how many promises God has made, they are 'Yes' in Christ. And so through him the 'Amen' is spoken by us to the glory of God.
(verse 20)

A great poet once said 'hope deferred makes the heart sick' (Proverbs 13:12). Some sickened Corinthian hearts questioned Paul's integrity because he changed his plans to visit them on his way to Macedonia. The sad truth is that, following the seemingly poor reception of 1 Corinthians, Paul made a hasty and ill-fated trip to Corinth that ended disastrously. Mentioned in chapter 2 verse 1, it was to forestall any further nasty scenes that he opted against his planned return. Paul assures his audience that his trustworthiness as a gospel envoy is derived from God's own faithfulness (1:17-20). He was not what we might call a 'fast-talker' – his intentions were honest, because they were God's.

As I write, the newspapers are replete with reports of mud-slinging between presidential candidates, revelations about the lurid vices of once respected and loved celebrities, and racism on football pitches. Opinions are divided, blame aimed at various parties and one question lingers – whom can we trust? As 2 Corinthians unfolds, the question of Paul's trustworthiness re-emerges at key moments. Is he a competent minister (3:1-5)? Can we trust such a poor speaker (10:10; 11:6), or an apostle who is constantly fighting his innumerable detractors (12:11-12)? Paul's answer also permeates the text: he cuts too frail a figure for the gospel's weight to rest on his shoulders. It can rest only on God, and this has the curious reverse effect of making the apostle confidently celebrate his shortcomings, for they accentuate the magnificence of God's powerful grace!

† God, whose answer is Yes in Christ, help me to live with courage and integrity.

For further thought

- Consider today whether you trust God with every part of your life.

Tuesday 10 June
You can't go home again

2 Corinthians 1:23 – 2:11

Anyone you forgive, I also forgive. And what I have forgiven – if there was anything to forgive – I have forgiven in the sight of Christ for your sake, in order that Satan might not outwit us. (part of verses 10-11)

The American writer Thomas Wolfe wrote a hugely successful book depicting his hometown of Libya Hill, North Carolina, in a way that outraged its residents – so much so they sent him death threats. It was entitled *You Can't Go Home Again* (1940), which meant, after leaving one situation for a new environment, nothing is ever the same again. The old habitat has changed and, more important, so have you. You could return physically but it would never be the place you left and you can never be the person who left. So, after the public humiliation he experienced upon his second visit to Corinth, Paul thought it best not to return without breaking up the fallow ground. So he wrote a letter.

This was, however, no easy letter to write. Paul sobbed as he wrote (2:4), remembering the broken relationships, hurtful comments and sadness caused by those supposed to know better, and love better. Unfortunately the letter has not survived, although thin evidence supports the theory that 2 Corinthians chapters 10 to 13 are actually that letter. What we do know is that the letter caused hurt temporarily, but led to change, so Paul had no regrets, as he makes clear in chapter 7 verses 8-9. Paul could never go home again, though a new equilibrium could be more mature and sober and learn from past errors. First, the disciples had to forgive the ringleader of Paul's opponents. So total was their turnaround that the Corinthians chose to make an example of the troublemaker as described in today's reading, until Paul said 'enough is enough'. We give the accuser victory if we turn our frustration on each other.

† Forgiving God, give me the strength to let go of past hurts, and forgive those who caused them from my heart.

For further thought
• Is there someone you need to forgive today?

Wednesday 11 June
A letter from Christ

2 Corinthians 2:12 – 3:3 .

You show that you are a letter from Christ, the result of our ministry, written not with ink but with the Spirit of the living God, not on tablets of stone but on tablets of human hearts. (verse 3)

In the ancient world, travellers carried recommendation letters from trusted sources who could validate their dependability. We have examples from Cicero, Pliny and even Paul himself – in 8:16-23 he recommends his co-worker Titus to the Corinthians. Here, Paul asserts that the church is the only recommendation he requires. However, he compares his letter (the church) not to those letters presumably carried by his opponents, but to the Ten Commandments. Paul's reference to tablets of stone and tablets of human hearts alludes to similar imagery in Exodus 31:18, Jeremiah 31:31-34 and Ezekiel 36:26-27. How do these prophetic texts demonstrate Paul's credentials to those questioning them?

According to the prophetic promises Paul hints at, the Law once written on stone would be written on people's hearts (Jeremiah 31:33) and God would place his Spirit in people's hearts (Ezekiel 36:27) to help them obey it. If the church displays the presence of God's Law in the heart under the auspices of Spirit, then Paul's ministry amongst the Gentiles has birthed the new covenant community: God is their God, and they are his people, as in the Jeremiah passage. With such divine endorsement, who needs the endorsement of people?

† God of the prophets, with your Law in my heart through your Spirit, help me to be Jesus' representative to the world.

For further thought

• With an all-sufficient God, what stops you being a witness for Christ?

Alive!

2 Corinthians 3:4-11

Such confidence we have through Christ before God. Not that we are competent in ourselves to claim anything for ourselves, but our competence comes from God. (verses 4-5)

Paul's answer to the quandary he has raised is not complex – we are not confident in and of ourselves, but through Christ. Only Paul employs this word for 'confidence' in the entire New Testament: in Philippians 3:4 he uses it to depict the confidence he once had in his religious pedigree. It is God, Paul writes, who qualifies him and his co-missionaries to be ministers of this 'new covenant'. As we saw in the previous reading, it is not a covenant of letter – that is, Law as written code – but of Spirit. This covenant of Spirit is the Law internalised in our hearts, as foretold by the prophets Jeremiah and Ezekiel.

It is controversial that Paul portrays a ministry that tries to bind people to the Law of Moses using the language of 'death' and 'kills' (here in 3:6 and 7 and in 2:16). Paul, however, had come to understand that the Law was temporary, which is why in verse 7 he writes of the fading of the shining glory on Moses' face. He is not denigrating the Sinai covenant, only expressing the all-encompassing glory of the Spirit. Here, 'life' is not to be understood as mere existence. To be made alive by Spirit is to be set in right relation to God. As we might say today, to be in a relationship with God through Jesus' death and Resurrection is to truly be 'alive'.

† God of life, our one boast is that you have made us alive!

For further thought

• Christians are called to be the aroma of life and healing where there is death and brokenness. Where does our competence for such a calling hail from?

Friday 13 June
Let there be light

2 Corinthians 3:12 – 4:6

For God, who said, 'Let light shine out of darkness', made his light shine in our hearts to give us the light of the knowledge of God's glory displayed in the face of Christ. (verse 6)

In the ancient world, secret knowledge was a trait of the so-called 'mystery religions', in which mysteries were unlocked by revelation only to a select few. Repeatedly in Paul, the mystery of the divine work is resolved, not in special knowledge but a special person, Jesus. For many in the synagogue, in Paul's view, hearing the Law was just like the Israelites hearing the Law from Moses. A veil remained, obscuring the glorious Jesus, the destiny of Torah. Only when someone turned to Jesus did the true glory of the Law shine.

So in 4:1-2 Paul reiterates the boldness he mentioned in 3:12: God has empowered Paul and the whole church to announce the new covenant, by which life comes through Spirit, so nothing need be under wraps, concealed or proclaimed nervously. Unlike the light that shone from Moses' face, the light that shines from Messiah's face is as permanent and luminescent as the light that first pierced the darkness (4:6, recalling Genesis 1:3). This 'light', Paul says, is the knowledge of God's glory; this light is also the gospel – that is, the true knowledge of God is found in the good news of Jesus Christ. That such knowledge cannot be hidden and kept secret is something Jesus himself declared in Matthew 5:14-16, but there were some in Paul's day, and ours too, blinded to this great radiance.

† God of all creation, may the light of the gospel help people to see your intentions for humanity.

For further thought

• How might the god of this age keep people from seeing and responding to the gospel?

Breakables

2 Corinthians 4:7-18

But we have this treasure in jars of clay to show that this all-surpassing power is from God and not from us. (verse 7)

My daughter turned to me and said 'Daddy, I'm shattered,' implying 'exhaustion as a result of hard work' (though I don't remember primary school being so taxing)! When something actually 'shatters' (like glass), it breaks into multiple cracked pieces. Indeed, the Greek word the NIV translates as 'jars of clay' in the verse above suggests something easily broken. If indeed the 'treasure' in that verse is essentially the gospel, then he and his team are the 'clay jars'. The apostle is once more asserting that his ministerial competence is from God.

We readily depict the human condition as fragile and susceptible, suggesting we are conscious of our need for help. Paul was not merely conscious of his need, but positively celebrated it! This is captured in the way he relates the dangers of ministry to Jesus' suffering: suffering was carrying the dying Jesus in his body; living through it was experiencing Jesus' life in the same body. In other words, Paul's ministry mirrored Jesus' death and resurrection, imbuing people with the life of Jesus even amid affliction. The quotation from Psalm 116 in verse 13 adds more brilliant colour: though fragile and afflicted, we, like the psalmist, keep speaking because we believe. Paul believed that, as his earthly ministry mirrored Christ's death and rising, his final judgement (and that of those to whom he preached) would mirror the same resurrection glory. In comparison, the present sufferings paled into insignificance.

† God of power, give me the strength to focus my vision on you so my problems don't seem so big!

For further thought

- Fixing our eyes on the unseen is often the only way to bring perspective to the difficulties of daily life.

June

2 Corinthians

2 Reconciled?

This week's notes are by **Lori Sbordone Rizzo**

 Lori Sbordone Rizzo has been an itinerant teacher of at-risk youth in New York City for the past 25 years. By the grace of God, she is currently transitioning to ordained ministry in the Episcopal Church diocese of Long Island. Theologically, she describes herself as a revolutionary evangelical mystic. She welcomes anyone who wants to discuss these texts to find her via social media, as she loves seeing how the Word of God pierces our hearts and changes us into God's likeness. She also really loves to fish.

Sunday 15 June
Joy lives around the corner

June

2 Corinthians 5:1–10

For while we are in this tent, we groan and are burdened, because we do not wish to be unclothed but to be clothed instead with our heavenly dwelling, so that what is mortal may be swallowed up by life. (**verse 4**)

When I first returned to relationship with Christ, a friend who did not share my faith claimed I was a 'death worshipper' because 'Christians can't wait to die so they can be with Jesus.' 'I'm happier than I've ever been,' I responded, 'Why would I want to die?' My friend replied, 'If you love him as much as you claim, you should want to be with him as soon as possible.' 'But I feel like I am with him right now,' I insisted, and it's still true. I think Paul would agree. He was too busy doing the Lord's work to miss him because, in the work, there is a sense of God's presence that is immensely satisfying.

The birth, death and resurrection of God's Son changed everything, but the full manifestation of Christ's work is ahead. The cross has recreated us; Christ's return will reveal us – we will finally get to be who we have always been, free from personal sin and social injustice. We will see God face to face. Do I long for that day? More than words. Paul calls it groaning (verse 4): we groan for 'what is mortal to be swallowed up by life'. So yeah, there's static, but joy lives around the corner. Run forward. You can't miss it.

† Thank you, Lord, that for now we see you as through a glass darkly, but one day face to face. Grant me the joy of serving you until that day.

New creation

2 Corinthians 5:11-21

God made him who had no sin to be sin for us so that in him we might become the righteousness of God. (verse 21)

Writing on the Incarnation, Saint Athanasius reached a scandalous conclusion: 'God became man so that man might become a god.' Not God exactly because we do not come by divinity naturally but, through the life and death of Jesus, we have become 'partakers of divine nature'. God is still wholly other, as different from us as life is from death, but in some way that is equally true, we are all kin. The Orthodox Church uses the word *theosis* – the process by which the Holy Spirit unites a believer to God. This is not an invitation to be a speck of potato in some great divine soup, rather it is a journey to discover the unique individuals God has always meant for us to be before this world of sin mucked up the divine image within us. Apparently the uncreated creator of all things wants to have a conversation with us that is deeper than master and pet, so God raises us into a relationship of essentially like beings. God has been longing to sit and chill with us, and God paid the very highest price to make this happen. The apostle puts it this way: 'God made him who had no sin to be sin for us, so that in him we might become the righteousness of God' (verse 21). We may sit in God's circle by grace – which is beyond amazing.

† Dear God, I confess that I do not experience myself as a new creation. Let me see all people as you do, and trust in the work you have been doing to unite us to yourself.

For further thought
• What could Paul mean when he implores us to be 'reconciled to God'? What do you think of the idea that God wants to sit and chill with us?

Tuesday 17 June
Unrequited love

2 Corinthians 6:1-13

We have spoken freely to you, Corinthians, and opened wide our hearts to you. We are not withholding our affection from you, but you are withholding yours from us. As a fair exchange – I speak as to my children – open wide your hearts also. (verses 11-13)

Paul is in love, but it's not a girl. He and Timothy have 'opened wide' their hearts (verse 11) to these Corinthians, but they are withholding their affections. Whenever Paul leaves, they run to preachers who are feeding them another gospel. They nod their heads when these other preachers bad-mouth Paul, calling him a loser. When Paul hears this, he is disconsolate; he rushes back to them with tears, reminding them of all he has suffered and begging them to 'open wide their hearts' (verse 13). It's as if, the more his opponents call him a fool, the more he is tempted to act like one.

My class this year did the same thing to me. Before they arrived, I cleaned the classroom, planted tomatoes and dragged in a tank for baby turtles. They came in angry. They were juvenile offenders 'sentenced' to six months. 'OK,' I admitted, 'the circumstances suck, but let's try to make it work.'

They wouldn't even pretend to pay attention. I broke down. I begged them not to blow up this opportunity to be something different. They were quiet for a minute but the next day it was back to the same-old. The false teachers say they will always be gangsters. They have record labels and clothing lines – it's hard to compete. Every day I'd bounce a ball against their fatalism and nag them to play a new game. In the end, I'm standing like some pathetic schoolyard clown. I'm a teacher. We're not supposed to take rejection personally. Except I opened wide my heart; I went all-in. I'll let you in on a professional secret – it hurts like hell.

† Lord Jesus, help me to open wide my heart to the people who love me, and to be foolish enough to believe the good news of your grace.

For further thought

• Who are the people to whom you open your heart wide? Has anyone ever given you a word you were reluctant to hear? How did you respond? By God's grace, how might you handle the situation better?

Wednesday 18 June
Unbelievers

2 Corinthians 6:14 – 7:1

Do not be yoked together with unbelievers. For what do righteousness and wickedness have in common? Or what fellowship can light have with darkness? (verse 14)

We have a tough word in today's reading: Paul's directive to 'not be yoked with unbelievers' (verse 14). There is a lot of disagreement amongst scholars about the origin of this passage or what Paul meant when he used the word 'unbelievers'. To further complicate this, we have 1 Corinthians, where Paul advises them to stay married to unbelievers (1 Corinthians 7:12-14) and not to refuse hospitality from strangers even if their meat may have been sacrificed to idols (8:1-6). Paul understands that, through relationships such as these, the church will grow. In this letter, however, Paul seems to have flipped the script. So what is the apostle saying to us and how can these verses speak to us now?

Most of my friends are 'unbelievers' – people who boast that they have no need for God in their lives. New Yorkers are supposed to be the most street-smart people in the world; it's hard for us to kneel. Once you do, though, you are different, for ever, and with this comes a tension with the rest of your world. My loved ones are those who have come to understand my need to pray before making decisions. I've lost friends too, and this is always painful, but it's important to stand for your truths. Honestly, I cannot see how I could be 'yoked together' – in a long-term partnership – with anyone who'd cringe whenever I brought God to the table. If Paul's caution sets me to take a moment and pray first, then that's a good word.

† Loving God, help me to stand for my truths and make room for others to stand as well.

For further thought
• You cannot surround yourself with haters. A single coal, separated from the fire, will soon go out. Seek out fellowship.

Thursday 19 June
Godly sorrow

2 Corinthians 7:2-16

Even if I caused you sorrow by my letter, I do not regret it … because your sorrow led you to repentance. For you became sorrowful as God intended and so were not harmed in any way by us. Godly sorrow brings repentance that leads to salvation and leaves no regret. (part of verses 8-10)

For a time, the Corinthians were led astray by false teachers, and this led the apostle to write a stern letter to them. His words created a space in their hearts for the Holy Spirit to produce 'godly sorrow' (verse 10).

Another prophet, Nathan, confronted King David when he murdered Uriah and took Bathsheba as his wife (2 Samuel 12). When David gets that his actions have left him utterly lost, he begs God's forgiveness. His prayer is recorded in Psalm 51: 'Have mercy on me, O God, according to your unfailing love' (verse 1). He is begging God for mercy, but he knows that he can ask this because God's love is bigger than our failings. He acknowledges that what he has done is reprehensible and that God taught him better than this. He misses the joy his relationship with God brought into every moment, but he knows he's too full of sin to dance in God's presence now. He just wants to be clean. 'Create in me a pure heart, O God, and renew a steadfast spirit within me. Do not cast me from your presence or take your Holy Spirit from me. Restore to me the joy of your salvation and grant me a willing spirit, to sustain me' (verses 10-12).

Finally, it hits him. If God could be satisfied with burnt offerings, he would have set his entire household ablaze, but what God wants is very different. 'My sacrifice, O God, is a broken spirit; a broken and contrite heart you, God, will not despise.' (verse 17)

† God, I know there are things in my heart that I make all sorts of excuses about, but which are not of you. Grant me the courage to let you do what is needed, so I might be a better vessel of your light.

For further thought
• Read Psalm 51, and try to imagine it as a prayer of David's, of one of these Corinthians, and for yourself.

Friday 20 June
The joy of swimming

2 Corinthians 8:8-15

Our desire is not that others might be relieved while you are hard pressed, but that there might be equality. At the present time your plenty will supply what they need, so that in turn their plenty will supply what you need. (part of verses 13 and 14)

Church, for most of us, means our parish or local congregation. Paul was not as parochial: for him, church meant all churches. Believers met together in local communities for prayer and worship, but the communion they shared was way bigger than the sum of their parts, which may explain the abundance of joy they experienced. Many churches even passed the eucharistic bread from one fellowship to the next to embody this truth. Individual parishes understood themselves as members of one body, so it was vital that all be strong.

I heard of an African bishop who addressed some worldwide Anglican shindig. He took out two bowls full of water and goldfish, then he slowly siphoned the water out of one bowl until the fish began to panic. The congregation pleaded for him to stop. 'I understand your concern,' said the bishop, 'because this is what life is like every day in my diocese.' Then he took a tube and began to siphon water from the full bowl into the almost empty one until the water was equal and all the fish were swimming happily.

If we are uncomfortable watching goldfish suffer, how much more unbearable must the suffering be of our own brothers and sisters? Take our water. Please! Can there be any other response? Paul is writing on behalf of Christians in Jerusalem where there was a severe famine, but we all know of churches within our own denominations who could serve breakfast for a month with what we spent on last Sunday's flowers. Our church bodies will not be strong until we fix this.

† Help us, dear God, to respond with joy to the needs of others, so we may all rejoice in you.

For further thought

• Jesus had everything, but he emptied his pockets for us. Do we really think we can come into his presence and swim happily if we are not prepared to do the same?

Looking out for your own

2 Corinthians 8:16-24

We want to avoid any criticism of the way we administer this liberal gift. For we are taking pains to do what is right, not only in the eyes of the Lord but also in the eyes of man. **(verses 20-21)**

Transferring money in the ancient world was not exactly point and click. This collection for the poor in Jerusalem had to be physically carried along dangerous roads. Paul is moved by Titus' offer to run the errand, and he arranges back-up. This companion brother provides a measure of protection: lone travellers were easy prey (remember the traveller helped by the Good Samaritan). The brother will also be another witness: he has an impeccable reputation, so no one will question his testimony. Paul still has enemies who would take any opportunity to create innuendos of financial discrepancies. 'We are taking pains to do what is right, not only in the eyes of the Lord but also in the eyes of man' (verse 21). When you are responsible for a ministry, it isn't enough to be right in God's eyes. You must also leave no room for the devil to attack your own – your people, your friends, your family.

What impresses me is how Paul continues to love them, never giving them less than his all. You feel as if he would trade his own salvation for theirs if it were possible. As I write this, I am transitioning from classroom to ordained ministry and, frankly, the example Paul sets here is beyond me. Am I really called to love God's people this much? God's words to us are wonderful, 'My power is made perfect in weakness' (2 Corinthians 12:9). Grace is sufficient.

† Lord, you ask us to love beyond our capacity. Expand our hearts until they look like yours.

For further thought

- Consider all the unnamed brothers and sisters who have made your own ministry possible. In what ways can you 'pass forward' the grace they have shown you?

2 Corinthians

3 Power in weakness

This week's notes are by **Joseph Duggan**

Revd Dr Joseph F. Duggan is founder of Postcolonial Networks (online at www.postcolonialnetworks.com) and series co-editor of Palgrave Macmillan's *Postcolonialism and Religions*. He is a priest of the Episcopal Church USA (Anglican), a scholar and a community organiser. A keen preacher, he learned from the Jesuits that the best sermons arise through attentiveness to the Spirit. He lives in Reno, Nevada (USA), with his wife, Revd Stefani Schatz.

Sunday 22 June

Open up your heart

2 Corinthians 9:1–15

They have freely scattered their gifts to the poor; their righteousness endures for ever. (part of verse 9)

Is Paul right that righteousness endures even when the giver lacks righteousness and authenticity? I have been given gifts that felt full of manipulation. There is a subtle difference between a gift, perhaps from a lover, that grows intimacy, and one given for deceptive gain. I have given my share of gifts by which, if I'm honest, I hoped to achieve this or that outcome. I was disappointed when my desires were not met, though my gift was great. Neither my gift nor my righteousness endured in these circumstances.

Gifts given even when we think we are innocent are not necessarily free of our sinful postures. Righteousness endures only when the gift given is rooted in the gifts of the Spirit. The gifts of the Spirit are implied for Paul throughout the Corinthians text but, as readers, we cannot innocently expect or trust that all gifts are freely given and Spirit-filled and that righteousness will endure.

We must examine our giver and receiver 'selves' that we may live up to Paul's standard and scatter gifts so that righteousness will endure. By doing so we will build up the kingdom of God where all power and glory is entrusted. The alternative is worldly power that manipulates innocence and shuts us off from all humanity.

† Lord, help me to examine the desire behind the gifts you give.

Monday 23 June
Let your real identity step forward

2 Corinthians 10:1-11

By the humility and gentleness of Christ, I appeal to you – I, Paul, who am 'timid' when face to face with you, but 'bold' towards you when away! (verse 1)

According to Paul, the Corinthians couldn't recognise the same person in Paul's writing as in his actions. This does not surprise me as much as it seemed to surprise Paul. I do not share Paul's confidence that 'we are in our letters when we are absent' and also 'in our actions when we are present' (verse 11). In my opinion, it was not the case in Paul's time and certainly not now in our age of social media.

Paul's defensiveness diminishes his awareness about his impact on his audience. Indeed he admits that he is partially conflicted in that he wants to model the 'humility and gentleness of Christ' as he demolishes arguments to make them 'obedient to Christ'.

Is the Christ who turns over the money-changer tables in the Temple only humble and gentle? If we are to follow Christ, we will sometimes be humble and gentle and at other times we will demolish arguments to reveal the power of God. When we are non-anxious about the complexity of Christ's personality then we are more likely to have greater influence in building up God's kingdom.

Perhaps social media allow for our true identities to come forward. Perhaps, in the possibility to construct multiple identities through social media, humanity is finally exposed in our attempts to be seen as other than conflicted.

† Pray to be a non-anxious presence in my relationships.

For further thought
• Take a moment to consider who you are before Christ.

Tuesday 24 June
What do you desire?

2 Corinthians 10:12-18

Let the one who boasts, boast in the LORD. (verse 17)

Charactistic of Paul is that, as we become less, Christ becomes more. How do we become instruments of Christ's voice in the world? For us to boast in the Lord, we must find our centre in Christ and be so full of Christ that we cannot but boast in the Lord. To desire to boast in the Lord is possible only if we are thoroughly in love with Christ! When we are in love with Christ, then we can abstain from our self-indulgent love of ourselves. It is love of our self in the name of Christ that distorts our vision and hearing by which we recognise Christ's image and voice.

Once I went on a four-week retreat to complete the Spiritual Exercises of Saint Ignatius of Loyola – a retreat that helps participants reflect on the life, passion, death and resurrection of Christ. The final week of the four is the week of joy. The purpose of the week of joy is to discover joy in Christ's Resurrection. It is a joy completely outside of and beyond ourselves. It may sound easy, but it is not! Grace is the only means to find joy in Christ. Grace is the only means to boast in the Lord and not to boast in ourselves.

Ignatian spiritual directors begin every conversation with their retreatants with the question, what do you desire? Do you desire to boast in yourself or do you desire to boast in the Lord?

† Pray to become less, so that Christ may become more.

For further thought
• What is stopping you from fully giving your life over to Christ?

Sticking together

2 Corinthians 11:1-15

And I will keep on doing what I am doing in order to cut the ground from under those who want an opportunity to be considered equal with us in things they boast about. (verse 12)

As a young aspiring Jesuit, I recall saying to a Jesuit priest who was making a bold defence of the Trinity, 'You don't need to defend God.' The priest responded, 'We must defend God.' I thought in that moment I became a Protestant, letting God's truth make its own defence.

It has taken me over twenty years to see that my rejection of that older Jesuit's defence was as much a participation in the ideology of truth as is the defence of the Trinity. I have come to see that often we see the same thing and call it something different.

I have marvelled over the need for some Episcopalians to leave the Episcopal Church over women's ordination or homosexuality and find a home in another church of the Anglican Communion. In their pursuit of truth and coherent unity, dissident Anglicans find churches that agree with their version of the truth. Yet the worldwide Anglican Communion loosely holds together that radical diversity of truth that no member church in the Anglican Communion is able to hold together on its own!

Humanity's need for a personal experience of unity in the middle of a more distant pluralism breaks up our communities. Paul and his opponents knew something of the struggle of the Corinthian community. Yet God stands above, below, and aside from our limited views to see the vast expanse of our partial truths. Neither Paul nor any of us has the vision of God to see over and past differences that polarise us. We with Paul proclaim that with which we struggle.

† Pray that our polarised differences make us laugh, so that our minds and hearts are opened to new possibilities.

For further thought

- In the midst of your church struggles, like the one dividing the Corinthians, consider these words: Here I stand alongside you.

June

Thursday 26 June
Weakness is our strength

2 Corinthians 12:1-10

*'My grace is sufficient for you, for my power is made perfect in weakness.'
Therefore I will boast all the more gladly about my weaknesses, so that
Christ's power may rest on me.* (verse 9)

My mother suffers from Alzheimer's, and I have attended many
Alzheimer's support groups. Sufferers of Alzheimer's forget
the names of their spouses and children, and it has been a
comfort to know that I was not alone in my struggles with my
mother's dementia.

Unless somebody has experienced this kind of loss of intimate
identity with a parent, it is hard to empathise with another.

The strength of support groups is the sharing in a common
experience. The compassionate support group leader intimately
knows the pain of being a child of someone with Alzheimer's but is
able to stay fully present with the pain of others. The members of
the support group find that their weakness is their strength.

Do we really believe that in weakness there is strength? Our
need for strong leaders does not cancel out Paul's celebration
of weakness. If that were true, strength and weakness must be
seen as opposites. But the weakness that Paul speaks of is not the
opposite of human strength.

To be a leader in any organisation one needs to be in touch with
one's own spiritual heart and the hearts of others. Many of us
find we are most in touch with our hearts when we are weak. In
weakness we are vulnerable. In our vulnerability we are broken open
to experience the full range of our feelings, emotional needs and
dependence on God. In our vulnerability we can be strong leaders.

† Pray that we celebrate and bless our weakness that we may see Christ in
our vulnerability.

For further thought
• Consider the question: Am I willing to be weak for Christ?

You will know me as I am

2 Corinthians 12:11-21

For I am afraid when I come I may not find you as I want you to be and you may not find me as you want me to be. (verse 20)

In the world of internet dating, people spend weeks or even months talking online without meeting in person. They build up a sense of the other person and a picture of the person in their head. When they finally meet, it can be a challenge to let go of their expectation to embrace the reality of the person before them. Meeting sooner rather than later helps us fall in love with the real person, not our fantasy of who the person is that we desire.

Over ten years ago, I met my wife-to-be after only three days on the internet exchanging emails. Over a three-hour lunch date we came to know each other as we shared stories, ideas, questions, hopes and losses. We established trust. An intuitive feeling of trust cannot be manufactured through the internet or any other distant kind of relationship. Ultimately we need to know each other, as we are, in real time.

Paul comes across as a schemer in relationships. He admits to being crafty. We see his loss of agency when he says, 'I have made a fool of myself, but you drove me to it' (verse 11). It is only when we meet one another that we have the privilege to know each other as we are.

This is true in our walk with Christ, as well. We should not wait too long to know Jesus as he is and not as we want Jesus to be!

† Pray to be known as we are in our complete dependence on God.

For further thought
• Take a moment to consider what holds you back from being known as you are.

Saturday 28 June
A model of authority and power

2 Corinthians 13:1-14

Finally, brothers and sisters, rejoice! Strive for full restoration, encourage one another, be of one mind, live in peace. And the God of love and peace will be with you. (verse 11)

Power and authority are intentionally intertwined in this passage, as they are in life. Paul writes, 'yet by God's power we will live with him' (verse 4) and he concludes with 'the authority the Lord gave me for building you up, not for tearing you down' (verse 10). Power and authority belong together. Authority without power leaves us cold. Power without authority leaves us hungry.

Communities that are sustainable in their life in Christ rely on both authority and power to flourish. The terms power and authority are not synonymous. Christian communities are established through the authority of Christ, but they are nourished and nurtured through the power of Christ. To establish and to nourish are two distinctive and necessary acts.

Sometimes those who have been given authority have power too. Sometimes those with power have been given authority. Perfection in leadership comes when authority and power can be held together non-violently. Too often, those with authority have no power and those with power lack the authority to bring change, in ways that leave our communities lifeless.

The choice we all have is whether we use authority and power as the means for violence, or as the means to Christ-like perfection. Christ has given us a model of authority and power. To flourish as Christian communities we must find ways to establish and nourish the communities for which we yearn.

† Pray to be perfect in authority and power.

For further thought

• In your roles as a leader, do you strive to bring together communities through your proper use of authority and power?

Journeys

1 Journeying out

This week's notes are by **Andy Nagy-Benson**

 Revd Andy Nagy-Benson is the pastor of The Congregational Church, United Church of Christ, in Middlebury, Vermont (USA). Prior to his studies at Yale Divinity School (M.Div., 1998), Andy worked on the salmon docks of Alaska, taught English in Costa Rica and New York. Since his ordination in 1998, Andy has served as pastor of three churches. Andy and his wife, Gwendolyn, have three daughters.

Sunday 29 June

I have no idea where I am going

Genesis 12:1-10

The Lord had said to Abram, 'Go from your country, your people and your father's household to the land I will show you ... So Abram went, as the Lord had told him. (verses 1 and 4a)

Last summer, friends and I traversed the Presidential Range in the New Hampshire's White Mountains, in the north-east of the US. It is a difficult, 15-hour hike in good weather, but our trek was complicated by dense fog. At one point, the visibility was so poor that we did not know which way to go. We were lost.

It is one thing to get lost during a wilderness hike. It is quite another to set out on a journey without knowing where you are supposed to go. Abram and Sarai and their nephew, Lot, leave home without a definite destination. This is not an episode of youthful adventure-seeking: 'Abram was an elderly man' (Genesis 12:4b). This is a peculiar journey, a journey of faith.

Faith is hope-in-action. It is active trust in God's goodness and guidance as we venture into an unknowable future. Perhaps the question is not 'Where are we going?' but 'How shall we go?' Perhaps getting lost has value to the spiritual life. Will we let go of the illusion of control and walk with confidence in God's blessings?

The journey of faith rests its head not on what we know but on 'assurance about what we do not see' (Hebrews 11:1). We'll take that journey of faith together this week.

† In the words of Thomas Merton: 'My Lord God, I have no idea where I am going ... But I believe that my desire to please you does in fact please you' (*Thoughts in Solitude*, London 1975). Amen

Monday 30 June
A journey not by (my) choice

Genesis 21:1-21

Early the next morning Abraham took some food and a skin of water and gave them to Hagar. He set them on her shoulders and then sent her off with the boy. She went on her way and wandered in the Desert of Beersheba. (verse 14)

I meet weekly with teens from the congregation I serve. The youth group enjoys hands-on community service projects and also likes discussing a range of topics – from friendship to climate change to the afterlife. Whether in active service or thoughtful conversation, the youth group has a tradition of sharing their highs and lows. When we gather, each teen in the group has the opportunity to share personal episodes from the past week: something good and not so good.

Of course, there are times when the students' lows are quite low. A university-bound member once told the group that her romantic relationship of several years had come to an abrupt end. That story is hers to tell, but suffice it to say the break-up was not her choice. She felt rejected and dejected. The more I listened, the deeper I was struck by the familiarity of it.

Haven't we all, at one point or another, been rejected, betrayed, under-appreciated? If so, then perhaps we find something of ourselves in Hagar's story. Hagar did not choose this leg of the journey. Who would? And yet, while we know not to underestimate the undertow of rejection, we also know that her story does not end there. In her despondency, Hagar experiences holy provision and presence. She and her son, Ishmael, will see better days.

† God, in your mercy, heal the hurt in my life and increase my faith in your tomorrow. Amen

For further thought

• What are your highs and lows this week? Have you sensed God's presence in those moments?

Tuesday 1 July
God is in this place

Genesis 28:10-22

When Jacob awoke from his sleep, he thought, 'Surely the Lord is in this place, and I was not aware of it.' He was afraid and said, 'How awesome is this place! This is none other than the house of God; this is the gate of heaven.' (verse 16)

During college, two friends and I decided to go to Montreal for the night. It was a spontaneous trip and a long drive. As we careened up the highway to the beat of our favourite songs, we had thoughts of a pub crawl in mind.

Along the way, something unexpected happened. From the backseat I saw late afternoon light illuminate a peeling red barn. In front of the barn, a mother swept autumn leaves into a pile with a broom. There were two children with her. One leapt into the pile of leaves. The other was turning round, arms raised, in pursuit of a falling leaf. I did not see if he caught it. The scene passed quickly.

At the time I was not a regular church-goer. But I would have sworn from that backseat that God had come near. God was in that place! Maybe it was the light – the light was perfect. What I do know is that God swung low in a strange way along the road to Montreal.

Years later, in Divinity School, I read the story of Jacob's ladder and it rang true. In that unlikely place, somewhere between Beer-sheba and Haran, something unexpected happened. God came near to Jacob. God was oddly accessible and present. It was awesome. It still is.

† God, swing low and into my life and grant me eyes to see the holy in the ordinary. Amen

For further thought:
• Two poems to fuel further reflection: 'The Bright Field' by R S Thomas; 'Look and See' by Mary Oliver.

Wednesday 2 July
A perilous journey

Exodus 12:37-42; 14:5-31

As Pharaoh approached, the Israelites looked up, and there were the Egyptians, marching after them. They were terrified and cried out to the LORD. They said to Moses, 'Was it because there were no graves in Egypt that you brought us to the desert to die? What have you done to us by bringing us out of Egypt?' (verses 10-11)

You don't need to have the ancient Egyptian army on your heels to know that life can be difficult. There are days that seem to last a decade. There are challenges that look impassable. There are moments that put us in touch with the fragility of our next breath.

This is the end. We can't overcome this. Whatever 'this' may be, we make a valid point. Left to our wisdom and abilities to act, we may come up short. But there is more to tell. As the Exodus narrative shows, the 'Dead End' signs we see are not all there is to see.

Have you ever braced yourself for a sure-fire ending that did not come? What words might we use to tell of such jaw-dropping reversals?

The word that came to mind on the shores of the Red Sea was 'Yahweh'. It was Israel's way of expressing what defied – and defies – explanation. God was not only in that place. God appeared to be the lead actor.

When Israel reached the limits of what it could do, it was invited to trust in a wisdom beyond its best ideas and a strength beyond its strength. There is still today much more than our eyes can see, more than we can reasonably explain. Sometimes, all we can do is say 'God'.

† In the words of African-American hymn writer Revd Thomas Dorsey, in his hymn 'Take my hand, precious Lord' (c. 1932): 'Precious Lord, take my hand, lead me on, let me stand.' Amen

For further thought

• Consider this line by American poet Wallace Stevens: 'After the final no there comes a yes/And on that yes the future world depends' ('The Well Dressed Man with a Beard', *Collected Poems of Wallace Stevens*, London 1945). What do you think it means?

July

Thursday 3 July
Are we there yet?

Exodus 16:1-19

*So Moses and Aaron said to all the Israelites, 'In the evening you will know that it was the L*ORD *who brought you out of Egypt, and in the morning you will see the glory of the L*ORD*, because he has heard your grumbling against him.'* (verses 6-7a)

'Are we there yet?'

'How much longer?'

'I feel carsick.'

I am bi-vocational by choice. I am a pastor and a father of three daughters. As a father, I subject my children to seemingly interminable car trips to see family members and to reach vacation destinations.

My wife and I have acquired strategies to alleviate road trip boredom. We have learned to engage our children in games, to play 'their' music as turbulence mounts, and to bring along plenty of food.

Nevertheless, like my siblings and me in years past, our children can take (and eat) only so much. There comes a point on the journey when they grumble.

There is biblical precedent for this. Israel complains on the wilderness journey. The people are not wholly dysfunctional. They are mostly hungry and tired. Hungry-and-tired can make it hard for us to see the value of what we're doing and where we're going. When will this trial end? Will this trial end? The tunnel's end is not always in view.

But along the way, there are moments of pleasant surprise. Moments of grace. Manna moments. 'Manna' means 'What is it?' As a pastor and parent, I'd say it's God's mercy seeing us through the long, dark hours on our way from here to there.

† God, our Father and Mother, give us this day, our daily bread. Amen

For further thought

• R S Thomas's 'The Moor' (from *Pietà*, London 1966) is a fine companion to this Exodus story.

Friday 4 July
A travel log

Numbers 33:5-49

The Israelites left Rameses and camped at Sukkoth. They left Sukkoth and camped at Etham, on the edge of the desert. (verses 5-6)

I remember an elderly woman in the first church I served. She died in the house in which she was born; she had one address for 94 years. In that same congregation, there was an adult son of a retired military officer. As a child, he went to four schools in four states in six years. Perhaps our own 'travel logs' fall somewhere between these two.

Town to town. House to house. In the course of a lifetime, we will probably have several addresses. And as we recall the names of the places we have lived, each one brings a host of memories. Each one lends itself to our backdrops and helps us frame our personal stories.

In Numbers 33, the author remembers key, if temporary, 'addresses' on Israel's journey to Canaan. The author's account reads like a military march, as Israel moves from camp to camp. Each place – more than forty of them! – triggers Israel's memory and tells part of its wilderness story. The sum of these parts makes an important point: Israel travelled from Egypt to Canaan on and with purpose. The author understands that God intended to give Israel a permanent address in the promised land.

Are we moving through life on and with a purpose beyond our own? In the late evening of our lives, we will perceive this?

† In the words of Dag Hammarskjöld, 'For all that has been – Thanks. For all that shall be – Yes.' (*Markings*, trans. L Sjöberg and W H Auden, London 1964) Amen

For further thought
• Where have you been? Do you have the sense that you life is being led by God?

Good company on the journey

Ruth 1

But Ruth replied, 'Don't urge me to leave you or to turn back from you. Where you go I will go, and where you stay I will stay. Your people will be my people and your God my God.' (verse 16)

Naomi is embittered by grief. Her name means 'sweet', but her life has been devastated by loss. Her husband and their two sons are dead. Naomi feels empty and abandoned by God. But there in the valley of the shadow of death, someone *is* with her. Is it God? Not exactly.

Her name is Ruth, Naomi's daughter-in-law. Ruth is loyal and loving. She is determined to stay with Naomi despite her mother-in-law's insistence that Ruth go. Ruth is not God, but she reflects God's faithfulness and lovingkindness. She helps Naomi – and us – glimpse what God is like.

Anyone who has endured the loss of a loved one knows too well the length and breadth of death's shadow. Likewise, anyone who has walked that long valley floor will not underestimate the ways good company can help heal a broken heart.

When my uncle died suddenly last summer, bitterness visited me like an unwelcome guest. I was quite close to my uncle, and the loss bored a hole in my life. The journey of grief is awful, but the kindness of others has given me the assurance that I am not alone.

Good company may not be God, but it surely gives us reason to believe in her.

† God, thank you for companions on the journey; grant me the heart to be one also. Amen

For further thought

- At the centre of the 23rd Psalm are the words 'with us'. Have you felt God's presence in the good company of someone like Ruth?

Journeys

2 Journeying towards

This week's notes are by **Mandy Briggs**

 The Revd Mandy Briggs is a Methodist minister based in North Somerset. A former journalist, she worked on newspapers in Weston-super-Mare and Bath before training for the ministry at Queen's College, Birmingham. She continues to be interested in how the church and the media can work together in a positive way.

Sunday 6 July
Different journeys

1 Kings 18:1-18

Elijah said, 'As the LORD Almighty lives, whom I serve, I will surely present myself to Ahab today.' (verse 15)

I love to travel and to explore new places when I get the chance. It's a pleasure to visit countries, cities, beaches – and yet I really hate packing! It makes no sense when I am excited about going on holiday, but I always procrastinate when starting to prepare for the journey. Maybe it's the ironing!

The readings we are going to look at this week are all about people making journeys, but not always easy or enjoyable ones. They are journeys that are often challenging and sometimes painful. Obadiah, for example, has been following a particular direction and doing what he believes is right and good, until a meeting with Elijah challenges him to do something more, something he is scared of. He has to face his fears but in doing so enables God's plans to move forward.

Sometimes the first step of a journey is the hardest to make: we worry about what the journey will be like and what we will have to face along the way. However, in the journeys we will look at together, God is not absent but present beside us and before us, and does not leave his people alone on the road.

† God, I always want to get to my destination safely, but thank you for reminding me I can learn from the journey too.

Monday 7 July
The power and the glory

1 Chronicles 13:1-14

'Let us bring the ark of our God back to us, for we did not enquire of it during the reign of Saul.' The whole assembly agreed to do this, because it seemed right to all the people. (verses 3-4)

When I was growing up, *Raiders of the Lost Ark* (Steven Spielberg 1981) was one of the biggest and most successful action movies around. Who could resist Harrison Ford as Indiana Jones in his iconic leather jacket, hat and bullwhip, tackling baddies in the search for the ark of the covenant?

This large holy box, made of wood and covered in gold, is said to have contained the tablets on which the Ten Commandments were written. It was stored in a set-aside position called 'The Holy of Holies' in a special place of worship called a tabernacle. It had been made when Moses and the Israelites were wandering in the desert and was a powerful symbol of God journeying with his people. When the Israelites saw the ark, they knew their God was with them.

Little wonder then that it was treated with awe and fear. This story of Uzzah losing his life while trying to protect it may seem unfair, but it just emphasises how incredibly holy and amazing this box was. That's why David wanted the ark back with him in Jerusalem – to show that God was there, with the king and with the people.

Sometimes we have the tendency to portray God as a 'best mate', a down-to-earth person who is always there for us. That is true, but these Old Testament images of awe and fear are a reminder of a God who is not to be messed with. That might not always be the most comfortable image we have, but we make God into a weakling at our peril.

† God, as I spend some time in your presence today, may I be filled with awe and wonder at your strength and might.

For further thought

• Is there a small item that you could carry with you as a symbol that God is always with you?

Tuesday 8 July
Words for the people

Ezekiel 2:1-10; 3:4-15

He then said to me: 'Son of man, go now to the people of Israel and speak my words to them.' (chapter 3, verse 4)

Recently a friend of mine posted a cartoon on her Facebook page. The picture was split into two sections. One had the caption '10 years ago' and showed a person with a pile of letters, looking at his computer and getting excited that one email had arrived. The second section was captioned 'now' and showed the same person looking at 436 emails on his computer, but then being overjoyed when one letter arrived in the post. Communication is always changing and developing and, in every generation, people find new and different ways to get their message across.

Ezekiel was chosen by God to be a prophet to the people of Israel, some of whom were in exile in Babylon. He was called to speak to his people, the community he was familiar with, but also used some outlandish methods to achieve this. During his time as a prophet, Ezekiel ate a scroll, lay on his left side for 390 days, and knocked a hole in the wall of his house. He used shock tactics and odd actions to get his message across because God had called him to speak directly to Israel, who were not always ready to listen.

In our society, where publicity stunts, flashmobs, Facebook pages and tweets are now common ways of communicating, how do we speak God's words so that those around us receive them in a new and fresh way? How do we avoid gimmicks and present the love of Jesus in a real and relevant way?

† God, when I speak, write, text or tweet, may my words be rooted in reality and relevance, full of your love and care for others.

For further thought

• If you use social media, how does your faith influence the way that you interact with others online?

Running away from God

Jonah 1:1-17; 3:1-5

After paying the fare, [Jonah] went aboard and sailed for Tarshish to flee from the LORD. (part of verse 3)

In the film *Evan Almighty* (Tom Shadyac 2007), Steve Carell plays an unassuming Congressman who tries to ignore increasingly urgent messages from God. Large quantities of wood mysteriously appear outside his house, a long beard sprouts from his chin and he is plagued by the number 614 – a reference to Genesis 6:14: 'So make yourself an ark of cypress wood, make rooms in it and coat it with pitch inside and out.'

As Evan tries hard to ignore God's promptings, the call becomes ever more impossible to avoid. Animals and birds follow him 'two by two' to the office and he is forced to cover up all these incidents as his fellow politicians wonder what is going on. Finally he listens to God and becomes a modern-day Noah, building his own ark and helping to avert a disaster.

Both Jonah and Evan try to run away from the things God wants them to do, but God makes it very clear that it is they, and only they, who can do the job.

If we feel we want to run away from something we know we should do, or are being called to do, the running may only take us round in circles. Putting our hand into the hand of God and saying 'yes' instead may lead to the peace and purpose we were trying to find all along.

† God, it is so easy to hear your call and run away because the job you want me to do seems too difficult. Help me to say 'yes' to your promptings and find peace in doing so.

For further thought
• 'You have made us for yourself, O Lord, and our hearts are restless until they find their rest in you' (St Augustine, *Confessions*, London 2013).

Christmas in July!

Luke 2:1-7

So Joseph also went up from the town of Nazareth in Galilee to Judea, to Bethlehem the town of David, because he belonged to the house and line of David. (verse 4)

I know of a church that once decided to hold its community Christmas dinner in the middle of summer. People got together and ate turkey and all the trimmings, decorated their hall with tinsel and held a celebratory carol service.

Congregation members explained that, as Christmas in December was now so focused on presents and 'buying stuff', they had decided to remember the real meaning of the season at a different time, so the emphasis on Jesus was not lost.

Reading about the birth of Jesus in July may seem strange, but actually it makes perfect sense. The amazing story of God becoming flesh and being born as a vulnerable little bundle of humanity does not just happen in a bubble during a few weeks in December.

The journey had begun years earlier with the promises of prophets (like Isaiah 7:14: 'the virgin will conceive and give birth to a son, and will call him Immanuel'). It continues with the personal journeys of Mary and Joseph, who are challenged to say 'yes' to this huge task that God asks them to undertake. They have to grapple with massive spiritual and emotional shifts in their faith and understanding as well as an actual, physical journey to Bethlehem. Even the Romans, unknowingly, play a part in history as they call people to journey to the census.

The twists and turns that occur in our own lives may be as unexpected as thinking about Christmas in July, but sometimes it is exactly those twists and turns that lead us into a deeper understanding of God.

† God of surprises, you called ordinary people like Mary and Joseph to embark on extraordinary journeys. Although I often feel very ordinary, may your Spirit guide me so that my life too may become extraordinary for you.

For further thought

- Take a moment to reflect on the image of Jesus as a tiny baby. Is this an image that is comforting or challenging for you?

Friday 11 July
Do not be afraid

Luke 2:8-20

An angel of the LORD appeared to them, and the glory of the LORD shone around them, and they were terrified. But the angel said to them, 'Do not be afraid. I bring you good news that will cause great joy for all the people.' (verses 9-10)

What is it that scares you? One insect that really gives me the shivers is the humble 'daddy-long-legs', or crane fly, which floats about looking for somewhere to land. I always think they are deliberately heading for me and I banish them from the kitchen as soon as possible.

Fears can be internal or external. It is one thing to be afraid of insects but it is quite another thing to be afraid of leaving the house. Sometimes enormous fears and phobias take years to overcome; sometimes special techniques are needed so the person who is afraid can leave what terrifies them behind.

The shepherds were probably not afraid of the dark but were terrified by the light of the angels singing glory to God. Fortunately, the heavenly host who sang their hearts out had instructions that would calm their fears: 'Do not be afraid. We have good news. A special baby has been born.'

It was the light that convinced the shepherds that something special had happened and motivated them to make the decision to leave their isolation and sprint down to the town to find Jesus. What does the visit of the angels to that hillside mean to us?

The words 'do not be afraid' are uttered many times to ordinary men and women in the Bible when they are confronted by the glory of God. We, too, may be fearful and want to hide in the murky corners of our own making. However, fear is not a place that God wants us to inhabit.

† God, you know the fears that I face each day and the doubts and worries that lurk inside me. Help me to hear the words of the angels – do not be afraid. Amen

For further thought

• 'Fightings and fears within, without – O Lamb of God, I come!' (from the hymn 'Just As I Am', by Charlotte Elliott, 1789–1871).

Saturday 12 July
Egypt and beyond

Matthew 2:13-23

When Herod realised that he had been outwitted by the Magi, he was furious, and he gave orders to kill all the boys in Bethlehem and its vicinity who were two years old and under … (part of verse 16)

When I think of Egypt, the first images that spring to mind are of swaying palm trees, pyramids and camels, with a couple of Pharaohs and Cleopatra thrown in for good measure.

These days it is more likely that visitors to Egypt opt for a boat trip on the River Nile or a tour to see the Sphinx, but in Matthew's Gospel the country takes on a very different role and becomes a refuge for Mary, Joseph and the infant Jesus.

There was very good reason for the family to flee. King Herod was powerful but he was also paranoid, and he would stop at nothing, even murder, as he tried to preserve that power.

His actions in sending soldiers to hunt down and kill small children are horrifying and we may wonder how to deal with this tragic Gospel passage.

It is easy to want to cry, 'Why God, why?' That cry echoes down the ages to today, where stories of terrible cruelty to children sadly still fill the media.

Herod's actions may shock us but there is nothing we can do to change them now. However, we do live in an age where it *is* possible to take action. We can support charities and campaigns that aim to help children forced into sex trafficking, slave labour or refugee camps and prisons. What else could you or your church do today?

† Compassionate God, every human being is precious in your sight. Today I pray for children trapped in trafficking and slavery; that they may know freedom and hope. I also pray for those who seek shelter and safety. Amen

For further thought

• How can I offer hope to a child in need today? How can I support a cause or charity that seeks to help children?

Journeys

3 Journeying in and out

This week's notes are by **Tim Yau**

Tim Yau spent 11 years in youth ministry before training as an ordained pioneer minister in the Church of England. He served his curacy in Peterborough, growing a church plant in a new housing development. He is now the Emerging Church Pioneer Minister for the Eastern Synod of the United Reformed Church. Most of his work time is spent in Ipswich, establishing fresh expressions of church in the town centre and waterfront area, but he also works more widely as a Fresh Expressions consultant.

Sunday 13 July
Go journey the kingdom

Luke 10:1-20

Go! I am sending you out like lambs among wolves. Do not take a purse or bag or sandals; and do not greet anyone on the road. (verses 3-4)

New job, new house, new town! All the familiarity and reassurances of position, place and people were suddenly stripped away as I headed off to Ipswich to pioneer fresh expressions of church. On leaving Peterborough, I had a similar conversation with different people, which went something like this: they'd ask, 'Where's your new church [building] going to be?' I'd reply, 'I don't have one.' They were puzzled. 'You must have a congregation then?' they'd enquire. 'No, just me and my family,' I'd answer. Furrowed brows, blank expressions or a simple 'Huh?' usually followed.

The appointed seventy-two head out on the road with lots to do but very little to do it with. Surely, that's not how you organise a mission: you need strategy meetings, resource management, an operations base and logistics. Apparently not! With Jesus, all you need is availability, co-workers and faith. When Jesus sends us out on his kingdom journey, everything goes topsy-turvy. What we think we need, we don't need. We travel light, as strangers, but we are not set adrift – we go with purpose, direction, and hope. The afflicted are comforted and the comfortable are afflicted. Few are called to be apostles. However, we are all called into the kingdom journey. Let's journey the kingdom together.

† What is stopping us going on the kingdom journey and letting God transform our world?

July

Whose journey?

Luke 10:30-37

'Which of these three do you think was a neighbour to the man who fell into the hands of robbers?' The expert in the law replied, 'The one who had mercy on him.' Jesus told him, 'Go and do likewise.' (verses 36-37)

I was preparing for a walking holiday in the Scottish Highlands, but earlier that season I'd sprained my ankle. I needed to get mobilised again to train for the hiking, so I set off alone on a twilight walk across local heathland. I could first negotiate a sprawling housing estate; alternatively, just a jump over my back fence and I'd instantly be in the wild. So I jumped. There was a crunching noise, slicing pain and everything went black. I came round to agony punctuated by waves of nausea and the certain realisation that the holiday was off. I shouted, I waited, I crawled until I reached a dark street. I called to some kids for help, but they ran away. A taxi driver arrived, but I was penniless, so he refused to take me anywhere. Finally, a lone female jogger ran past my desperate self and took pity on me. A lift to the hospital for the wreck of a man, salvation in Lycra, and I never even found out her name.

What happens when our kingdom journey is hijacked, whether by external forces, unforeseen circumstance, or – in my case – stupidity? In this well-known parable, it's obvious to put ourselves in the position of the Samaritan, an ethnic outsider rejected by the religious majority, but willing to cross the cultural divide to be a good neighbour. Yes, that's what we want, to be a role model, a hero, a healer. However, how many of us are actually the wounded traveller, dying in the dirt and wondering what happened to our journey?

† 'Man plans, God laughs' (Yiddish proverb). Lord, enable us to hand you our life plan and allow it to become your kingdom journey, where calamity leads to transformation and healing comes from the unexpected. Amen

For further thought
• What life plans have you made that are being frustrated? Do they fit with God's kingdom journey? Are you willing to be helped by the outsider?

Tuesday 15 July
The King's journey is our journey

Luke 19:28-40

Go to the village ahead of you, and as you enter it, you will find a colt tied there, which no one has ever ridden. Untie it and bring it here. If anyone asks you, 'Why are you untying it?' say, 'The LORD needs it.' **(verses 30-31)**

The minister looked with weary eyes at the congregation and asked, 'Is anyone willing to clean the church on Saturday?' I looked around at my friends – they were chatting, and no one in the congregation was giving him eye contact. Who'd want to clean on a weekend? I was 16 and I didn't even help clean my own house! But, I felt an inner nudge and my hand shot up. I wasn't a great cleaner, I have to say, but that insignificant incident of recognising and responding to God's quiet call began a transformational journey into his kingdom. Years later, I found myself at a selection conference for ordained ministry in the Anglican Church. 'Why do you want to be a priest?' asked the vocational adviser. 'I don't!' I replied, 'I'm here because I feel God wants me to be a priest.' OK, that sounds like semantics, and I wonder how many times he'd heard that before. Was I just sidestepping the issue, a pre-emptive blame strike, allowing me to point the finger at God in case it all went horribly wrong? Or, did it remove me from centre stage and allow God to take the limelight?

Two of Jesus' disciples were sent on an errand to organise transport. It's not glamorous and it's away from the excitement and buzz of the Jerusalem paparazzi. Who'd want to miss the big pre-triumphal entry party? Did they realise that their seemingly insignificant chore would be transformed into Jesus' momentous moment – something that fulfilled ancient prophecy and forced the hand of the powers that be?

† John the Baptist declared of Jesus: 'He must become greater; I must become less' (John 3:30). Lord, make us humble to take the lowly tasks, to be faithful in their execution, and willing to let *you* ride the colt.

For further thought

• Try listening to God today. Sometimes we're asked into his kingdom journey in very obvious ways. Is someone around you asking for help?

Wednesday 16 July
Kingdom versus certainty

Acts 9:1-9

As he neared Damascus on his journey, suddenly a light from heaven flashed around him. He fell to the ground and heard a voice say to him, 'Saul, Saul, why do you persecute me?' 'Who are you, LORD?' Saul asked. 'I am Jesus, whom you are persecuting,' he replied. (verses 3-5)

A high-pitched siren rang out and a disembodied voice harangued me across the petrol station forecourt: 'Will the driver at pump three please replace the nozzle and immediately step away from the pump.' I looked around to see who the offender was and realised all accusing eyes were on me. That potent mix of panic, humiliation and self-justification coursed through my brain, but what had I done wrong? I can only begin to imagine the confusion that must have gone through Saul's mind on the road to Damascus. With all his power he'd been pursuing what he thought was God's work and here was Jesus with all the heavenly manifestation of God telling him he wasn't – gutted!

I spent several years as an evangelist in schools, doing assemblies and lessons and running breakfast, lunchtime and after-school clubs. It was hard work, but young people started to come to faith. However, this early growth would more often than not wither, as the methodology of trying to integrate unchurched young people into local churches did not work. The young people felt that they just didn't fit. The epiphany that I'd been wrong and all that strategy and energy had been misguided was hard to swallow. But realising that all people require an expression of church suitable to their culture and context was liberating. What might church look like for Goths, new-agers or commuters? Admitting you've been in the wrong and having your worldview put back together is humbling yet formational. God is in the kingdom business of forgiveness and transformation. Mistakes are mistakes only if we don't learn from them.

† A 'road to Damascus experience' is a phrase now firmly part of our language. However, few get to see Jesus' heavenly glory in this life. Instead, may we hear and be attentive to his call.

For further thought

• Are there areas of 'certainty' in your life that are closed to God's challenge? Have you ever asked yourself the question: 'What if I'm wrong?'

Kingdom clash

Acts 10:17-35

*So I sent for you immediately, and it was good of you to come. Now we are all here in the presence of God to listen to everything the L*ORD* has commanded you to tell us.* (verse 33)

The week before I was ordained, I went on semi-silent retreat. I threw myself into the quiet to contemplate and make sense of the vows I was going to make. This was an understandably difficult discipline for an extrovert like me; nonetheless, I embraced the stillness, and strived to stick to the regime. On the ordination day, I wanted to smarten up and thought I could fit in a quick haircut before the ceremony started. I strode into town in my new clergy collar, found the nearest barber's and sat in the chair. The cape was wrapped around me and then came the questions: 'So you're a vicar? What does a vicar do? Why are you a vicar? What is the gospel in a nutshell?' I had a rapt audience who were genuinely interested and all I kept thinking was 'I shouldn't really be here; I've got somewhere else I should be.'

Peter, too, was distracted. God had shown him a vision of the kingdom and he was trying to make sense of this new information. He found himself summoned by a Gentile, a non-Jew, someone with whom it was culturally taboo to mix and, to top it, Cornelius was an agent of Rome – the occupying enemy of the Jews. But he wanted to know the gospel. I wonder if Peter was thinking, 'I shouldn't be here; I've got somewhere else I should be.' Nevertheless, that's exactly where God did want him to be, and that encounter helped him make sense of the vision God had revealed to him: The kingdom is open to all.

† Could the focus on our own theological points of view sometimes cloud God's kingdom intentions for the journey he wants us to make? Lord Jesus, in our spiritual distraction let us find your kingdom attention.

For further thought

• How do you make sense of the sometimes conflicting priorities that you encounter? If you're being distracted, is God trying to say something to you?

Kingdom guide

Acts 16:6-12

Paul and his companions travelled throughout the region of Phrygia and Galatia, having been kept by the Holy Spirit from preaching the word in the province of Asia. When they came to the border of Mysia, they tried to enter Bithynia, but the Spirit of Jesus would not allow them to. (verses 6-7)

'Great idea, but the answer's no,' frowned the Bishop's representative. I stared at them in disbelief, feeling confused, frustrated and pessimistic. I'd researched the demographics, consulted with churches, and explored the ins and outs with Christians who had a passion to reach this people group. In my mind, it was obvious that there was an opportunity to plant a fresh expression of church, but the diocese said 'no'. Being a pioneer means that sometimes you see what no one else sees and you go where no one else goes. The danger with that is you can end up being so focused on your vision you end up pushing forward into new territory, presuming it's God's will.

Even though Paul and his companion's itinerary was set, with provinces to travel to and people to reach, God stopped them in their tracks. We don't know how God said 'no', but we do know why. God had another kingdom journey in store for them and the vision came in the night. Kingdom journeys start slow and faltering, but we learn to have faith in God and, before long, we stride out with a sense of purpose and direction. However, if we're not careful we can end up trusting our trajectory more than trusting God. Sometimes God has something else for us, so he stops us in our path. He says 'no' and it feels like being in the dark. Will we trust God for the next step? Do we believe that God has something else for us to do? Will we wait in the darkness for the new vision to dawn?

† Lord God, wherever you take us and whatever we go through on our kingdom journeys, help us to trust your guiding Spirit, knowing that Jesus promised to be with us always. Amen

For further thought

† If the journey forward is closed, don't despair, but – like Paul – seek companions to help you discern God's mind and wait for the new direction.

Saturday 19 July
Birthing the kingdom

Acts 8:26-40

Then Philip ran up to the chariot and heard the man reading Isaiah the prophet. 'Do you understand what you are reading?' Philip asked. 'How can I,' he said, 'unless someone explains it to me?' So he invited Philip to come up and sit with him. (verses 30-31)

Hundreds of people dancing around a muddy tent at night with scintillating lights and smiling faces – but something was wrong; it was silent. As I gawped from the periphery at the silhouetted bodies shuffling and leaping around in their wellies to rhythms unhearable, several thoughts crossed my mind: 'Is this some kind of joke? Are these people mad? I just don't get it!' My train of thought was suddenly broken as the crowd punched the air in unison and sang out the chorus from a familiar song. As I stood there with an obviously perplexed look on my face a steward came over handed me some headphones. 'Wear these,' she said, with a knowing smile. I put them on and instantly understood – it was a silent disco and everyone was wearing headphones. I felt the beat, leapt for joy and joined the dance.

Being on the outside looking in on God's kingdom is bewildering. The Ethiopian, with all his wealth, power and knowledge couldn't seem to penetrate its mystery. Even with all the world's resources at our disposal, we can't buy our way in, force ourselves through or learn a secret entrance. The kingdom journey is open to all, but we need the revelation of God to gain access. Philip sees a man seeking divine direction and points the way. Like a midwife, Philip recognises a soul in labour and helps him into spiritual new birth. Philip can't make it happen but accompanies the Ethiopian as God's kingdom is birthed in the eunuch. They're just both in the right place, at God's right time.

† Lord God, open our senses to the reality of your kingdom journey, to join in the dance of the Trinity; the Spirit song of creation; and the joy of good news of Jesus. Amen

For further thought

• Look for people around you who are pregnant with the kingdom. Be willing to go with them to help them realise the kingdom journey.

Ecclesiastes
1 Is all vanity?

This week's notes are by **Aileen Few**

 Aileen Few is an Anglican layperson who is interested in facing the sharper edges of scripture, and of life. She has previously written a blog entitled *Scripture This* in which she chronicled her attempt to read the Bible in a year. She has a Master's degree in Cultural History from the University of Manchester. Aileen has a passion for working with and inspiring young people and is currently mentoring students at Xaverian Sixth Form College, Manchester. She is the lead singer in the band The Beat Keepers.

Sunday 20 July
A new way of being

Ecclesiastes 1:1-18

'Meaningless! Meaningless!' says the Teacher. 'Utterly meaningless! Everything is meaningless.' What do people gain from all their labours at which they toil under the sun? Generations come and generations go, but the earth remains for ever. (verses 2-4)

Earlier this year I visited Sachsenhausen, a concentration camp on the outskirts of Berlin. It was winter and, wrapped up against the bitter wind, I was confronted by the horror of the Nazi regime on a visceral level. I could find no meaning, no hope in what I saw. Returning home, I felt profoundly shaken. Words that may have once offered comfort seemed insulting, trivial. This could not be 'a mysterious way' in which God worked.

The writer of Ecclesiastes, traditionally King Solomon, is courageous enough to be open with the reader. His wisdom has not given him answers. No pithy words of comfort are offered. Rather, he has learned not to turn his face from the spikier truths of human existence. Instead of insisting that each moment of our lives holds some kind of cosmic significance, he invites us to look upon life with a profound humility and a maturity that accepts 'the more knowledge, the more grief' (verse 18).

Are we brave enough to open ourselves to the possibility of meaninglessness? To face the idea that we tiny beings may never know 'why'? This is the call and also the comfort of Ecclesiastes. The writer calls us to a new way of being with ourselves and with God: a place of acceptance and presence.

† In a moment of honesty with God, hold in your heart those parts of your life where you struggle to find meaning.

July

Preparing to live

Ecclesiastes 2:1-17

Then I said to myself, 'The fate of the fool will overtake me also. What then do I gain by being wise?' I said to myself, 'This too is meaningless.' For the wise, like the fool, will not be long remembered; the days have already come when both have been forgotten. Like the fool, the wise too must die! (verses 15-16)

There are some great rhetorical questions in the Bible. This has got to be up there with the best: 'what do I gain by being wise?' (verse 15). The writer takes great care throughout the book to emphasise the fleeting nature of life – a fool's or a king's. So what's the point?

On the surface this question smacks of defeatism; it feels more grumpy than anything else. But it also does what much of scripture does so devastatingly well: it exposes something very basic about human nature.

The idea of 'gain' is firmly embedded in our reading of the world. Wisdom for its own sake, light in the darkness, is contrasted here with the human desire to conquer, to accomplish. Where does wisdom take me? What does it get me? That's what we want to know. Yet true wisdom sees that gain is meaningless and impermanent. Truly to have wisdom is, perhaps, to accept that it will not give you anything. Wisdom is its own reward.

Again there is a sense that the text of Ecclesiastes calls us to be with what is. The writer declares that he hates life when faced with its transience. He is testing pleasure instead of taking pleasure, measuring life instead of living it. Yet in his conclusion that it is all meaningless perhaps he's also setting himself free from his search for meaning. Is he finally preparing himself to live?

† In a moment of solidarity with God, hold in your heart those parts of the world that have been destroyed by humanity's obsession with gain.

For further thought
• Where are thoughts of gain casting shadows over your life?

Tuesday 22 July
Seasons of the Great Rhythm

Ecclesiastes 3:1-22

There is a time for everything, and a season for every activity under the heavens: a time to be born and a time to die, a time to plant and a time to uproot, a time to kill and a time to heal, a time to tear down and a time to build, a time to weep and a time to laugh, a time to mourn and a time to dance. (verses 1-4)

Last autumn I was given one of those lamps that simulate sunlight. This one doubles as an alarm clock, mimicking sunrise even in deepest winter. For someone who wishes she could disappear for the whole of January, it was the perfect present – yet part of me is still in rebellion. Why should I trick my body into waking up? Why can't I just rest?

Whatever the time of year, most of us work the same hours. Whether it's cold and dark or it stays light until 10 pm, that 9 to 5 lifestyle remains a year-round reality for most people in the Western world. However many sermons we may hear about 'times and seasons', we rarely apply this lesson to ourselves in any radical way.

This familiar passage of Ecclesiastes continues the book's theme of acceptance, of being present with what is, rather than yearning after what has been or might be. There is a time to be born and a time to die. Similarly, there is a time to waken and a time to rest. But few of us are comfortable with our more dormant seasons. Why am I not productive? Or vibrant? Or innovative?

The truth is that we cannot constantly create, any more than the ground can constantly yield a harvest. Urban, post-industrial lifestyles rarely make allowances for subtle, personal seasons; many of us live our lives to somebody else's rhythm. The call to prayer is a call to align oneself again with that Great Rhythm, the one that whispers to us of our own seasons.

† In a moment of honesty with God, hold in your heart those times when you have ignored the seasons of your life or the lives of others.

For further thought

• Do I make space for the ebbs and flows of my own energy? What season am I in right now?

July

205

Called to comfort

Ecclesiastes 4:1-16

Again I looked and saw all the oppression that was taking place under the sun: I saw the tears of the oppressed – and they have no comforter; power was on the side of their oppressors – and they have no comforter.
(verse 1)

If I want to test the climate of my heart, there is no better barometer than to notice my feelings as I walk past someone begging on the street. There are times it feels natural to exchange a smile and a kind word. Other times I automatically reach into my purse or offer to help in some way. I wish these were all the times. But sometimes I see that person from the corner of my eye and I clam up, averting my gaze. I feel an imaginary hand tighten around my purse strings and offer a furtive half smile or, worse, no acknowledgement at all. I scuttle off to whatever appointment it is I need to keep, or even to buy myself some superfluous piece of clothing. A twinge of guilt may flicker in my belly, but that's all. This is when I know my heart is cooling and, if I can catch it, asking myself why, then I can bring it into prayer and quiet and invite it to warm up once more.

In today's reading we are challenged to see the tears of the oppressed. Here, again, is a moment when scripture calls us to look upon what is cast aside, just as Jesus does so often. The repetition of 'they have no comforter', which appears twice in verse 1, haunts me. It reads almost as an accusation, challenging those of us who are comfortable. Why are we not offering comfort?

† In a moment of optimism with God, hold in your heart the possibility that you might offer someone radical comfort today.

For further thought
• Whom or what is my gaze avoiding today?

Let my words be few

Ecclesiastes 5:1-20

God is in heaven and you are on earth, so let your words be few.
(verse 2b)

As I sit down to write, the verse above resounds in my head. It reminds me that there are no words that I can write that will communicate even a fraction of that sweet peace that occurs when we sit in silence with God. It seems ironic to write a whole week on 'Meaning and Meaninglessness' without acknowledging that these words, too, in the end, have no meaning. So today I invite you to spend what few minutes you would have spent reading my words sitting quietly, perhaps turning over some words from today's reading in your heart.

† In a moment of honesty with God, rest a while…

For further thought
• 'Go quietly amid the noise and remember what peace there may be in silence' ('Desiderata', Max Ehrmann, 1872–1945).

July

The ability to enjoy

Ecclesiastes 6:1-12

I have seen another evil under the sun, and it weighs heavily on mankind: God gives some people wealth, possessions and honour, so that they lack nothing their hearts desire, but God does not grant them the ability to enjoy them, and strangers enjoy them instead. (verses 1-2a)

There are some very well known statistics about wealth that float around churches and other socially aware institutions. They go something like this:

'If you have food in the refrigerator, clothes on your back, a roof overhead and a place to sleep, you are richer than 75 per cent of this world. If you have money in the bank, in your wallet, and spare change in a dish, you are among the top 8 per cent of the world's wealthy.'

When considering readings such as today's, we do well to remember this. We may be the people with wealth, possessions and honour – but how many of us enjoy it? In fact, how many of us know what enjoying it means? Advertisements that bombard us would have us believe that to enjoy wealth means to spend money, to get more stuff. But I don't think owning pretty clothes and gadgets is what this passage is getting at.

Many of us have heard the phrase 'count your blessings' but how many of us have ever done it? Today I invite you to do just that. Sit down and make a list of all the wealth, possessions and honour you are blessed with. Can you enjoy it? Can you override the natural reflex of guilt and heed the call of Ecclesiastes 6? I hope so.

† In a moment of thankfulness to God, hold in your heart all that you have to be grateful for.

For further thought

• What could you enjoy today that you usually take for granted?

Saturday 26 July
Wisdom in the midst of things

Ecclesiastes 7:1-12

Frustration is better than laughter, because a sad face is good for the heart. The heart of the wise is in the house of mourning, but the heart of fools is in the house of pleasure. (verses 3-4)

What has made you who you are? What experiences have shaped you? When I begin to answer that question, I turn to the traumatic events in my life. Though laughter and love have no doubt nurtured me, without the darker times I would be a very different person. I would have less empathy with those who suffer, less appreciation of the complexities of human experience.

On first glance, today's reading seems counter-intuitive. Frustration is better than laughter? Death is better than birth (verse 1)? It is one of those wonderful pieces of inverted logic that appears so many times in the Bible. Jesus suggesting that the poor are blessed would be equally disconcerting were it not so familiar a phrase. Yet who hasn't been shaped by life's struggles? I don't really believe the old adage 'what doesn't kill us only makes stronger'. There are some traumas in life that rob us of more than we can ever regain. But the wisest, most remarkable people I know have all looked upon life's tragedies. If nothing else, this passage reminds us that we cannot avoid suffering – and so invites us to welcome it.

Again the theme of acceptance arises. We have little control over the twists and turns of our lives. Perhaps our only choices lie within, in our reactions to what we experience. Maybe this is the wisdom that offers shelter. May it be a solace to us all in the darker seasons.

† In a moment of honesty with God, hold in your heart those times in your life that have taught you the most.

For further thought
• Where would an attitude of acceptance allow you to go deeper into the wisdom of God?

Ecclesiastes
2 What is wisdom and who is wise?

This week's notes are by **Anthony Loke**

Revd Dr Anthony Loke is an ordained minister in the Methodist Church in Malaysia. He is an Old Testament lecturer and Academic Dean in the Seminari Theoloji Malaysia, the largest ecumenical seminary in the country. He is married to King Lang, who is a Doctor of Education candidate in Christian Education and a teacher in a private international school. They have two teenage children, Charis and Markus, who are studying in the US. Anthony and his wife regularly play badminton and volleyball and the family members are cat lovers. Anthony has written five books and is currently writing on Song of Songs.

Sunday 27 July
Consider God's wisdom

Ecclesiastes 7:13-29

Consider what God has done. (verse 13a)

In the original Hebrew text, Ecclesiastes 6:9 is considered the midpoint of the book. Thus, verses 10-12 introduce the second half of the book, and here the Teacher poses two questions that sum up the rest of the book: Who knows what is good for a person in life? And: Who can tell people what will happen under the sun? Chapters 7–12 are devoted to these two questions.

In the reading today we turn to the first of these questions. The Teacher reminds us that we may not have all the answers to life but there is still 'relative' good in this world (verse 14). We should enjoy the good while we can before adversity comes our way. In times of trouble we should remember the good times so that we can look ahead with hope and encouragement.

Maintaining a right balance in life is essential. Do not be over-righteous or overwicked (verses 16a and 17a). Do not be overly hard on yourself or on others. Absolute objective wisdom is beyond our reach (verses 23-24) but even the little that we know is far better than madness and folly (end of verse 25). In this vain short life that we have on earth we will fare better if we have wisdom and reason on our side.

† Lord, help me to consider your wisdom that I may learn to live life fully. Amen

Who is wise?

Ecclesiastes 8:1-17

No one can comprehend what goes on under the sun. (verse 17b)

At the start of this chapter, the Teacher asks two good questions: 'who is like the wise man?' and 'who knows the explanation of things?' The rhetorical questions demand the answer: 'very few' or 'no one'!

We live in a world filled with enigmas and riddles. In this life we struggle with the enigma of authority and obedience (verses 2-9). A world without authority would be a chaotic world and yet we often find it difficult to submit to authority. We struggle with the enigma of death (verse 10). Even in death, a wicked man is given a decent proper burial and praises are sung about him. We struggle with the enigma of injustice (verses 11-13). There is a general injustice all over the world where people are oppressed and there is no one to defend them. We struggle with the enigma of misfortune (verse 14). Sometimes life is not fair! In death, even our hard-earned benefits go to someone who does not deserve it.

In this vain life on earth, we sometimes have to live with injustice and misfortune. But we should remember that there are always God's good gifts: mercy and justice.

† Lord, it is difficult to live with deep mysteries in life, but give me wisdom to know what can be overcome and what has to be lived with. Amen

For further thought
• In what form have God's gifts of mercy come to you, yesterday or today?

July

A common destiny

Ecclesiastes 9:1-10

For the living know that they will die ... (verse 5a)

The Latin phrase *memento mori* means 'remember your mortality'. In other words, remember that all must die one day; this is the common destiny that awaits all humans and animals. No one can escape this despairing certainty, except Enoch and Elijah in the Old Testament. They say there are two things that are certain in life: death and taxes! This is the type of life 'under the sun' (verse 3). How we choose to live our life depends on us: we can make the best of it or waste all the years of our life.

The Teacher enjoins us to go and enjoy life (verses 7-10). The simple things in life such as eating and drinking should not be underestimated, for one day to eat and drink may be a struggle! Dress occasionally in your best, anoint your head with fragrant oil, and enjoy time with your spouse. This is not a hedonistic call to 'wine, women, and song' but rather a celebration of life itself. A 1950s' song entitled 'Enjoy Yourself (It's Later than You Think)', by Herbert Magidson and Carl Sigman, aptly sums up the issue at stake: one day it may be too late for many of us to enjoy life.

† Lord, do I find my life like a half-full glass? Help me to make the years in my life count for eternity. Amen

For further thought

• If you knew you would die tomorrow, what would you do today?

Wednesday 30 July
Wisdom, not folly

Ecclesiastes 9:11-18

The quiet words of the wise are more to be heeded than the shouts of a ruler of fools. (verse 17)

There are two word pairs in this portion of scripture that grab my attention: time and chance (verses 11-12) and wisdom and folly (verses 13-18). The hard reality of life 'under the sun' is that things may not always work out the way we expect or desire. One can be wise but still remain a poor person. One can be strong but may not win the battle. Why is life sometimes like this? This is because time and chance even out the playing field. We can make careful plans for our lives but there is no absolute guarantee that everything will work out exactly the way we planned (verse 11).

In this life 'under the sun', wisdom definitely has its advantages over folly. The wise are those who can remain calm and cool in the face of trials and adversities while the foolish may react too quickly and in their haste say or do things they may later regret. Abraham Lincoln once said, 'Better to remain silent and be thought a fool than to speak out and remove all doubt.' One foolish thought or one ill-conceived act can destroy a whole lifetime.

† Lord, sometimes I know I am not getting enough out of life. Help me to find significance, purpose, meaning and enjoyment in the remaining days of my life here on earth. Amen

For further thought

• Who are the softly-spoken people near you whom you could listen to better? What can you learn from them?

Thursday 31 July
Beware of multiplying words

Ecclesiastes 10:1-20

If a snake bites before it is charmed, the charmer receives no fee.
(verse 11)

A quick glance through chapter 10 shows that it is a collection of disparate sayings and proverbs but, as in the previous chapter, two word pairs stand out: here, the wise and the fool (verses 1-3, 12-15), and princes and kings (verses 4-7, 16-20). The theme of the fool is a common one in the book and here a little folly is shown to be able to undo a lot of good (verses 1-3). Plato once said, 'Wise men talk because they have something to say; fools, because they have to say something.' Avoidance of the behaviour of the fool, revealed in empty and vain words, is what constitutes the wise and their wisdom. The second pair, princes and kings, is linked with wisdom and folly basically to show that even those in high places can sometimes behave and act like fools! On the contrary, if princes and kings know how to act appropriately and govern wisely, the land and her people will be blessed.

That leaves verses 8-11, which seek to argue that there is no real advantage even with wisdom (verse 11). As Old Testament scholar C L Seow, Professor of Old Testament at Princeton Theological Seminary, says, 'Wisdom may have its advantages but wisdom guarantees one nothing.' Do a little folly and everything becomes undone.

† Teach me to walk the path of neither depending too much on wisdom nor foolishly neglecting it. Amen

For further thought

• What have you spent your money on in the last week? What does that say about the health of your relationship with wisdom?

Friday 1 August
Invest wisely

Ecclesiastes 11:1-10

Ship your grain across the sea; after many days you may receive a return.
(verse 1)

Are you willing at times to take risks? This passage is a challenge to us. What may look like an unprofitable venture may end up reaping a good harvest in the end. A person who comes to us for help may not look like a good candidate for our time and energy, but who knows whether this person may turn out to be our most successful disciple! The theme of taking risks and yet investing wisely constitutes the first part of chapter 11. No one can predict the future but, if we procrastinate or are not willing to try, we may never get to see the outcome. 'Nothing ventured, nothing gained.'

The second part (verses 7-10) enjoins us to enjoy all the years of our life. We often live as if we have many more years ahead of us but death is no respecter of persons. When it is time for us to go, we will have to leave everything behind, including unfinished business and unfulfilled dreams. Be happy while we are young (verse 9). George Bernard Shaw cautions us, 'Youth is such a wonderful thing. It is a shame to waste it on young people'! The period of youth is the prime years of our lives but there are many young people who find life boring and a waste of time.

† Teach me, Lord, to trust in you at all times. Amen

For further thought

• What are you storing up in barns? What in your life needs the risk of shipping out?

Keeping God's command

Ecclesiastes 12:1-14

Remember your Creator in the days of your youth... (verse 1a)

Some scholars think that the book initially closed at 12:8: 'Meaningless! Meaningless!' says the Teacher. 'Everything is meaningless'. Such a conclusion fits very well with the opening cry in 1:2, which is very similar. The book then begins with a sense of pessimism about life in general and ends with the same pessimism. The truth is that there is nothing great about this vain life since it must ultimately end in death. Our human bodies are not made to last for ever. They will slowly decay and break down like a rundown house (verses 3-4). From dust we came and to dust we will return (verse 7).

To diminish the harsh pessimistic tone, some scholars suggest that the editor of the book added verses 9-14 to 'soften' the impact of the original conclusion. The editor tells us that the Teacher was like other wise men compiling wisdom to impart knowledge to his people, and the words will benefit the later generations who read them (verse 9). The Teacher wrote in an upright and truthful manner about the things he encountered and experienced in his life (verse 10) and we ought to learn from him. The book ends with the same call to 'fear God' (verse 13c) as in the book of Proverbs (1:7). The fear of God will lead us to wisdom.

† May I love you more, thank you more, and enjoy you more, day by day. Amen

For further thought
• What will give your life meaning and purpose today?

War and peace

1 Making war, longing for peace

This week's notes are by **Sister Paula Fairlie OSB**

Paula is a Benedictine nun and lives Chester, England. She has been catching glimpses of God in nature, through prayer, in the world and people around her from the time of her birth in 1940 in Germany, just after war had been declared. This awareness of the 'Other' has been deepened by the monastic life. Paula was brought to England in the winter of 1947 after her mother had remarried. She is deeply grateful for her English upbringing, especially for the loving-kindness of her teachers. She spent four years in Italy before entering an English Benedictine monastery in 1970.

Sunday 3 August
East of Eden

Genesis 4:8-10

Now Cain said to his brother Abel, 'Let's go out to the field.' And while they were in the field, Cain attacked his brother Abel and killed him. Then the LORD said to Cain, 'Where is your brother Abel?' 'I don't know,' he replied. 'Am I my brother's keeper?' (verses 8-9)

Some of the readings for the week are influenced by early oral biblical traditions, as well as history and mythology. The Book of Genesis tells us that we were created to love and care for creation, allowing ourselves to be guided by the word of God. The exercise of free will disrupted our relationships, human and divine, and brother murdered brother.

However, was Cain really so culpable when God aroused his jealousy against Abel? Both offered what they could according to their means, the one a lamb and the other crops from the field. Cain wanted to be appreciated as well, and sibling rivalry still exists!

The story of Cain and Abel originated in the rivalry between settlers and nomadic people: Cain tills the soil as a settler would, and Abel keeps flocks on the move. As the narrative ends, the roles of Cain and Abel are reversed: Abel is consigned to the soil, and Cain becomes the fugitive. Pardoned, Cain becomes the founder of cities, later seen as places of evil, while Abel becomes the forerunner of the Good Shepherd.

† Let us ask God to help us remember that we were created to be our 'brother's keeper' and to live accordingly. Amen

August

Monday 4 August
Who will fight for us?

Judges 1:1-11

When Judah attacked, the LORD gave the Canaanites and Perizzites into their hands, and they struck down ten thousand men at Bezek ... Adoni-Bezek fled, but they chased him and caught him, and cut off his thumbs and big toes. (part of verses 4 and 6)

War strategies are based on certain principles: the forging of alliances for mutual benefit, imprisoning captured enemies, and finding a plausible reason for making war. The usual cause is self-interest, although sometimes it is described as a divine mission. The religious history of Israel is one long search for the promised land, in which the chosen people could live in peace, worshipping the Lord. The achievement of this entailed much hardship, courage and barbaric cruelty. In the reading today, Adoni-Beek was able to accept the justice of retribution; he admitted he had been guilty of the same cruelty himself.

A different kind of retribution is still demanded from conquered people, whether innocent or guilty. Even so-called 'just wars' are initially harmful, although long-term consequences may be good. Women become chattel, children are orphaned, whole populations are displaced. This happened in Germany at the end of the Second World War. The land was split between the Allies: Britain, the USA and Russia. Retribution was made through the seizure of machinery from factories, leaving the Germans with the incentive to rebuild. Our small town was full of refugees from the Russian Sector. We shared our flat with three generations who had fled. Once the atrocities committed in concentration camps were made known in the early 1950s, most of us felt deeply ashamed. The horror and revulsion remain.

† Let us pray for all those who are still suffering from the consequences of war. Amen

For further thought
• How has war impacted your community? Your family?

Tuesday 5 August
A divine promise

1 Samuel 31:1-13

Saul said to this armour-bearer, 'Draw your sword and run me through, or these uncircumcised fellows will come and run me through and abuse me.'
(verse 4)

The tragic death of Saul, God's anointed king, personifies deterioration through disobedience to God and the wrong use of power. Saul's reign began with hope: the Israelites finally had a king and were now like other nations! Throughout the centuries all great empires succumbed to corruption and disintegration through the eventual weakness of their leaders and slow infiltration by other peoples. The Davidic dynasty, established after Saul's defeat, became *a divine promise* for the future rather than a stable succession in time.

Many military leaders have died ignominiously. Some were captured and imprisoned; others were executed after horrendous tortures; some were betrayed and killed by political opponents; others committed suicide to avoid personal degradation. Saul was in this latter category.

His dead body was abused by the Philistines but the valiant men of Jabesh Gilead, having burned the bodies of Saul and his sons, 'took their bones and buried them under a tamarisk tree … and fasted seven days.'(verse 13)

European wars were usually initiated by power-hungry rulers (basically dictators) who sought personal aggrandisement clothed in political ideals. The First World War was fought between related dynasties, brother killing brother. The Second World War was initiated by a fanatic who desired ethnic cleansing, and he committed suicide. The end of war did not lead to peace. Family life was seriously disrupted for winners and losers alike. Europe was permanently changed, despite the forming of a European Union.

† Lord, forgive us for all the harm we have unwittingly done and help us to forgive ourselves. Amen

For further thought
• Do you think this century will be more peaceful than the last one, or less? What will help the cause of peace?

Wednesday 6 August
Father, forgive

Lamentations 5:1-18

Remember, LORD, what has happened to us; look, and see our disgrace.
(verse 1)

This poignant passage says all that needs to be said by those who have suffered the depredations of war:

Our inheritance has been turned over to strangers, our homes to foreigners.
We have become orphans and fatherless, our mothers are widows.
We must buy the water we drink; our wood can only be had at a price…
we are weary and find no rest…
Our ancestors have sinned and are no more, and we bear their punishment…
Women have been violated…
Princes have been hung up by their hands; elders are shown no respect… (part of verses 2-12)

Add to this the attendant horrors of more modern warfare: blackouts; sirens; curfew and the drone of aeroplanes; the goose-stepping German foot-soldiers passing by, marching on cobbled streets; the fear of informers; the required Nazi salute; the bombing of Hamburg, our nearest town; nights spent in air raid shelters, sleeping fully clad on top of beds, with rucksack and boots on a chair; letters from soldiers almost deleted by the black tape of censorship; the strange fear that the enemy was black-skinned, and the relief that the Tommies were (it seemed to us) ordinary and kindly men. What more can one who was a very young child say, except that our 'enemies' were kinder than our feared fellow-men with their stern faces? We were all wary but came to no harm, although a few men committed suicide. I saw a man throw himself under the wheels of our local train, in which I was a passenger: he was rescued but succeeded in killing himself later.

† Have mercy, Lord, on all who still carry the wounds of war in mind and body.
Amen

For further thought

• Where is there conflict in the world today? Ask God to look and remember.

Conflict above and below

Revelation 12:7-9

Then war broke out in heaven. (verse 7a)

This can come as a shock to those of us who pray the 'Our Father' every day: 'Thy kingdom come, thy will be done on earth as it is in heaven.' We think of heaven as a calm and peaceful place, failing to notice that spiritual warfare is part of heaven.

So, can 'religion' really be the 'opium of the people'? False religion perhaps, but not the spiritual life. We believe that God is everywhere, and he is in heaven, while on earth we are aware of spiritual conflict in ourselves, here and now. Is the text for today reminding us that Satan is in our midst, leading the whole world astray? This is not a comforting thought. On whose side are we going to fight, and for whom are we going to die? In this battle we cannot be true to God and be pacifists at the same time. We may have to be martyrs (witnesses) prepared to shed our blood for our belief. This is something I have never wanted to do, and would not (or could not) commit myself to Christianity in my teens – I did not want to be a missionary and die for the faith. I am inherently a coward who very much admires those who go out to preach the gospel in wild places.

Yet there are wild places within us, too, as the Desert Fathers discovered in the early centuries of Christianity, to which we can fear going. We all need to pray 'Forgive us our trespasses as we forgive those who trespass against us'.

† Let us remember the importance of the words 'and lead us not into temptation but deliver us from evil'. Amen

For further thought
• Consider where in your own heart you are conflicted.

Friday 8 August
Hand in hand

Micah 4:1-5

Come, let us go up to the mountain of the LORD, to the temple of the God of Jacob. He will teach us his ways, so that we may walk in his paths. (part of verse 2)

This prophecy about the last days is at the heart of our hopes for the future, a future when many nations will walk together in peace. Humankind has a deep longing for peace – but on our own terms. We know in theory that true peace must include all people, and the whole creation. We also know that this ideal cannot be reached through divided human aspirations. How can we ever agree about anything? The absurdity of this is described in the ancient Indian story of the blind men and an elephant, which can be interpreted as the incompatibility of the range of truths and fallacies found in various religious traditions. It can also be applied to Christianity. We have only a fragment of knowledge as individuals and need to have the humility to listen to the insights of others. Only God knows the whole!

An image used by the sixth-century theologian Dorotheus of Gaza illuminates this. We know that we all have to follow our own paths, the path prepared for us by God. But walking separately ever upwards we come closer both to God and each other. On the summit, in the house of God, we shall attain both union with God and communion with each other. Our ascent brings us to unity. Were we to turn back, our paths would diverge as before but the memory of the communion would remain.

† Let us pray that, as we follow our God-given path, we may experience the love and communion for which we were created. Amen

For further thought
• Is peace more than the absence of war? If the answer is yes, what else is peace?

Saturday 9 August
New heavens and a new earth

Isaiah 65:17-25

They will build houses and dwell in them; they will plant vineyards and eat their fruit. No longer will they build houses and others live in them, or plant and others eat. For as the days of a tree, so will be the days of my people; my chosen ones will long enjoy the work of their hands. (verses 21-22)

Christians are called to forget the past while retaining an awareness of the grace it contained. In the Bible there are many symbolic events. God 'repented' of having created human beings. Noah became the saviour of the animal kingdom. In Isaiah the Lord repented creating heaven and earth. The envisaged new creation is to be everlasting, with the whole of creation at peace, with God listening to our prayer.

I think we realise that this vision of Isaiah will not be fulfilled here on earth. God sent his only Son into the world to show us another way. In the new creation 'The wolf and the lamb will feed together, and the lion will eat straw like the ox, and dust will be the serpent's food. They will neither harm nor destroy on all my holy mountain' (verse 25).

In this life we can accept the guidance of the Good Shepherd as we pass through this fleeting world to 'the holy mountain'. We must be prepared to be nomads like Abel, passing through the darkest valley of Psalm 23 until we can 'dwell in the house of the Lord for ever'.

† Our new life begins when we accept the good news in our hearts: let us pray for this acceptance. Amen

For further thought
• After reflecting on war and peace this week, do you think peace is possible in our world? How will it come about?

War and peace

2 Peace begins with God

This week's notes are by **Kat Brealey**

Kat Brealey developed a passion for justice and equality as an undergraduate theologian at the University of Manchester, where she studied feminism and liberation theologies. In 2012 she worked with Coventry Cathedral's reconciliation ministry team during the Cathedral's Golden Jubilee year. More recently she has been exploring interfaith encounter in higher education, working as chaplaincy assistant at the University of Bristol's multifaith chaplaincy. In her spare time she enjoys cycling, dystopian fiction and gospel music. Her favourite colour is green.

Sunday 10 August
Called to witness to peace

Matthew 5:9

Blessed are the peacemakers, for they will be called children of God.
(verse 9)

I find the Beatitudes both beautiful and bewildering – making them the perfect place to begin this week on peace, with its tendency to elude us! The morning after the Luftwaffe destroyed Coventry Cathedral, Provost Howard stood amidst the rubble and scratched 'Father forgive' on the charred wall. In doing so he acknowledged that fault lay not only with the bombers; the sentiment was not 'Father forgive them' but, rather, 'Father forgive us all' for our failure to find peaceful means to address our differences. For many who had witnessed the devastation of their city, this call for reconciliation rather than revenge seemed like betrayal. Speaking out as he did, in faithfulness to the gospel's call to be peacemakers, was a courageous act. Today, Coventry Cathedral is a symbol of hope for communities around the world, inspiring them to work for reconciliation – whether at local, national or international level. Blessed are the peacemakers – not because their words will be applauded; the message of peace is still met by confusion and resistance – but because their actions reflect the character of God. As we stand in the ruins of our broken world, asking for our Father's forgiveness and committing ourselves to peace, we show ourselves truly to be his children.

† Loving God, give us eyes to see and hearts to recognise situations and relationships where we can choose to be people of peace this week.

Monday 11 August
Called to peace before the sword

Matthew 10:34-39

Do not suppose that I have come to bring peace to the earth. I did not come to bring peace, but a sword. For I have come to turn 'a man against his father, a daughter against her mother, a daughter-in-law against her mother-in-law ...' (verses 34-35)

As a Christian advocate for peace, it is not long before this passage comes up in conversation, with its seemingly clear message rendering it perfect ammunition (excuse the phrase) to oppose the case for Jesus the peacemaker. The context of these verses means that there are no legitimate grounds for arguing that Jesus was an advocate of physical violence. The parallel passage in Luke clarifies that the 'sword' Jesus is talking about is not a weapon but rather division – primarily of families. Yet, however tempting it is to execute some hermeneutical gymnastics and come up with an analysis that makes this verse central to the case for peace, this is no more faithful to the text. As is often the case with controversial passages of scripture, neither side can truly claim this passage as proof of its argument. It is difficult to avoid the fact that Jesus believes his message will inevitably lead to conflict. Reading this passage in light of our focus on peace, it occurs to me that Jesus foresees that, if there is violence, his followers will be victims, not aggressors. The sword is not ours to take up; it is ours to expect. Thus this passage does not override Paul's instruction that 'as far as it depends on you, live at peace with everyone' (Romans 12:18). But it does remind us that the gospel is offensive and divisive, and it is in the light of this that our call to be people of peace is truly tested.

† Crucified Christ, you bear on your body the marks of violent opposition to your message. Make us strong and courageous to bear them too, that they may lead us deeper into the way of peace.

For further thought
• Think of those in our world for whom the rejection by family and violence are a reality.

Tuesday 12 August
Called to more than 'Peace''

Luke 19:41-44

As he approached Jerusalem and saw the city, he wept over it and said, 'If you, even you, had only known on this day what would bring you peace – but now it is hidden from your eyes.' (verses 41-42)

A constructive, if potentially uncomfortable, way to explore these verses is to turn their challenge on ourselves. Each of us is engaged in the continuous process of discerning what will bring us peace. Yet often I know I'm sold short, fobbed off with a shallow imitation of the peace of which Jesus speaks – a peace that can be equated with God's coming. Have I bought into the idea that peace is financial security, and job security will ensure I sleep at night? Or the belief that peace is mental well-being: fresh air and positive thinking? Or the notion that peace is tranquillity, obtained only on spa breaks and tropical beaches? While none of these things is objectively bad, Jesus' words suggest that they are inadequate definitions of what peace is and where we find it. In a world where the pursuit of peace has been co-opted as a marketing tool by a multiplicity of different industries, let's not allow ourselves to be persuaded to seek peace apart from the Prince of Peace. For peace is not merely protection against or absence of poverty, stress, or busyness – it is not an end in itself, but a means to a far greater end. It is a state in which I embrace God's presence, and in doing so create space for the things of God to flourish in my life.

† Jesus, Prince of Peace, lift my sights above the peace the world offers, and cause me first and foremost to look for the time of your coming.

For further thought

- How can decisions on the horizon for you be made so as to render you more readily able to recognise and welcome God into your life?

Wednesday 13 August
Called to a community for peace (1)

James 3:13-18

The wisdom that comes from heaven is first of all pure; then peace-loving, considerate, submissive, full of mercy and good fruit, impartial and sincere. Peacemakers who sow in peace reap a harvest of righteousness. (verses 17-18)

In this passage we read about earthly and godly wisdom, with the former leading to disorder, and the latter to peace. Eugene Peterson's rendering of verse 18 in *The Message* (Colorado 2003) is beautifully practical: 'you can develop a healthy, robust community that lives right with God and enjoy its results *only* if you do the hard work of getting along with each other, treating each other with dignity and honour.'

Community living is a perfect example of the fact that selfishness breeds disorder. For a year I lived with two other girls from my internship programme at Coventry Cathedral, and we decided early on that we wanted to commit to living as a community, rather than just occupying the same house. We wanted to cultivate a common life through eating together regularly, exploring life and faith, and being honest about any issues we had with one another or the running of the house. We came from different countries, with different perspectives and life experiences, and it took time to create routines and ways of doing things that worked for us. We soon found that, in order to develop a healthy community, we had to do the hard work of getting along with people, which this passage talks about, each putting the harmony of the group before our individual desires. Over time, in the minutiae of life together, our little community became more than a group of housemates. Our efforts to live in peace enabled us to reap the harvest this passage promises – in the form of a smooth-running household, and friendships that outlasted our time there.

† Threefold God, give us the courage to share our lives with others, the patience to commit to relationships, and the humility to recognise how much we can learn in doing so.

For further thought

• Which of our communities – family, work, church – needs us to commit to doing the hard work of getting along for it to flourish?

Called to a theology for peace

Ephesians 2:13-18

But now in Christ Jesus you who once were far away have been brought near by the blood of Christ. For he himself is our peace, who has made the two groups one and has destroyed the barrier, the dividing wall of hostility. (verses 13-14)

When I started working at Coventry Cathedral, one of the biggest challenges was to get my head around what reconciliation was – and it was this description of its dual nature, tucked away in Ephesians, that was really helpful. Paul explains that, in its vertical dimension, humanity is reconciled to God through the death and Resurrection of Jesus, as we are 'brought near by the blood of Christ' (verse 13). However, the cross has horizontal implications too, as in Christ divisions are destroyed and we can find peace with our neighbour across the boundaries of ethnicity, class or culture. My experience tells me that we all have a tendency to emphasise one of these above the other, depending on our church background and theological leanings. However, if we are truly to grasp the nature of reconciliation, then we must avoid creating this false dichotomy – they are in fact two sides of the same coin, as each flows naturally from the other. It is *because* we are reconciled to God in Christ that we can extend a hand of peace to our neighbour, in the knowledge of the gift we have received; for she who has been forgiven much, loves much. Yet it is as we work for peace and see relationships develop across divisions that we gain a renewed understanding of the work of Christ, as the relational reflects the cosmic. The challenge of Christian maturity is to understand Christian faith in a non-defensive, non-reactionary way that honours the full depth and nuance of the gospel message.

† Jesus, your death brings about reconciliation with God and with others. Help us to grasp again the glorious complexity of the cross, that we might love you more than our doctrine.

For further thought

• Take time to reflect on whether your faith has developed more in response to those you agree with or reaction to those you don't.

Friday 15 August
Called to peace – and a placard?

Ephesians 6:10-17

For our struggle is not against flesh and blood, but against the rulers, against the authorities, against the powers of this dark world and against the spiritual forces of evil in the heavenly realms. Therefore put on the full armour of God, so that when the day of evil comes, you may be able to stand your ground ... (part of verses 12 and 13)

I'm sure I'm not alone in having strong memories of this passage from attending, and later teaching, Sunday school – the imagery lends itself so well to action songs and craft activities! Returning to it now, I'm struck by the encouragement to recognise that our enemy is not 'flesh and blood' – as a feminist, I don't find it difficult to see systems of power at work in our world today that are the enemy of the values of God's kingdom. Sin is not just individual human actions, but is systemic, creating power structures that are oppressive. Followers of Jesus are called to challenge these unjust structures, in the manner described in Romans; 'do not be overcome by evil, but overcome evil with good' (Romans 12:21). Yet how often do we read passages like this and think of opposition to Christianity as religious practice, in terms of workplace regulations on wearing crosses, rather than opposition to the message of Christ and the values of his kingdom? This is in part because we tend to see political involvement as a 'worldly' concern, or protest as inappropriate for Christians. The radical lives of people such as William Wilberforce and Josephine Butler suggest otherwise. They recognised that their claim to follow Jesus could not be authentic while they condoned the slavery and abuse of other humans, equal bearers of God's image. In today's world where rulers, authorities, powers and forces continue to oppress, our faith equips us to respond – clothed in the non-traditional armour of truth and righteousness – by pointing to a better way.

† Liberating God, renew our minds that we might be quick to recognise and swift to challenge powers that are in opposition to the peace, justice and joy of your kingdom.

For further thought
• As you watch or read the news today, ask God to reveal the rulers and forces that cause brokenness and despair in our world.

Called to a community for peace (2)

Colossians 3:12-17

And over all these virtues put on love, which binds them all together in perfect unity. Let the peace of Christ rule in your hearts, since as members of one body you were called to peace. And be thankful. (verses 14-15)

Over the past few years I've been somewhat nomadic, living in various places across the UK. Along the way I've been part of churches with huge spectrums of theology and worship styles represented within their membership. I've learned that unity doesn't always mean agreeing on things, but rather refusing to let our disagreements divide us. As members together of the body of Christ, Paul tells us we are called to peace. Yet the metaphor of clothing oneself with virtues illustrates that behaving in ways that are compassionate, kind and gentle is a choice – these things don't come naturally to us! Perhaps this is particularly true in a church setting, which is, as the saying goes, not a museum for saints but a hospital for sinners. Where broken human beings create a new family on the basis of their identity as children of God, we need to make an active decision to override the inevitable negative attitudes, however qualified these may seem. Give up the bitterness that stems from past hurts. Let down the barriers that serve to isolate you from those you're not comfortable being in community with. Let the peace of Christ trump it all. This peace must be our priority, above our loyalty to liturgy or spontaneity, the choir or the band. As we let the peace of Christ reign and are united as his body, the gospel will indeed dwell among us richly in all its colour, texture and nuance – a gospel that speaks to our pain as broken people, and of the hope that is embodied in our gathering.

† Living God, empower us by your Spirit to make ourselves vulnerable, deciding against division and letting the peace of Christ rule in our relationships with our sisters and brothers.

For further thought

• From the passage, pick one virtue that doesn't come easily, and choose to clothe yourself with it in your conversations with fellow Christians this week.

Nearer God's heart in a garden?

This week's notes are by **Jane Gonzalez**

Jane Gonzalez is a Roman Catholic laywoman and works as a pastoral assistant in a parish in Hertfordshire, UK. She was awarded an MA in Pastoral Theology in 2012. She has a keen interest in studying scripture and is a visiting preacher at a local Anglican church. Her other interests include singing, gardening and sewing – although she doesn't have as much time for these as she would wish – and she looks forward to an active retirement one day, provided the government doesn't axe the bus pass. Ambitions for the future: visit all the English cathedrals and walk the Camino de Santiago.

Sunday 17 August
The garden of the soul

Genesis 2:8-17

Now the LORD God had planted a garden in the east, in Eden; and there he put the man he had formed. … The LORD God took the man and put him in the garden of Eden to work it and take care of it. (verses 8 and 15)

Gardening takes many forms and each person's plot is different. I'm what they call a natural gardener. I prefer informality and I am forgiving of the plants that others call weeds, especially when they are beautiful or attractive to the wildlife who share my garden.

I realised on my return from a five-week holiday that such a laissez-faire attitude has serious drawbacks: my garden, after the wet and warm weather, is hidden under a tangle of weeds and brambles. It will be a mammoth task to get it back to the manageable disorder that I like! I see that I have neglected my garden over some time; I have not been ruthless enough in getting rid of the weeds or the brambles. I haven't really cared for my garden. Pride, the sin of Adam, has made me mistake laziness for kindness.

Taking care of the garden is what Christian living is all about – the 'garden' that constitutes the soul, the physical body we inhabit and the graced space that is the world we live in. Each aspect deserves attention and care. The call to conversion is like gardening – a labour of love that is painstaking and requires attention and time; and the courage to root up and eradicate the often attractive weeds of sinfulness.

† How does my garden grow? What areas of my spiritual life am I neglecting and how can I attend to them?

August

231

Monday 18 August
A garden is a lovesome thing

Song of Songs 4:9-16

Awake, north wind, and come, south wind! Blow on my garden, that its fragrance may spread everywhere. Let my beloved come into his garden and taste of its choice fruits. (verse 16)

A favourite film of mine is *Into Great Silence* (directed by Philip Gröning, 2005) – a depiction of the daily lives of the Carthusian monks of La Grande Chartreuse, with no commentary or musical soundtrack, except when the monks are singing during prayer and worship. It is an immensely moving film showing their austere lives of work, prayer and solitude but the overwhelming impression is of joy. Those who have persevered in this most arduous of callings, who have surrendered themselves to God in this way, find intense peace and happiness. A phrase from the prophet Jeremiah (20:7) in the New Jerusalem Bible version punctuates the scenes and highlights their vocation: 'You have seduced me, O Lord, and I have let myself be seduced.'

We read in scripture that God is love (1 John 4:8) but we use the image of God as lover sparingly. The physical and sexual connotations of *lover* may feel uncomfortable.

Yet human love, articulated in the poetry of the Song of Songs, is a gift from our creator, an aspect of our humanity that we suppress at our peril. God is the passionate lover of humanity whose love brought about our redemption, through the Incarnation. As the third-century theologian Tertullian said, 'the human body is the hinge of salvation'.

What would it mean to our spiritual life, to the garden of our soul, to be seduced by the lover God? To surrender ourselves totally to him? To allow ourselves to be as intimate with God as he desires to be with us? The temptation is to keep him at arm's length, to protect our personal space – because complete surrender means really 'dying to ourselves'.

† Lord, I want to let go of myself in love to you. Give me the grace to accept your loving embrace.

For further thought

• Have we the courage to allow God full access to the garden? What choice fruits would he find?

The art of hope

Jeremiah 29:1-9

Build houses and settle down; plant gardens and eat what they produce.
Marry and have sons and daughters; find wives for your sons and give your
daughters in marriage. (part of verses 5-6)

I remember reading an article some years ago about a diplomat's wife who had planted over 20 gardens in the course of more than 25 years. Everywhere her husband was posted she set about creating a garden, irrespective of how long the placement lasted. Her energy and optimism never failed her even though she rarely saw the fruits of her labours.

Planting a garden implies stability and roots – or at least the desire for these. Gardening is the art of hope. Jeremiah's exhortation to his people to build and plant, settle and put down roots may seem to be a despairing resignation but is actually a call to trust in God and in his providence. Exile is part of the plan, not the object of the exercise.

Hope is not an easy virtue to cultivate in the garden of our soul. It requires patience and trust, qualities that can sometimes be difficult to nurture in our frenetic world. We want instant response to our problems, quick answers to our prayers. We want the weekend garden makeover so beloved of television programmers rather than concerted effort and graft in the garden! Christian hope is not the easy optimism of the world but the inner certainty that God is at work in things and there is a meaning to it all. Like the farmer in the passage in Mark, we can be sure that God is on the case – while we sleep, and while we are awake, the seed is growing (Mark 4:26-29).

† Lord, help me to be patient and to persevere. Give me the grace to work to your timetable and no one else's.

For further thought

- 'To create a little flower is the labour of ages,' wrote William Blake (1757–1827). What does it mean to say that I place my trust in God?

The grass on the other side?

Luke 13:18-19

Then Jesus asked, 'What is the kingdom of God like? What shall I compare it to? It is like a mustard seed, which a man took and planted in his garden. It grew and grew and became a tree, and the birds perched in its branches. (verses 18-19)

One of the most exciting things about gardening – for me – is looking at seed catalogues and imagining my garden full of lots of colourful and fragrant plants. And growing from seed is an immensely satisfying, if scary, thing – watching and waiting for the first appearance of the shoot; nurturing the seedling; pricking out and jealously guarding the tender plant while it matures; mourning the loss of fragile young plants if conditions are not right for them.

Sometimes, also, the final product does not quite resemble the picture on the packet. As in the parable of the sower (Mark 4:2-9), seeds do not always enjoy optimum conditions for growth, in spite of the efforts of the gardener. Wind, drought, frost, sun – too much or too little – can affect matters. But with care and patience a seed can be encouraged to realise its potential.

The crux of Jesus' words, it seems to me, is that the mustard seed – called elsewhere in scripture 'the smallest of all seeds' – has the potential for greatness and achieves this through the process of being planted and reared. In our lives as Christians, we too have potential to become the unique and special person that God wants us to be. Fear inhibits us and we spend our time trying to be someone else, despising our own gifts and talents through wanting those of others, looking over the fence at the other person's greener grass … we resist being planted! We want to be the picture on the packet rather than the living growing plant.

† Lord, give me the faith I need to be the person you want me to be.

For further thought
• Reflect on these words of James: 'Humbly accept the word planted in you, which can save you' (James 1:21).

Thursday 21 August
Nearer to God in a garden

John 18:1-12

When he had finished praying, Jesus left with his disciples and crossed the Kidron Valley. On the other side there was a garden and he and his disciples went into it. (verse 1)

I went to the Holy Land on pilgrimage some years ago and we visited the Garden of Gethsemane, where Jesus went to pray on the night he was arrested. The garden is actually an olive grove, rather than a formally cultivated plot. It is small now, but with ancient and venerable trees, some of which may well have been, as our guide said, present to witness the agonising hours that Jesus spent there. It was an uplifting experience to be there – to tread where Jesus had trodden. We felt part of that history and his story.

Gardens are places that reflect the cyclical nature of human existence – birth, growth, maturation and death. It seems fitting that gardens frame the accounts of God and his creation in the Bible, and feature so strongly in the major events of salvation history. It is fitting too that the olive grove is where Jesus makes his decision to accept the cup of suffering. Like the olives coming to fruition around him on the trees, he will be gathered and crushed. Olives give us oil for our use in both the sacred and secular areas of our lives – the oils of anointing and strengthening and the oils with which we cook or dress our salads. Oil is a sacramental – something that is part of making the ordinary into something holy. The oil of redemption will be the gift that Jesus expresses in his beaten and broken body and with which he anoints the world.

† Lord, give me the grace to harvest the failures that crush as well as the successes that uplift.

For further thought
• Where have I felt crushed and beaten? Can I see these experiences as possibilities for growth?

The circle of life

John 19:41 – 20:18

Early on the first day of the week, while it was still dark, Mary Magdalene went to the tomb and saw that the stone had been removed from the entrance. (verse 1)

I like the seasonal aspects of gardening because they connect me to the basic rhythms of life, and because there is beauty and grace even when nothing appears to be growing. There is always something happening even in the darkest days of winter.

Something happens as Jesus is buried in what is called the garden tomb. A cycle, or circle, is being completed. What appears lifeless and barren and dead is just that – mere appearance. Jesus, the new Adam, as Paul calls him, achieves new life for the human race through his death and his Resurrection. The fall takes place in – and its consequences are redeemed in – a garden. The transformed and transfigured Jesus makes his first appearance in a garden.

We can only imagine how Mary Magdalene had passed her Sabbath, longing to be near Jesus, to tend to him in death, wondering what it had all been for. We are privileged in knowing, before she does, the end of the story and the joy that she will experience when she recognises him as he speaks to her.

Our hearts have seasons as well, when all seems hopeless and barren. God is still at work, however, and we can be sure that nothing is outside the compass of his compassion and companionship. Can we use the blessing of this knowledge when our own lives are full of pain and doubt?

† Lord, I do have faith. Help me to grow that faith even more.

For further thought
• Reflect further on your prayer using Mark 9:24-29.

Saturday 23 August
God's re-creation and fulfilment

Revelation 21:1-4, 22-27

I saw the Holy City, the new Jerusalem, coming down out of heaven from God, prepared as a bride beautifully dressed for her husband. And I heard a loud voice from the throne saying, 'Look! God's dwelling place is now among the people, and he will dwell with them.' (verses 2-3a)

This summer we went to the wedding of our god-daughter. She looked as beautiful and radiant as every bride should be; the sun shone; and family and friends celebrated with great joy this new step along the way for the marital couple. The bride had planned and prepared just about everything. It was all well organised and supervised, revised and tweaked, so that a good time was had by all. Insofar as any human endeavour could be, it was perfect.

Perfection is our goal and our destiny. As Joni Mitchell tells us in her song 'Woodstock', 'We've got to get ourselves back to the garden'. The desire for a return to Eden, for a world of peace and love and eternal dwelling with God, is part of the restlessness of human nature. The sense of loss and of imperfection is deeply engrained in us. The Book of Revelation gives us a vision of the restored creation: Eden revisited, restored and renewed – the perfect garden. It is what God has planned and is preparing for us and towards which we journey.

In the meantime, though, we have responsibilities. We are required take care of and work the garden that is the here and now. We have to prepare, like a bride, for the biggest day of our lives – the day when we are reunited with God. We know that God's unconditional love is there for us whatever, but our response to that needs to be to strive for perfection so that we come to him joyful and excited as a bride.

† Lord, give me joy as I labour and prepare for the day when I will return home to you.

For further thought
- '[T]he old order of things has passed away' (verse 4b). What bits of the old order do I need to let go of?

Readings in Matthew 8 – 16
1 Jesus went about in all cities...

This week's notes are by **Katie Miller**

Katie Miller is an Anglican lay minister working in an area of social housing in the west of the city of Norwich. She has worked for a number of years in urban church settings, including with Youth with a Mission in Belfast and Derry, Northern Ireland, during the years of conflict. She is a speaker for the Church Urban Fund. In her day job Katie has worked as a paleooceanographer, studying past climates by analysing microfossils in ocean sediments. She is married to Bill and they have three teenage children.

Sunday 24 August
Jesus and the man with leprosy

Matthew 8:1-4

When Jesus came down from the mountainside, large crowds followed him. A man with leprosy came and knelt before him and said, 'Lord, if you are willing, you can make me clean.' Jesus reached out his hand and touched the man. 'I am willing,' he said. 'Be clean!' (verses 1-3a)

This week we are looking at encounters Jesus had with people in cities. Our little church is situated in an area of government housing in the west of our city. I love this area – it is a vibrant urban community. To some people it is a place of social deprivation, but I think it is all a matter of what you look to see. The encounters we will look at this week show Jesus seeing beyond the immediate, beyond the obvious, to individuals and their needs: a paralysed man, a centurion, a woman, a bereaved father, and many others. Cities are full of diverse people and Jesus meets their individual needs.

In today's reading he heals a man with leprosy. Leprosy made people outsiders, unwelcome. Many people in our urban community feel like outsiders, not welcome, but Jesus sees beyond the disease or the situation and heals the person. When we are feeling rejected and pushed out and cry out for help, Jesus says, 'I am willing'. He engages with us, draws us back into relationship with himself and others.

† Dear Lord, thank you that you see beyond outward appearance to our hearts, and meet each of our needs. Help us to see beyond the outward appearance of others. Amen

The faith of the centurion

Matthew 8:5-13

When Jesus had entered Capernaum, a centurion came to him, asking for help. 'Lᴏʀᴅ,' he said, 'my servant lies at home paralysed, suffering terribly.' Jesus said to him, 'Shall I come and heal him?' (verses 5-7)

Every Tuesday a friend and I prayer-walk the whole community around our church, praying for the homes, the schools, businesses and agencies working in the area. One morning we were walking past the small parade of shops praying when a woman came running out to greet us. She dashed across from the other side of the road, waving to attract our attention, and shouting apologies for interrupting us. When she caught up with us and gathered her breath she asked if we knew if there was a church in the area. Of course we explained that we were from the church, told her when and where we met and that she would be most welcome. This woman has become a faithful member of our congregation, attending regularly to this day.

The incident always reminds me of the centurion running out to greet Jesus in his need, without hesitation, without worrying what others would think. He knew that Jesus could meet his greatest need, to heal his beloved servant. That was all that mattered. And Jesus commended the centurion for his great faith.

† Dear Lord, we thank you for the faith of the centurion who sought you out knowing that you alone could meet his needs. Help us also to be bold and seek you out in faith. Amen

For further thought
• What do we need to run up to Jesus and ask him today?

Tuesday 26 August
He touched her hand

Matthew 8:14-17

When Jesus came into Peter's house, he saw Peter's mother-in-law lying in bed with a fever. He touched her hand and the fever left her, and she got up and began to wait on him. (verses 14-15)

Recently Jenny, a woman we met first through our choir, starting attending our church. She had been coming for only a few weeks when she brought along someone we assumed was a friend. It turned out this friend was in fact her sister, a committed Christian who had been praying for her family for years. The sister was so full of joy and delight at Jenny finally coming to church and asking questions about faith. Before she left to go home, we prayed with Jenny's sister for their family. A very short time after this, Jenny asked for a Bible and for guidance as to how to read it. Soon she volunteered to help with our work with mothers and children, where she is now a much-loved and valued helper.

Jesus cares about whole families. Jesus knows the needs of our families and he knows that those needs sometimes worry and trouble us. He knows that sometimes we can feel our families are very far from him. Jesus walks into the house and sees that Peter's mother-in-law is unwell. He immediately attends to her. He heals many people that day, but there is nothing more important to do before attending to Peter's mother-in-law.

† Dear Lord, thank you that you know and care for our whole families. Help us to entrust our loved ones into your hands, knowing you see their needs. Amen

For further thought
• Let us offer up our whole family to God's care today.

Wednesday 27 August
The demon-possessed men

Matthew 8:28-34

Those tending the pigs ran off, went into the town and reported all this, including what had happened to the demon-possessed men. Then the whole town went out to meet Jesus. And when they saw him, they pleaded with him to leave their region. (verses 33–34)

Sometimes we need God to be powerful in our lives. The troubles we have can seem so great that only our powerful God can bring about the change we need. A lady we have known for a long time confessed to me recently troubles in her family that seemed totally overwhelming. No amount of just telling her 'it will be all right' was going to make the situation better for her. I did not know what to say except how very sorry I was that she was facing such a difficult time and that we would pray for her and her family.

A few of us were meeting that evening about general church business and, as we closed the meeting in prayer, we lifted up this woman's situation to God. I was amazed to get back that night and find a message from her, even though it was very late. She wrote to say that she had gone home and had already seen unexpected and wonderful answers to our prayers that very evening.

I am not sure I believed when I prayed that she would find answers so quickly. I was reminded what a powerful God we serve. The people in this story were in awe of Jesus when he drove out the demons so much so they begged him to leave. There is no situation too difficult for our God. There is nothing we cannot bring to him in prayer.

† Dear Lord, help us to know that there is nothing we cannot bring to you in prayer. You are a loving and powerful God doing more than we can ask or imagine. Amen

For further thought
• What overwhelming situations can we hand over to God today?

Thursday 28 August
Jesus and a paralysed man

Matthew 9:1-8

Jesus stepped into a boat, crossed over and came to his own town. Some men brought to him a paralysed man, lying on a mat. When Jesus saw their faith, he said to the man, 'Take heart, son; your sins are forgiven.' (verses 1-2)

Recently I noticed one of the mothers who comes to our mums and toddlers group reading some leaflets she had brought with her to the group. I asked her about them and she explained that she wanted to become a foster carer for children who had had a difficult start in life. She had already gone as far as making some enquiries about what fostering would involve, and collecting the leaflets. I have known this woman for a number of years. I know she herself had a difficult childhood. I know she is a wonderful mother to her own children and cares for others, so I asked if there was any way we as a church could help her in her desire to become a foster parent. I was wondering if there was anything practical that we could do. She told me, 'You already have. You have seen me as someone who can help.'

A fresh start is one of the greatest gifts that God can give us. Without it we can feel as paralysed as the man in this story. He had nothing to give until Jesus brought forgiveness and healing into his life. With a fresh start from Jesus we can bless and help others.

† Dear Lord, we bless and thank you that you give us a fresh start through forgiveness and grace. Help us never to forget that you are our help and our hope. Amen

For further thought

• Where do we need God's healing and forgiveness and a fresh start?

Friday 29 August
From death to life

Matthew 9:18-26

Just then a woman who had been subject to bleeding for twelve years came up behind him and touched the edge of his cloak. She said to herself, 'If I only touch his cloak, I will be healed.' (verses 20-21)

Some years ago a decision was made to close the small church building in the area where we work as it was considered no longer financially viable to keep it open. This was a cause of great bereavement to some for whom it had been their place of worship for many years – people who had faithfully polished its floors, painted its walls, tended its gardens and given sacrificially for its upkeep. Since that time we have been something of a nomadic collection of worshippers. We have met in the school and the community centre for worship. We need space for our community choir and our work with mothers, so we shared those with other agencies in the area. We held our meetings in the local café. The powerlessness of having no place to meet has caused us to build many new relationships in the area where we work – relationships that we did not need to develop when we had our own building.

This story tells of two very different people who were driven to a point of powerlessness: a sick woman and a bereaved father. But it was at that point of powerlessness they met Jesus and he was able to change their lives.

† Dear Lord, we thank you that in our powerlessness you are powerful. Help us to give you our powerlessness so that you can break through in our lives. Amen

For further thought

• What areas of powerlessness in your life can you offer to God to see his power break through?

Saturday 30 August
He touched their eyes

Matthew 9:27-31

Then he touched their eyes and said, 'According to your faith let it be done to you'; and their sight was restored. Jesus warned them sternly, 'See that no one knows about this.' But they went out and spread the news about him all over that region. (verses 29-31)

One of our great joys as a church has been our community choir. It was a simple idea, born out of a few of the mothers in the community mentioning that singing made them happy. 'What if we simply invite people to come and sing?' Having no great resource of musicians, we simply play backing tracks to popular songs and sing along together to printed word sheets. Everyone gets to suggest songs, and no one has to pass an audition; all are welcome whether they can sing in tune or not and whether they attend church or not.

The choir has become a caring community, looking out for each other, helping each other through times of difficulty. One of the highlights of the evening is always coffee, cake and sharing stories. We have not asked people to bake but someone always seems to bring goodies to share. Repeatedly someone in the choir will say, 'Is it OK if I ask my friend? Do you mind if they come to choir, too?' It is humbling to have people ask if it is OK to bring people to a church event because they enjoy it so much. You cannot keep good news quiet, it seems.

This story of Jesus healing the blind men can seem a little strange. Jesus heals the men then tells them not to speak of it, but you can't keep good news silent.

† Dear Lord, thank you that the good news that you bring into our lives is impossible not to share. Give us opportunities to tell others of your goodness, we pray. Amen

For further thought

- What good news about Jesus do you just have to tell someone today?

Readings in Matthew 8 – 16
2 ... proclaiming the good news of the kingdom

This week's notes are by **Elizabeth Whitehorn**

Elizabeth Whitehorn grew up in Edinburgh and has lived and worked in various parts of Scotland and England. A former schoolteacher, adult educator and editor, she and her husband moved to Cambridge, UK, on retirement. There she has been able to revive and develop various interests, including French, reading and music. She is a voluntary tutor for the University of the Third Age, sings in a choir and is an active member of her local United Reformed church.

Sunday 31 August
A transformed life speaks loud and clear

Matthew 9:32-38

[A] man who was demon-possessed and could not talk was brought to Jesus. And when the demon was driven out, the man who had been mute spoke. (part of verses 32-33)

What does it mean to proclaim the good news of the kingdom? This week we observe Jesus' methods: sometimes he addressed large crowds, but at other times he spoke quietly to an individual or gave practical help. These notes aim to encourage you to enter imaginatively into the readings and then reflect on their relevance today. Ask God to speak to you afresh. Listen, reflect prayerfully, then go and live out what you have discovered.

I wonder what the formerly mute man said. Did he thank Jesus? Did he praise God? Perhaps he rushed off to spread the good news, starting with his family. Try to picture the scene and what might have happened next. In what ways would the lives of the man and his family be different from now on?

What experience do you have of being unable to speak? Perhaps a throat problem prevented you from talking. Perhaps you were not allowed to speak for yourself or were ignored when you did speak. Perhaps you find yourself tongue-tied when you try to talk to others about God. Wherever God has placed you and whatever your personality or situation, God can speak through your life, character and actions and possibly also through your words.

† Loving God, please may my life, character and actions, as well as my words, speak to others of you and your good news.

Monday 1 September
People versus rules

Matthew 12:9-14

[Jesus] went into their synagogue, and a man with a shrivelled hand was there. Looking for a reason to bring charges against Jesus, [the Pharisees] asked him, 'Is it lawful to heal on the Sabbath?' He said to them … '[I]t is lawful to do good on the Sabbath.' (verses 9-10, 12b)

Jesus' compassion overrode concern for his personal safety, even when it exposed him to further opposition from the Pharisees. The way Matthew tells this story, the man with the shrivelled hand did not ask to be healed but was singled out by the Pharisees in order to cause trouble for Jesus.

Try to picture the scene. In what ways is the man's life restricted by his shrivelled hand? How might he feel when he sees Jesus coming into the synagogue? Listen to the discussion between Jesus and the Pharisees. In what ways will the man's life be different as a result of his encounter with Jesus? What thoughts and emotions do you experience while this episode is happening? Is there any good news for *you* in this story?

It can be easier to live by a set of detailed rules than to use our freedom to choose how to behave. It can be tempting to find a Bible verse that supports our opinion rather than to wrestle with seemingly contradictory passages. For example, even within my lifetime there have been enormous changes in the way British Christians observe Sunday. Families can find it particularly difficult to decide on priorities when, for instance, children's sports activities are routinely held on Sunday mornings. What can your church or Christian community do to help people who are wrestling with questions about priorities? In what ways can this passage give guidance relevant to your particular situation?

† Compassionate God, please forgive me when I put rules before people. Help me to sort out my priorities in the light of your love.

For further thought

- Spend time reviewing how you spend Sunday. In the light of today's reading, do you need or want to make any changes?

Tuesday 2 September
Encouragement for the flawed

Matthew 14:22-33

*'Lᴏʀᴅ, if it's you,' Peter replied, 'tell me to come to you on the water.'
'Come,' [Jesus] said. Then Peter got down out of the boat, walked on
the water and came towards Jesus. But when he saw the wind, he was
afraid and, beginning to sink, cried out, 'Lᴏʀᴅ, save me!' Immediately Jesus
reached out his hand and caught him.* (verses 28-31a)

Imagine you are one of Jesus' disciples. You have just witnessed
Jesus feeding 5000 men plus women and children, using five
loaves and two fish. How do you feel when Jesus sends you and
your companions on ahead before the crowd has dispersed? What
do you think when Jesus appears in the early morning darkness
(between 3:00 and 6:00 am)? How do you react to Peter's
behaviour? What good news is there for *you* in this incident?

This is one of several stories in the Gospels where Peter is shown
to be impulsive and flawed but also courageous and full of faith.
As a fisherman, he knew it was physically impossible to walk on
water, yet at Jesus' invitation he climbed out of the boat. When
he focused on his surroundings, his faith faltered and he began
to sink. What experience do you have of setting out full of faith in
response to Jesus' invitation and then finding it impossible to keep
going? Can you identify why this happened?

God calls and uses us in spite of our flaws and inconsistencies.
Perhaps you have begun to have doubts about a task you believed
God had called you to. Or perhaps you feel overwhelmed by
a situation. Whatever your circumstances, spend some time
reflecting on this passage and listening for what God is saying to
you through it.

† Talk to God about any aspect of your life in which you feel at a loss or
overwhelmed, or pray for someone else in such a situation.

For further thought
• Find a Bible verse that can encourage you in times of difficulty
and learn it by heart. Then remember to meditate on it in time
of need.

September

Wednesday 3 September
Close enough to touch

Matthew 14:34-36

[W]hen the men of that place [Gennesaret] recognised Jesus, they sent word to all the surrounding country. People brought all who were ill to him … and all who touched [the edge of Jesus' cloak] were healed. (part of verses 35-36)

Imagine you live in the Gennesaret area, a fertile plain north-west of the Sea of Galilee. What makes you come to see Jesus? Do you come alone? Do you bring someone who is ill? Does someone else bring you? Try to picture the scene and how it develops. What does Jesus say to the people around you? What does he say to you? What do you want to say to Jesus? Do you feel able to reach out and touch him yourself?

There is a lot of deliberate movement in this passage: the local people 'sent word' of Jesus' arrival in their area; people 'brought all who were ill'; they 'begged Jesus'; the sick had to touch Jesus. I am particularly struck by this last detail, that people had to reach out and touch Jesus. Usually it was Jesus who reached out and touched others, even those considered untouchable. One thing this says to me is that we can bring others to Jesus but it is up to them to respond to him. Another thought is that there are times when Jesus waits to be asked to change me or to work in my life. What does this passage say to you?

Reflect on how you came to Christian faith. Who shared the good news with you? In what sense was it good news for you at that time? What insights does this give you for how you might share the good news with other people?

† Generous God, thank you for the people who helped me find faith. Gentle Jesus, I invite you to work in and through me, too.

For further thought

- If God seems silent and distant, might it be that God is waiting to be invited to act in my life?

Thursday 4 September
Good news for everyone?

Matthew 15:21-28

The woman came and knelt before [Jesus]. 'LORD, help me!' she said. He replied, 'It is not right to take the children's bread and toss it to the dogs.' 'Yes, it is, LORD,' she said. 'Even the dogs eat the crumbs that fall from their master's table.' Then Jesus said to her, 'Woman, you have great faith!' (verses 25-28a)

Imagine you are one of Jesus' disciples. What do you think of the way the woman behaves and talks? Are you surprised, shocked or challenged by the way Jesus reacts to her? Do you think he is right to heal her daughter?

I wonder why Jesus appears to have been reluctant to help this woman. Wasn't he supposed to welcome everyone, regardless of who they were? Was he refining his understanding of his mission? Did she actually persuade him to change his mind or was he testing her? The disciples clearly believed that she, a Gentile, was beyond the scope of the good news of the kingdom. Do we, in our churches and Christian communities, behave as if we think this way about other people?

A few years ago I attended a Sunday evening service where a group of young people, obviously not used to church, suddenly came in and sat down. After a while they left, presumably because what was happening seemed irrelevant to them. If they had kept coming, I wonder what changes the congregation would have been willing to make in order to make it easier for them to feel welcome. If we really do believe that the good news of God's kingdom is for everyone, in what ways do we need to change? Who are the people that are missing from your church or Christian community?

Perhaps, on the other hand, you feel that there are barriers that keep you outside the church, if not outside God's kingdom. What is God saying to you through today's Bible passage?

† Welcoming God, I am glad that you welcome everyone. Please keep me from putting up barriers for myself and for others.

For further thought

- What barriers, both obvious and hidden, exist in your own church or Christian community?
- Should they be removed? If so, how?

Giving and receiving help

Matthew 15:29-31

[Jesus] went up on a mountainside and sat down. Great crowds came to him, bringing the lame, the blind, the crippled, the mute and many others, and laid them at his feet; and he healed them. The people were amazed … And they praised the God of Israel. (part of verses 29-31)

I wonder why Jesus did not go to those who wanted to be healed but sat down and waited for them to be brought to him. Would it not have been kinder to settle everyone down and move among them? Instead there must have been a lot of picking up and putting down, jostling, murmuring and so on. Try to picture the scene. Imagine you are there in the crowd. Have you brought someone else to be healed? Whom have you brought? Have you been brought by friends or family to be healed by Jesus? Who has brought you? Why have you agreed to come? What has the journey been like? How do you feel when you see the crowds who have got there before you? What goes through your mind while you await your turn? Visualise what happens when you and your companion(s) meet Jesus. What effect does this have on you?

How might this apply in our daily life? We can get so used to helping others that we find it hard to accept help for ourselves. We can be so conscientious about fulfilling our various roles and responsibilities that we become stressed, exhausted and burned-out. 'Better to burn out than to rust out', the saying goes; but does that really honour God? Whether you are concerned about your own state of mind and health or about someone else's, what is God saying to you through this passage and your reflections on it?

† Healing God, I lay before you my concern for ___. Please help.

For further thought

• There are times when we need someone else to support and pray for us: a friend or a spiritual director, perhaps. Who takes you to Jesus?

Saturday 6 September
No contribution is too small

Matthew 15:32-39

Jesus ... said, 'I have compassion for these people; they have already been with me three days and have nothing to eat ... His disciples answered, 'Where could we get enough bread in this remote place to feed such a crowd?' 'How many loaves do you have?' Jesus asked. 'Seven,' they replied. (parts of verses 32-34)

Try to picture the scene. Perhaps you would like to continue in yesterday's role; perhaps you would prefer to choose a different character. Watch and listen to what happens. Are the disciples surprised when Jesus asks how many loaves they have? Do they give him the loaves gladly or reluctantly? Why have they not eaten the loaves and fish already? How do the people near Jesus react when they see him blessing and breaking the food and then asking the disciples to distribute it? How do you feel as you receive and eat your share?

I wonder why people stayed for three days when they, their friends or their relatives had been healed, especially as they had no food or shelter. What was it about Jesus, his words and his actions that kept them there? This challenges me: do I spend enough time in Jesus' presence? Do I recognise the value of spending time with him?

I am also challenged about how I react when God asks me to do something, especially if it means making some sort of sacrifice. However reluctantly I do it, however small my contribution seems, God can bless and multiply it as he did the small amount of food in this story. Perhaps, on the other hand, this passage speaks more to you of Holy Communion (the Eucharist). Spend some time reflecting on what this sacrament means to you. What is God saying to *you* through today's Bible passage?

† Nurturing God, keep me close enough to you for you to be able to feed others through me.

For further thought

• What is God inviting *you* to do?

Faithful and fruitful
1 Vocation of faith

This week's notes are by **Jember Teferra**

Jember Teferra is from Ethiopia and is a widow with three children and four grandchildren. She works with very dedicated team in some of the poorest slums in Addis Ababa. Her ministry, known as the Integrated Holistic Approach Urban Development Project, fights poverty as a Christian agenda and promotes social justice.

Sunday 7 September
A faithful God

Psalm: 31:1-23

Love the LORD all his faithful people! The LORD preserves those who are true to him, but the proud he pays back in full. Be strong and take heart, all you who hope in the LORD. **(verses 23-24)**

This week's theme addresses and focuses on faithfulness, trustworthiness, prudence and wisdom, in our stewardship. This week we will also consider the need for the responsible use of the gifts of God in his service. The New Testament selection we will read together is clearly addressed by our Lord himself to teach us to be wise stewards and take responsibility to carry out what we are assigned. Paul also stresses the point of absolute trustworthiness.

Although all who follow the Lord know how faithful God is, those who have gone through suffering know it more deeply and realistically. The only hope and confidence David had during his hiding from Saul, who wished to kill him, was his confidence and trust in being protected by God. 'In you, LORD, I have taken refuge … deliver me' (verse 1). David, as we know, was not let down. He was privileged enough to be a king and served God as a chosen man and king.

† Heavenly Father, please give us the confidence and faith to trust you completely and serve you faithfully.

Monday 8 September
When will you come to me?

Psalm 101:1-8

I will sing of your love and justice; to you, O LORD, I will sing praise. I will be careful to lead a blameless life – when will you come to me? I will conduct the affairs of my house with a blameless heart. I will not look with approval on anything that is vile. (verses 1-3a)

This portion of the Psalm is thought to describe the 'Davidic ideal' – be it personal, household or public standards. Controversial as David's personal life is, it appeals to all of us sinners who, like David, have been forgiven for what we have done. Jesus gave his life to make us blameless; and God honoured David's best intentions and described David as a man of his own heart. What a privilege! Do we aspire to reach that standard? We have to plead with David, saying, 'When will you come to me?' (verse 2). All human beings are equal in God's eyes, and God is just. God will certainly come to us when we call upon him; God favours the faithful.

† Almighty God, as we choose to follow you, give us the blessing of your Spirit to live justly and blamelessly, and to serve you and honour you every second of our lives, for you are worthy!

For further thought
• Consider keeping a prayer journal to record how often the Lord has shown his faithfulness.

Tuesday 9 September
A refuge

Psalm 11:1-13

*In the L*ORD *I take refuge. How then can you say to me: 'Flee like a bird to your mountain. For look, the wicked bend their bows; They set their arrows against the strings to shoot from the shadows at the upright in heart.'* (verses 1-2)

As I am writing, our ministry to the poorest slum dwellers is going through a hard time – but nothing as bad as David's situation with Saul! At times work can be full of trouble and distraction. People who see us struggling, with the voice of worldly prudence keep telling us to just give it up and go. I can understand how people feel. However, my repeated response is that when God calls you to any ministry God also equips you with adequate tolerance, wisdom and persistence. With the help of the Lord, my team will take refuge in God who enables us. It is only through the help of God that we have survived for 22 years of service and ministry. How is God a refuge to you?

† Thank you, Lord, for giving us patience, confidence and the ability to keep trying.

For further thought

- How do you cope with trouble and distractions in your work, whether paid or voluntary, or at home?
- What lessons do you take from David's response in his circumstances?

Wednesday 10 September
Who is faithful?

Matthew 24:1-13

At that time many will turn away from the faith and will betray and hate each other, and many false prophets will appear and deceive many people. Because of the increase of wickedness, the love of most will grow cold, but the one who stands firm to the end will be saved. (verses 10-13)

Verse 13 answers the question we were left with yesterday. In the past few weeks I have been paying attention to world events as they come through the media in Ethiopia. The more I listened, the more world events seemed to confirm these verses of our Lord's warning: horrific events, wars, natural disasters, betrayals, unusual crimes – it was too much to take in. Those of us who know the Lord just pray even harder; but on the other hand we desire the coming of the Lord in justice and peace. Come, Lord Jesus!

† Our King and our Lord, the life we live is worth living only if we know you, follow you and obey you. Help us to share this joy with others in words and deeds, and keep us faithful to the end.

For further thought
• Will you be faithful to the end, come what may?

Thursday 11 September
Faithful with a few things

Matthew 25:14-30

His master replied, 'Well done, good and faithful servant! You have been faithful with a few things; I will put you in charge of many things. Come and share your master's happiness! (verse 21)

This parable points out different spiritual opportunities that are given to different people in whatever context God wishes it. If we take them on, we have to look beyond our limited understanding.

The choices of whom to utilise and give the opportunities to are the Lord's to make! When I became a political prisoner, in the first two days I found it hard to understand why God wanted me to be there. I went through a spiritual struggle until God enabled me to see that I could serve my fellow prisoners with my health background, education, and counselling training. I was able help others in many different ways, and I was sad to leave. I remember the head of the prison guard saying to me, when I was released, 'You came in upset – and now that you are being released you look as though you are upset! You are an odd woman!' God uses our talents in different ways and contexts – if we are ready to be used.

† God of all wisdom, open our eyes to see where you wish us to use our talents to serve you and bring glory and honour to you.

For further thought
• God always knows how best we can use our talents. Are we always open to see how God wishes to use them?

Friday 12 September
Shrewd for God's sake

Luke 16:1-15

Whoever can be trusted with very little can also be trusted with much and whoever is dishonest with very little will also be dishonest with much. So if you have not been trustworthy in handling worldly wealth, who will trust you with true riches? And if you have not been trustworthy with someone else's property, who will give you property of your own? (verses 10-12)

This parable is confusing. Is Jesus approving dishonesty? Or is shrewdness something different? We should look further to understand Jesus' words.

Jesus makes it clear that it was the steward's morality and not his shrewdness that was condemned. It is challenging for all who are in places of responsibility: the worship of money leads to dishonesty, and is not a Christian value. Our Lord points out that we cannot serve both God and money for, as the scriptures indicate, the love of money is the root of evil. Honesty, accountability and integrity are the values promoted here. How about through our words and actions?

† Giver of all good things, help us to put the value of money against what money can't buy – and so honestly and with integrity share with those who are very poor.

For further thought
- How do we use our wealth?
- Are we being shrewd in our kingdom work?
- Let us ask ourselves and examine our values with the scale our Lord wishes us to use.

Judge of all

1 Corinthians 4:1-13

This, then, is how you ought to regard us: as servants of Christ and as those entrusted with the mysteries God has revealed. Now it is required that those who have been given a trust must prove faithful … It is the LORD who judges me. Therefore judge nothing before the appointed time; wait until the LORD comes. (part of verses 1-5)

Paul here stresses to Christians the need to be absolutely trustworthy. As we all know, it is only God who can rightly assess our motives.

After my political imprisonment during Ethiopia's military Marxist era, I went to work in a slum area identified by the World Bank as among the world's poorest. As I was assessing and filling out forms for mothers and babies, I lost my voice. One of the military local officials noticed me. He asked my friend and colleague, 'Why is your colleague who comes from the oppressing class pretending to care for the oppressed poor? She is a hypocrite. Does she think they don't know her? Or is she hoping that this will help towards her husband's release from political imprisonment?' Thankfully, my friend defended me. She replied, 'Oh! Sir, you cannot understand her motives – her values and motives are only understood by the Good Lord above.' Luckily he walked away. But three months later the official approached me again. I said to him that my friend had answered adequately on my behalf – so there was nothing more to say.

† God almighty, only you can understand, judge and assess the faithfulness, motives and values of your servants – what a privilege to be your servant!

For further thought

- How do we measure who a faithful servant is?
- What scale do you use?
- Does it matter anyway?

Faithful and fruitful
2 Fruitful living

This week's notes are by **Sister Christopher Godden OSB**

The wide-open skies over the coastal village in her native Lancashire have given Sr Christopher a great love of space and silence. Following her schooling she attended a College of Education for 18 months before moving into the electricity industry. Thirteen years later, having become a Catholic in the intervening years, she entered the Benedictine monastery at Talacre, remaining with the same Community when it moved to Chester.

Sunday 14 September
Beginnings

Colossians 1:1-10

We have not stopped praying for you … so that you may live a life worthy of the LORD and please him in every way: bearing fruit in every good work, growing in the knowledge of God. (part of verses 9-10)

For both plant and animal life, certain maturity has to be reached before fruiting occurs. Learning to cope wisely and well with life, its problems and glories is the route. Paragraph 2 of the Prologue to the Rule of St Benedict (*Households of God: The Rule of St Benedict*, ed. David Parry, Darton, Longman & Todd Ltd, 1980), which guides my religious order, begins 'First of all, whenever you begin any good work, you must ask God with the most urgent prayer that it may be brought to completion by him …'. In order to be able to bear fruit for the gospel it is essential we be well grounded in prayer and also rooted in a firm and deep relationship with God.

Asked to define prayer, the late Cardinal Hume said, 'Relationship'. This is what prayer is all about. Building up a live, personal relationship with God. It takes time, space, fidelity and work. Also the conviction that, even when we are not 'with God', he is always 'with us' and can transform the unlikeliest situation into one of grace. We may never see or know the fruit of our efforts – but that's not the point.

† Lord, at the start of a new week we ask a blessing on our lives in the days ahead. We also remember all who look ahead with fear and dread to the next seven days. Lord, in your mercy, give them strength and hope.

September

Monday 15 September
Good dirt

Luke 8:5-15

But the seed on good soil stands for those with a noble and good heart, who hear the word, retain it, and by persevering produce a crop.
(verse 15)

When I was a Novice and in what is called 'Formation', it was the custom that twice a year I had to ask to be 'allowed to persevere' in the monastery. It was a sort of stocktaking. I could review things and decide if I wanted to go on, and the community could review me and see if they thought I was a suitable candidate.

Perseverance is not a popular word or concept these days. We live in an age when it seems easy to change career, job and partner all on a whim when one feels the old one has become boring and stale. Instead of sticking things out and trying to make them work, the idea seems to be to cast off the old and begin again. Yet it is through sticking things out and making them work to the best of our ability that we mature and grow stronger.

Do you take the soil for granted? I tend to. It is 'just there'. Yet, from time spent in the garden, I have come to realise that soil maintenance is important if one wants a good crop. Weeds need to be pulled up, stones and rocks removed, compact earth broken up and the soil periodically turned over and composted. This happens in our lives, too, mostly through the daily events we meet and cope with. We may not realise it at the time. It can be achieved by focusing on God and what God might be asking of us, which is better than becoming introspective or taking ourselves too seriously. We have the best gardener of all.

† We pray especially today for all whose mission it is in life to spread the gospel by their words and lives. Encourage them by your presence and may their toil not be in vain.

For further thought

• You are asked to tell someone about the Christian gospel and way of life. Where would you begin and what would you suggest the person does next?

Tuesday 16 September
Be not hasty

Matthew 13:24-32

Let both grow together until the harvest. At that time I will tell the harvesters: first collect the weeds and tie them into bundles to be burned; then gather the wheat and bring it into my barn. (verse 30)

In the first parable we read today, the servants saw only the weeds; the owner saw both weeds and wheat. It is easy to see only the negative and immediately try to eradicate it. However, this is not always the best way. As the story says, more serious damage is then done and the entire crop lost. Better to wait and see.

War is evil and yet it seems there will always be wars. But from the carnage of war have come some incredible advances in medicine and surgery as doctors have learned to treat the damaged and injured. There also have been peace movements, movements for racial justice, the creation of the United Nations, and many other developments, all of which have come about as a result of war and injustice. It is good these things have come into being – just very sad that it has taken violence of some sort to generate them.

In England we do not have the sort of mustard seed mentioned in our second parable, but we do have conkers, which grow into huge horse chestnut trees, and acorns that make large oaks. I have often marvelled that these fruit, each no bigger then a plum, will grow into such large trees. But there is a warning here and a timely reminder. A hasty word spoken in anger may kill a friendship or damage a relationship whereas a smile or kind word of encouragement can make someone burst into flower! Am I being openhearted or small-minded? A moment's thought can make all the difference.

† Help us, Lord, to see the positive in all the situations we face today. When we make an unwise choice, show us the way it can be redeemed.

For further thought

- Go out and look at a tree. Imagine it in seed form.
- Think of a tree mentioned in the Bible.
- If you can, plant a seed today.

September

261

Gardening inside

Galatians 5:13-24

For the entire law is fulfilled in keeping this one command: 'Love your neighbour as yourself.' (verse 14)

There are people who seem to go through life making lists: things to do, books to be read, friends to contact, and so on. I am one myself, and I think St Paul was one too. (See also 1 Corinthians 13:4-7.)

Today's reading contains two lists, each of which names seeds already planted deep within us. Some of these seeds will have already grown into plants. There are 'the weeds' of verses 19-21 (a member of our community always maintains that weeds are just 'flowers in the wrong place', and that many of them are also herbs), and the flowers of verse 22. We have to encourage the flowers and deal somehow with the weeds.

In Chapter 4 of the Rule of St Benedict, he equips his monastics with seventy-four 'tools' (of good works) to use on their 'inside' gardens. Nothing fancy: just ordinary sensible things such as the Ten Commandments, the Golden Rule of Jesus, and others such as 'Not to give way to anger' (Tool 22), 'Not to return evil for evil' (Tool 29), 'Not to indulge in envy' (Tool 67). All very mundane, but needed in society in general as well as in a monastery.

Tool 74, the wisest tool of all, states 'And never to despair of God's mercy'. We are to try to do our best when circumstances are difficult, remembering God sees and knows all and is a merciful judge. God helps us not to be downhearted or tempted to give up when the weeds seem to be flourishing, but to keep on digging for victory.

† Lord, help me to balance the day so I get the mixture of work, prayer time and relaxation right. When the unexpected comes along, may I deal with it fairly and with common sense.

For further thought

- Sometimes the urge to 'put someone right' is almost beyond one's strength to cope with, so what do we do then?

Thursday 18 September
True love goes wide and deep

1 Corinthians 13:1-13

For now we see only a reflection as in a mirror; then we shall see face to face. Now I know in part; then I shall know fully, even as I am fully known.
(verse 12)

John Chrysostom writes: 'And where I am, there also are you: Where you are, there too am I: we are one body. We are separated by space, but we are united in love' (*The Homilies of St John Chrysostom*). Those words finished our reading at midday office today. It's an incredible thought, isn't it! Most of us reading this do not know each other, have never met and never will, yet we are united in love. Scattered over the planet we may be, but together in love.

Love is hard. Love is a state of mind rather than a feeling. Love involves objectivity, effort, focusing correctly, vigilance, trust and discipline. At times it can involve going against your own or another's will, sometimes maybe becoming unpopular. Do you really want to love? You will have tears, frustration and be misunderstood. But you will also know peace, joy, happiness. It was love that made Jesus cry over Jerusalem (Luke 19:41); it was love that made Jesus so frustrated when the Pharisees attacked and tried to trap him; it was love that made Jesus unpopular (John 6:66).

St Paul gives us some of the 'is and is not's of love, today. Within each negative lies a small seed of positive we need to discover and help grow. Good and bad days, both can be utilised; there's nothing that cannot. That's one of love's secrets; it is everywhere waiting to be discovered. Love is something continuous. Learning to love is the journey of a lifetime.

† Thank you for your love of us, O Lord. We pray for the unloved, unwanted, discarded, despised and rejected. May each one receive some help and consolation before the sun goes down.

For further thought

• How does one explain and illustrate the real meaning of love in a world that looks in the wrong place and wrong direction to find it?

Friday 19 September
Joy beyond words

Philippians 4:4-9

Finally, brothers and sisters, whatever is true, whatever is noble, whatever is right, whatever is pure, whatever is lovely, whatever is admirable – if anything is excellent or praiseworthy – think about such things. (verse 8)

For at least fifteen terms of my schooling, the headmistress read this famous passage at the last school assembly of term. Rejoice? We certainly did, end-of-term report permitting. Did we know joy? I don't think so; we were too young.

Joy is a deep thing, more akin to a state of being rather than just an emotion or good feeling. It has a sense of permanence and security that, even when life has gone all pear-shaped, noisy and horrid, it can still be there buried inside us and giving us hope of better things to come. St Paul has come to experience this and wants to share it.

Joy is a facet of peace, that deep peace mentioned in verse 7: 'the peace of God which transcends all understanding' and which can be won only by hard work, sweat and tears (Churchill). How can we too come to find the joy he alludes too? As plants grow and naturally turn towards the light, so must we keep our eyes on Jesus and the path to God, concentrating beyond ourselves and not turning our gaze inward to inspect any progress we may or may not have made. The important part comes after all the words are read and we begin to practise and live them so they become alive and real in us.

As St Benedict writes in the Prologue to The Rule, 'through the continual practice [of monastic observance] and the life of faith, our hearts are opened wide, and the way of God's commandments is run in a sweetness of love beyond all words'.

† So many people in the world feel no joy, O Lord. Help each of us to be able to communicate and share its secret to just one person we will meet today.

For further thought

• Which is your favourite piece of scripture? Why?
• What parts of the Bible do you find it hardest to accept and cope with? Why?

Saturday 20 September
Apples for eating

John 14:15-31

Whoever has my commands and keeps them is the one who loves me. The one who loves me will be loved by my Father, and I too will love them and show myself to them. (verse 21)

Words sometimes fail me. What is the Holy Spirit? What does it look like? What does it do? I have no idea what the Holy Spirit looks like but I do believe in it and have felt it.

The disciples are full of fear. Jesus has told them he will soon be leaving them (John 13:33). He has been with them from the beginning of their time together and they cannot imagine life without him. (We know the feeling. When someone or something we have relied on is suddenly no longer there, one can feel very exposed, frightened and vulnerable.) Jesus is suddenly speaking in riddles; suddenly not making sense with all this talk about a Spirit of truth that lives with them but that cannot be seen – that they 'know' but the world doesn't … He will go from them but then will come back to them …. It is all very confusing! However, throughout his ministry Jesus has been preparing the disciples for this moment. They are the soil he has nurtured and prepared; he has sown the seeds of the gospel within them and they have taken root and grown. Now the disciples have matured and it is their turn to go out, prepare new ground, and sow seeds so others can continue the mission of spreading the good news.

A man called Joseph Smith wrote a carol called 'Jesus Christ the Apple Tree'. What a wonderful illustration there is in this title – from Adam to Jesus to us. Friends, whoever you are, wherever you are, we have gardening to do: 'Come now; let us leave' (John 14:31).

† Lord, we thank you for the past week, ask you to forgive any blunders we have made and, in your own way and time, help them to be turned around so good things may come from them.

For further thought

- Have you been able to speak openly and freely about your faith in the past week? Pray for all who have heard the gospel for the first time this week.

Faithful and fruitful
3 On bearing good fruits

This week's notes are by **Lesley George Anderson**

 Lesley G Anderson is the Superintendent of the North Trinidad Methodist Circuit in Trinidad, a leader in the Caribbean Conference of Churches and a member of an ecumenical World Council of Churches' Pentecostal consultative group. He was President of the United Theological College of the West Indies, Jamaica; past District President of the Caribbean Conferences of the Methodist Church; and a former Area Secretary of the British Methodist Church, serving the Americas, Caribbean and Europe.

Sunday 21 September
Cultivating the fruit of patience

Romans 5:1-5

We also glory in our sufferings, because we know that suffering produces perseverance; perseverance, character; and character, hope. (part of verses 3-4)

Paul, an apostle, was called and chosen by Christ to proclaim and spread God's word. In exercising leadership over the churches, he motivated believers to bear good fruit – the theme we will be considering together this week.

Empowered by the Holy Spirit, Christians are challenged to bear fruit. To bear fruit we must live connected to the vine, Christ himself. This connectedness is what gives life and vitality to our spirituality. The fruits of the Spirit are Christian values and virtues. We must practise and root them into our lives as spiritual habits, for God wants from us a bountiful harvest.

Today we begin with *patience*. How do you cope with severe and painful sickness? Are you slow to anger? Barbara from Belize was a young Methodist local preacher, hymn writer and poet, committed to Christ and dedicated to the church. Born with one kidney and afflicted with diabetes, she suffered severely but without complaint. Like Paul in the verse above, Barbara, who was always joyful, kept hope alive. Patiently she faced the daily trials of her sickness and faith with courage. Patiently and victoriously, she endured to the end.

† Lord Jesus, in the trials and tribulations of our lives, give us courage and strength to endure patiently to the end. Amen

Monday 22 September
Cultivating the fruit of kindness

Ephesians 4:31 – 5:2

Get rid of all bitterness, rage and anger, brawling and slander, along with every form of malice. Be kind and compassionate to one another, forgiving each other, just as in Christ God forgave you. (verses 31-32)

Kindness is the fruit of the Spirit that binds us together in love. Our love is manifested in God's love for us – a love that is continuously pointing us to others. Kindness as a result highlights the quality of our relationships.

The word kindness evokes thoughts of love, mercy and goodness; in essence, it is love in action for and towards others. Kindness is the visible evidence of God's steadfast love, God's tender mercies and God's extraordinary goodness in the world. Kindness points us in the direction of the cross and Christ.

There is a climate of violence pervading the world today. We seem entrapped in r+age, anger, rudeness and much unkindness. To forgive and forget appear to be impossible. Paul calls on us to cultivate this virtue of kindness. In order to do so we must faithfully imitate God's loving kindness in the world; and internalise Christ (in Greek, *Christos*) and kindness (*chrēstos)* in our lives.

Once, on a visit to a remote village in Mexico, I was introduced to a poor old Christian woman well known for her kindness. She made soup for us with water from a nearby polluted creek. It was unthinkable to refuse such kindness. Her act of kindness embraced us all. It was kindness born of the fruit of the Spirit.

† Almighty God, teach us how to accept in humility all acts of kindness. Amen

For further thought
• Think about kindness. What comes to your mind? Do an act of kindness to someone this week. Cultivate the fruit of kindness in your life.

Tuesday 23 September
Cultivating the fruit of goodness

Romans 15:1-7, 13-16

Each of us should please our neighbours for their good, to build them up. For even Christ did not please himself ... **(part of verses 2-3)**

God is good. We know from a variety of experiences that God is always good. What about us?

Are we good? What does it mean to be good? Are we able to cultivate the fruit of goodness in our lives in light of our sinful nature? When the Spirit of God lives in you, you desire to live the good life. The quality of your life in the Spirit allows you to grow in character. The quality of your relationship with God allows you to depend on God to strive only for the good. The quality of your relationship with your neighbours requires you to seek only their good.

The fruit of goodness is not a virtue we can produce. Goodness is not just acts and deeds of kindness. Goodness is not just an absence of badness in our lives. Goodness is a virtue that can grow in us only as a quality of life in the Spirit. The fruits of goodness and kindness stand as equals.

I have met many good and kind persons all over the world – particularly in Trinidad and Tobago. God, the initiator of all goodness, is the sole standard of goodness.

Goodness compels us to be compassionate with the suffering poor.

Goodness reaches out to serve the hungry, thirsty and naked.

† Gracious God, you are good. Help me to grow in goodness. Amen

For further thought

• Begin your day with God, the chief example of all goodness.

Wednesday 24 September
Cultivating the fruit of faithfulness

2 Timothy 1:1-14

What you heard from me, keep as the pattern of sound teaching, with faith and love in Christ Jesus. (verse 13)

Throughout the Caribbean and the Americas one is still able to see the graves of some of the early Methodist missionaries. Their graves bear witness to their steadfastness and faithfulness in the face of tribulations, sufferings and death. Many came during the days of slavery. They endured harsh laws, beatings and stonings. They battled with many diseases. They were obstructed in proclaiming the gospel by the planters. They were ridiculed by some priests of the established churches. Work conditions were severe: some churches were forcibly closed while others were burned. Yet, they remained faithful to their task. When one died, the question was raised in London, 'Whom shall I send? And who will go for us?' Someone always volunteered, using the words of Isaiah: 'Here am I. Send me!' (Isaiah 6:8). There was an urgency to proclaim the gospel of Christ. There were no fears, obstacles or barriers that could deter them. They remained faithful to God and God remained faithful to them.

Faithfulness is an attribute of God. It describes the character of God. It reminds us that we have a covenant relationship with God – a relationship that requires faithfulness from us. God who is faithful calls us to bear the fruit of faithfulness in our lives. He challenges us never to quit at any time and in any circumstance. To this commitment, let us burn an inextinguishable flame of faithfulness in our lives.

† Great is your faithfulness, O God. Allow your Spirit to cultivate the fruit of faithfulness in my life. Enable me to be faithful always. Amen

For further thought
- What are some of the consequences of unfaithfulness?
- What are some challenges or difficulties you have encountered in cultivating the fruit of faithfulness in your life?

September

Cultivating the fruit of gentleness

2 Timothy 2:22-26

Opponents must be gently instructed, in the hope that God will grant them repentance leading them to a knowledge of the truth. (verse 25)

Gentle persons are often mistaken for being 'soft' and 'weak'. The world seems to have a greater appreciation for dominant, aggressive, ambitious and powerful persons. We need to rediscover the value and importance of gentleness as a virtue of strength.

Jesus embraced in his own life gentleness and humility as manifestations of his love for us; in his mercy, Jesus gently saved and forgave a woman caught in adultery, in the Gospel of John, chapter 8. He told her to sin no more, and that in him she became a new creation. On another occasion, Jesus gently transformed the messed-up life of the Samaritan woman he met at the well (John 4). Experiencing salvation, she went back to the town to witness for Jesus.

Here, Paul is charging Timothy to grow gentle in character, exercising humility and meekness. He tells him to be considerate and not show signs of arrogance or display power over those who oppose him. 'By the humility and gentleness of Christ, I appeal to you,' Paul writes in 2 Corinthians 10:1. Let us, too, imitate Christ, who is gentle.

† In all my relationships, help me to be gentle with others, O Lord. Renew in my heart and mind the fruit of gentleness. Amen

For further thought

• Be gentle. Are you able to be gentle? Do you like being gentle? What are some positives and negatives (if any) of gentleness?

Friday 26 September
Cultivating the fruit of self-control

Psalm 51:1-19

My sacrifice, O God, is a broken spirit; a broken and contrite heart you, God, will not despise. (verse 17)

The psalmist reminds us here that sacrifices require a commitment of the self. The worshipper with his sacrifice is required to commit his will to the will of God. This commitment of the self to God requires full surrender. Full surrender requires self-control. Self-control requires the strength of God.

Do we need to have more self-control? Do we need to make more sacrifices? What are the spiritual implications? We have discussed so far this week five fruits of the Spirit: patience, kindness, goodness, faithfulness, gentleness. As attributes of God they are directed towards others. Self-control is directed towards the self, for the sake of the self and others.

Some years ago I was invited to give a lecture in Bristol on 'John Wesley's View on Alcoholism'. Some persons did not appreciate Wesley's position of total abstinence from alcoholic drinks. Some argued for moderation. Wesley argued for abstinence and self-control. In the words of Proverbs: 'Who has woe? Who has sorrow? Who has strife? Who has complaints? Who has needless bruises? Who has bloodshot eyes? Those who linger over wine, who go to sample bowls of mixed wine' (Proverbs 23:29-30).

Many young and mature lives have been lost or ruined by reckless sex, alcohol, disease, drugs and guns. Every day we need God's grace and strength to exercise self-control. Every day we need the Spirit's guidance on our uncontrolled lives. Let us hold on to Jesus – he is the solution to all our challenges and problems.

† Lord, give me the will and the strength to cultivate the fruit of self-control in my life. Amen

For further thought

• Give reasons why some people lack self-control. Why is self-control so difficult to cultivate? Can we rely on God's strength to achieve self-control?

Saturday 27 September
Harvesting the fruit of righteousness

Philippians 1:1-11

… so that you may be able to discern what is best and may be pure and blameless for the day of Christ, filled with the fruit of righteousness that comes through Jesus Christ – to the glory and praise of God.
(verses 10-11)

Paul prays that the Philippians may have a genuine experience of being in Christ. He wants them to discern what is best. He wants them to live pure and righteous lives. Righteousness is rooted in God. When we are bewildered by grief and sorrow, it is not because God has changed. God still loves and cares for us.

When I was younger, I remember well a fateful telephone call. Rita, my mother, answered. 'Drunk?' she asked. The caller responded, 'No, drowned!' My mother screamed and then fainted. At 13 years of age, my little brother, Guillermo, was dead. He slipped from a canoe, hit his head against the dock and drowned in shallow waters in Colon City, Panama. My mother testified at church that Christ became her source of comfort. He provided her with the strength to endure the ordeal of sorrow. A few years later, my cousin Alfonso died by drowning after saving a man. My nephew Luis died by drowning after being thrown into the sea by friends who thought he should have a swim.

My mother believed that in all circumstances of death, sorrow, distress, discomfort and tribulations, righteousness informed her that God is always near to lift us up. She believed that God would be with us in all storms of life. She believed God was never wrong, God was always right. Her belief in God's Son, Jesus, made a difference in her life. Allow this same Jesus to make a difference in your life.

† Give me, O God, peace and righteousness in Christ and, in your mercy, cleanse me from sin and all unrighteousness. Amen

For further thought

- Read Galatians 5:22-23. The fruit of the Spirit implies a single growth pattern. What kind of harvest are you reaping from Jesus, the Vine?

Amos and Habakkuk
1 'The Lord roars from Zion'

This week's notes are by **Jules Gomes** (see page 21).

Sunday 28 September
The Lion King

Amos 1

He said: 'The LORD roars from Zion and thunders from Jerusalem; the pastures of the shepherds dry up, and the top of Carmel withers.' (verse 2)

Who does not wait with bated breath on hearing the roar of the world's most famous lion? On screen, when the lion roars we know a Metro-Goldwyn-Mayer movie has begun. Encircled by the Latin motto *Ars Gratia Artis*, the 'roaring lion' is MGM's trademark. The roaring lion is also Amos' trademark. If the motto of MGM's lion is 'Art for art's sake', the motto of Amos' lion is: 'Religion is not for religion's sake'. Religion is for the sake of justice and righteousness! MGM's lion roars – a movie has begun. Amos' lion roars – Israel's end has begun.

Israel's end will come through exile and earthquake – a national calamity and a natural catastrophe. The roaring of the lion causes the cosmos to quake; it calls the nations to account; it compels the prophet to prophesy. From Zion's mountaintop it reverberates to Carmel's mountaintop, from south to north and, like the thunderous drumming of the timpani at the crescendo of a boisterous symphony, it rolls across the nations and then boomerangs back to Amos, loosening his tongue for God. God is a lion, not a pussycat. When Amos' God roars, the universe quakes and the nations tremble.

† Almighty God, whose word is like the roaring of a lion: forgive us for every attempt we make to domesticate you, dumb you down, plug our ears to your roaring, and gag our mouths to speaking for justice. Amen

September

Prophets of justice versus profits of injustice

Amos 2

This is what the LORD says: 'For three sins of Israel, even for four, I will not relent. They sell the innocent for silver, and the needy for a pair of sandals.' (verse 6)

Amos' vision is panoramic, not parochial. He hails from Tekoa, south of Jerusalem. But God calls him north, to Israel. There he issues a rapid-fire salvo of prophetic outbursts against foreign nations that have committed bloodcurdling war crimes. Six nations (Damascus, Gaza, Tyre, Edom, Ammon and Moab) receive a red-hot tongue-lashing for their human rights abuses. But does Amos spare his own people – God's own people? Far from it! His seventh oracle is directed against Judah: the south. Judah is guilty of breaking the Torah and flirting with other gods. Is their crime as heinous as the war crimes of their neighbours in God's eyes? What do you think?

Imagine the scene. Amos is delivering this address in Israel: the north. The Israelites must have been applauding, after all, their enemies were getting their comeuppance. Even their cousins from down south were getting kicked in the teeth. And as the applause gets louder and reaches its climax with the seventh oracle, Amos' audience must have assumed he would stop – 'seven' was the number of completion. But Amos does not stop! With devastating rhetorical effect, he now points his finger at his audience – Israel. They, too, are guilty! They have committed sickening crimes of social injustice.

The prophets of justice challenged the profits of injustice. It was God's will that wealth should not be monopolised by a few. The widow, the orphan, the stranger and the landless were to have access to an abundant life. What sharp words might Amos be directing at our world today?

† God of justice, grant us the courage to sing Mary's song and work for the day when the hungry will be filled with good things and the rich will be sent empty away. Amen

For further thought

• When was the last time you heard a sermon or a Bible study on economic injustices or on the prophet Amos?
• Ask your non-Christian friends if they are aware that the biblical prophets speak out against social and economic injustices.

Fresh from the Word 2015

It may seem early, but *Fresh From the Word 2015* is now available to order.

Order now:

• with your local IBRA Rep*

• in all good bookshops

• direct from IBRA

To order direct from IBRA

• website: shop.christianeducation.org.uk

• email: sales@christianeducation.org.uk

• call: 0121 472 4242

• post: using the order form at the back of this book

Price £9.00. If ordering direct you will be charged postage and packaging.

Ebook versions priced at £7.49 inc.VAT are available from our website.

Become an IBRA rep

*If you purchase 6 or more print copies, and you live in the UK, you can sign up as an IBRA Rep and claim the 10% IBRA Rep discount on all IBRA products. You will also receive a free poster and samples to help you share IBRA more easily with family, friends and others in your church. Contact staff at IBRA to sign up now!

Would you consider leaving a legacy to IBRA?

What's valuable about a gift in your will to the International Bible Reading Association's International Fund is that every penny goes directly towards enabling hundreds of thousands of people around the world to access the living Word of God.

IBRA has a rich history going back over 130 years. It was the vision of Charles Waters to enable people in Britain and overseas to benefit from

the Word of God through the experiences and insights of biblical scholars and teachers across the world. The vision was to build up people's lives in their homes and situations wherever they were. His legacy lives on today in you, as a reader, and the IBRA team.

Our work at IBRA is financed by the sales of the books, but from its very start 100 per cent of donations to the IBRA International Fund go out to benefit our international readers. We guarantee not to spend any of it on general administration costs or our day-to-day overheads.

But to continue this important work would you consider leaving a legacy in your will?

Young IBRA readers in Nigeria

Find out more

Leaving a gift in your will to a Christian charity is a way of ensuring that this work continues for years to come: to help future generations and reach out to them with hope and the life-changing Word of God – people we may never meet but who are all our brothers and sisters in Christ.

Through such a gift you will help continue the strong and lasting legacy of IBRA for generations to come!

To find out more please contact our Legacy Adviser on 0121 472 4242, by email admin@christianeducation.org.uk or by writing to International Bible Reading Association, 1020 Bristol Road, Selly Oak, Birmingham B29 6LB.

- To read more about the history of IBRA go to page 20.
- To find out more about the work of the IBRA International Fund go to page 370.

Tuesday 30 September
Exile is the reversal of exodus

Amos 3

You only have I chosen of all the families of the earth; therefore I will punish you for all your sins. (verse 2)

Amos now addresses the entire people of God (Israel and Judah, north and south), the 'whole family' God rescued from Egypt. God intends to reverse his rescue operation and send his people back into captivity. Yesterday, they were in the promised land. Soon, they will be in a foreign land. Yesterday, they stood and sang by the waters of the Red Sea. Soon, they will sit and weep by the rivers of Babylon. Yesterday, they were the chosen people. Soon, they will be like Lennon–McCartney's 'Nowhere Man', in 'a nowhere land, making nowhere plans, for nobody'. But weren't they the chosen people? How could this be happening to them? They were chosen for privilege not for punishment! They were to be recipients of blessing not curse; exodus not exile.

Does God punish his chosen people? We can ask the question with two very different emphases. Does God punish his chosen people? Here the emphasis is on the people. To be chosen by God is both an awesome privilege and an awful responsibility. If being chosen implies covenant, or mutual commitment, then breaking the covenant must have its punitive consequences. We cannot take our covenant relationship for granted. Or, the emphasis can be on the agent of punishment. Does God punish his chosen people? This puts punishment in a very different light. Can we see punishment as a privilege of being within God's gracious care?

† Almighty God, you are an all-consuming fire. Forgive us for so often taking you for granted. Forgive us for settling for cheap grace. Discipline and disciple us as a loving parent. Amen

For further thought
- How often have you deliberately committed a sin knowing that you can go to God and ask his forgiveness and be forgiven?
- How might this be a form of 'cheap grace'? Compare Romans 6:1-2.

Wednesday 1 October
Who do you think you are?

Amos 4

Hear this word, you cows of Bashan on Mount Samaria, you women who oppress the poor and crush the needy and say to your husbands, 'Bring us some drinks!' (verse 1)

This scene would have been almost obscene in the ancient world. Women were expected to be the face of public decency. Women were supposed to submit to their husbands. But fair is foul and foul is fair among the wealthy women of Israel's consumerist elite. They binge, booze, and bully their husbands. They stamp on the poor and grind them beneath their heels. They attempt to sanitise their sins by sacrificing at the sanctuaries. Amos likens them to physically and metaphorically fattened cattle, ready for slaughter. They have forgotten who they are because they have forgotten where they came from. Once they were slaves in Egypt. Now they suffer from historical amnesia and live in the drunken stupor of the present.

Amos jolts them into remembering history. He reminds them of the covenant curses that have been unleashed against them – famine, drought, crop failure, war, exile and earthquake – consequences of covenant violation. The biggest shock is Amos' announcement that their worst punishment is no different from God's judgement against God's worst enemies: Sodom and Gomorrah and Egypt. They have failed to learn from history. They are now God's worst enemies! The great Henry Ford once quipped, 'History is bunk!' Not so for those whose faith is rooted in the Bible. 'Those who forget history are bound to repeat its mistakes,' said the philosopher Santayana. History reminds us who we were and who we are. It gives us identity. It is used for illustration. It imparts inspiration. It provides instruction. It also indicts us when we go astray and redirects us to God.

† Lest we forget your mercies, lest we forget your judgements, O Lord, prod us lovingly through the words of the prophets, restore to us the remembrance of your mighty acts and open our eyes to your hand in history. Amen

For further thought
• What era of your country's history could teach it lessons today?

Thursday 2 October
Singing in the ruins

Amos 5:1-17

Hear this word, Israel, this lament I take up concerning you. (verse 1)

God's people are dead. This is their funeral. Amos now sings a funeral song of mourning. This is his last resort. Will this finally get their attention? Will the consciousness of their own mortality as a nation shock them into repentance? This section begins with lamentation, but the lamenter is ambiguous. Is it God weeping? Or is it Amos weeping? Perhaps it is both. After all, Amos is speaking on behalf of God. The section ends with the entire nation weeping.

Lament is one of the most poignant and powerful forms in the Hebrew Bible. Over one-third of the Psalms contains laments. It is only the liturgy of lament that can counter the culture of self-congratulations, denial, cover-up, spin, canned laughter, synthetic and mind-numbing entertainment and the privatisation of pain – a counter to every seduction that seeks to deny or explain away the reality of sin, suffering and death. If we do not lament our losses, we will pretend that nothing ever happened. And our situation will get worse, not better. Unless we plumb the depths of lament, we will never ascend to the mountaintops of praise. There can be no reliving, rethinking, redoing, and renegotiating our faith unless we weep when we remember Zion. If Jesus wept at the grave of his friend Lazarus, we ought not to be ashamed to weep. If Amos wept over the nation of Israel, we ought to weep over the brokenness of our own people.

It was the African-American spirituals that inspired the slaves to move from lamentation to liberation. God weeps. Amos weeps. Jesus wept. Let's make lament part of our prayer and protest.

† Keep us, O Lord, from the temptation of happy praise that leaves no room for lament. Amen

For further thought

- What percentage of the hymns or songs in your church's worship is laments?
- Why is there such an emphasis on praise in much of today's worship?

Independence Day or Judgement Day?

Amos 5:18-27

Woe to you who long for the day of the Lord! Why do you long for the day of the Lord? That day will be darkness, not light. (verse 18)

Every single tradition God's chosen people have doggedly clung to Amos is now turning on its head. Here, he pulls the carpet of conceit from under their feet by upending the tradition of the 'Day of the Lord'. This is the first time in the Bible that this idea occurs. This would be the day, Israel hoped, when God would destroy her enemies and bring victory to God's chosen people. Amos contradicts Israel's expectations. They believed this day would be light; Amos predicts it will be darkness. They believed it would bring judgement against the nations; Amos predicts it will bring judgement for Israel.

What will save Israel? Will worshipping God at Bethel, Gilgal or Beersheba do the trick? Far from it! Amos does not attack these northern shrines for their allegedly counterfeit religion. The problem is that they have become places where music is of the highest order and sacrifices are punctiliously offered but where injustice and corruption are whitewashed and laundered. The finest choral and orchestral music, whether classical or contemporary, when devoid of justice, is cacophony in God's ears. Privilege brings peril. Judgement begins in the house of God. And worship without justice is a detestable oxymoron.

† God of Amos, may we never dare to substitute worship for works of justice. As we strive to walk the way of Jesus, may we seek the overflow of justice and righteousness in our world. Amen

For further thought

• What is the modern definition of justice that prevails around us? Try asking friends and family this question.

Saturday 4 October
The cancer of conspicuous consumption

Amos 6

Woe to you who are complacent in Zion, and to you who feel secure on Mount Samaria, you notable men of the foremost nation, to whom the people of Israel come! (verse 1)

The global economy is on a roller coaster. Capitalism is getting its comeuppance. The walls of Wall Street have come tumbling down. The big banks have imploded with big bangs. Like Humpty Dumpty, global capitalism has had a great big fall. The splurge-now-pay-later party is over. Welcome to our brave new economy! It is an economy where the forces of good have been substituted for forces of greed; where the new religion is the monotheism of the market. But are we justified in passing the buck and blaming the bankers? Are we mere victims or unwitting accomplices? For the past decade or so, was materialism not our mantra; consumption our creed; the supermarkets our cathedrals; the credit card our ticket to paradise? And did we not think we were invincible and utterly secure?

Amos' world was no different. Shameless self-indulgence stalks the streets of Israel and Judah hand in hand with cocksure self-confidence. God's people are 'complacent in Zion' and 'secure on Mount Samaria'. These capital cities had become centres of conspicuous consumption: beds of ivory, expensive cuts of meat, exclusive wines, exquisite perfumes, and extensive entertainment. Amos debunks the myth and might of the twin cities. He points to the cities of Calneh, Hamath and Gath, reminding God's people that they are no better or worse than their pagan neighbours. Again, Amos turns privilege on its head. Because Zion and Samaria are the capital cities, they will be the 'first to go into exile'. In God's eyes, opulence amounts to obscenity if justice is thrown to the winds. And now, we too, in the Western world have been exiled into an economic recession.

† Almighty God, who through your Son cautioned us that it would not profit us if we gained the whole world, but suffered the loss of our souls: help us to live simply that the poor and less fortunate might simply live. Amen

For further thought

- Look around your house. List five purchases that were unnecessary or made on a whim.

Amos and Habakkuk
2 'I heard and my heart pounded'

This week's notes are by **Clare McBeath**

 Clare McBeath is a Baptist minister working with Urban Expression to develop new ways of being church in East Manchester. She works as a community fundraiser and in-house liturgist with Church Action on Poverty, which campaigns on issues of poverty and injustice in the UK. With a PhD in contextual theologies, Clare writes on inclusive worship and spirituality and has keen interests in poetry, art, urban regeneration and mental health. She is co-author of *Crumbs of Hope: Prayers from the City* and of the worship resource website www.dancingscarecrow.org.uk.

Sunday 5 October
Setting the standard

Amos 7

Then the LORD said, 'Look, I am setting a plumb-line among my people Israel; I will spare them no longer.' (part of verse 8)

This week we hear from the prophets Amos and Habakkuk as they hold a mirror up to our world and ask us to compare ourselves against God's standards. How often do we listen to the news on radio or TV and hear the same stories repeated over and over again? Stories of war, famine, flood and climate change. Stories of people going hungry, suffering illness because of a lack of medical care, or being homeless while others live in comfortable housing. Stories of religious tension and atrocities committed in the name of religion. And of course *our* religion is not like that. We are not extremists. We would not walk by on the other side while people suffer, would we? But do we really, to paraphrase the prophet Micah, 'act justly, love mercy and walk humbly with our God' (6:8)?

In Amos 7 we are presented with graphic imagery of a prophet pleading for mercy for the people of Israel before God's vision of calamity. And God finally says, 'Enough is enough. I am setting my plumb-line, my standard among the people.' Needless to say, Jeroboam, the king of Israel, does not like what he hears and sends Amos packing.

As we consider issues of social justice this week, take some time to read a newspaper and hear God's voice setting a plumb-line.

† For the sake of justice, gracious God, do not spare us, but in love refine us.

Monday 6 October
Measuring up

Amos 8

Hear this, you who trample the needy and do away with the poor of the land. (verse 4)

Amos doesn't pull his punches. God shows him a basket of ripe fruit, fruit that to all intents and purposes looks good enough to eat. But we all know that ripe fruit can go bad overnight. Outwardly all looks fine, and this is where Amos sticks in the knife. Outwardly Israel is keeping up appearances and congratulating itself on its religious observance. But once the Sabbath is over, a very different picture emerges, of a people who trample the needy and do away with the poor, skimping with dishonest scales and selling the sweepings of the wheat.

In 2012, Church Action on Poverty and Christian Aid campaigned together under the banner 'Tax dodging hurts the poor'. We organised a Tax Justice bus tour of Britain and Ireland to highlight the injustices of our tax system: for example, while the lowest-earning 10 per cent of people in the UK pay 39 per cent of their income in tax, the top 10 per cent pay just 35 per cent. Wealthy individuals and companies can avoid paying much of their tax altogether, illegally through tax evasion or legally through tax avoidance, all of which means there is less public money to spend, which hurts the poor the most.

What Amos is describing here is not just the occasional act of injustice towards the poor, but a whole system that benefits the rich *at the expense of* the poor. Not only does Amos highlight the corruption that lurks beneath the outward appearance of the basket of fruit, he warns of the dire consequences of allowing the system to go unchallenged.

† Set up a bowl of fruit, as a reminder throughout this week, that our faith calls us to stand up for the poor and challenge systems of injustice.

For further thought

• How can you show your commitment to a just society for all by where and how you spend your money?

Held to account

Amos 9

For I will give the command, and I will shake the people of Israel among all the nations as grain is shaken in a sieve. (verse 9a)

We like to think of our churches as places of sanctuary. Somehow it seems doubly unjust if an earthquake or unprovoked attack strikes in a place we have marked out as sacred. And yet here we have Amos' vision of God standing at the altar, right in the heart of religious life, raining down destruction and terror. This is just one of many texts from scripture that just seem too appalling to contemplate. And yet, in our anxiety to explain away texts that do not seem to fit with a more contemporary understanding of God as a God of compassion, are we missing something? Is this not justice raining down on the unjust? Is this not the dire consequences Amos warned us about? Is this not what happens when systems of oppression and injustice come crashing down?

But this vision, appalling though it is, is also tempered by the image of the sieve in which the unrighteous are caught and destroyed but the righteous descendants of Jacob flow through. It is here God speaks a vision of restoration as one day the remnant will be returned from exile. But, be clear, the vision is one of justice *and a sustainable livelihood for all*. 'They will rebuild the ruined cities *and live in them.* They will plant vineyards *and drink their wine.* They will make gardens *and eat their fruit*' (verse 14, emphasis added).

Far from being a place of safety where we could hide from the troubles of the world, our churches can be places where we see God's justice and God's good news for the poor in action.

† Use the newspapers and fruit from earlier in the week as a focus for reflection on Amos' vision. Are there signs in the newspapers of God's restoration, too?

For further thought

- Are there behaviours that we need to catch in a sieve and 'throw away'?

Wednesday 8 October
How long?

Habakkuk 1:1-11

How long, Lord, must I call for help, but you do not listen? Or cry out to you, 'Violence!' but you do not save? (verse 2)

In 1983, Irish pop band U2 released a now famous song that shocked the world partly for its uncompromising political message, and partly for daring to use a swear word in its title. 'Sunday B***** Sunday' begins where we began this week, with news of destruction and violence – in the song's case in Northern Ireland, where outrage boiled over in Derry after British troops had opened fire on unarmed protesters and bystanders. The song is a lament, before God and before the world: How long? How long …?

'How long?' are also Habakkuk's opening words. Rather than being a prophet who speaks to us words of God's justice, Habakkuk echoes our words of lament back to God. But rather than answering Habakkuk, and us, with words of comfort or hope, God's response to Habakkuk is a vision of the Babylonians, the outsiders, sweeping across the earth, destroying all in their path. They are like the refiner's fire, leaving nothing in their wake.

And so in the face of much of what we hear in our news – of war and conflict, of environmental destruction, of hunger and disease – we, too, take up the lament to God, and to our world: How long? How long …?

† How long will you ignore the cries of the Earth, as ice caps melt and the climate changes? How long will you ignore the cries of people as hunger eats away and disease causes despair?

For further thought
• We are very quick to ask the 'How long?' question of God. What happens when God asks the same question of us?

October

God's silence in the face of suffering

Habakkuk 1:12-17

Why are you silent while the wicked swallow up those more righteous than themselves? (verse 13b)

Habakkuk's second complaint goes to the heart of the matter. First we cry 'How long?' And when we do not receive an answer, we rail against God's silence. Moreover, God is silent while the *wicked* Babylonians destroy the *righteous* Israelites. It is so easy to see ourselves as righteous and to demonise the other. After all, surely God is on our side? Isn't part of the problem inherent in all religions to see God as *our God,* an exclusive God. We then rail against God when God seemingly fails to back us in support of others.

But maybe God's silence is telling us something else? Maybe God's silence is holding a mirror up to our own lives, our own behaviour? Maybe God's silence is a refusal to be owned by one side or another? Maybe God's silence is the silence of the cross, God's sharing in the pain and death humanity wreaks on humanity.

And maybe, hard as it is, we need to sit with the silence, to feel the pain, to accept that God is an inclusive God, a God of all of humanity; a God who does not necessarily ride in to rescue but instead opens arms wide to embrace the pain of the crucifixion: the pain of broken humanity.

† How long, you ask us, will *we* ignore the cries of the Earth, as ice caps melt and the climate changes? How long, you ask us, will *we* ignore the cries of people as hunger eats away and disease causes despair?

For further thought

• Try sitting with the newspaper today or really listening to the news and give yourself permission to feel, to pay attention to, your own emotional response.

Living the consequences

Habakkuk 2

Because you have plundered many nations, the peoples who are left will plunder you. For you have shed human blood; you have destroyed lands and cities and everyone in them. (verse 8)

Habakkuk has made his complaint against God. Now it is God's turn to answer; and just in case we are left in any doubt, God's answer is clearly spelled out. It is not so much that God is punishing Israel, but that Israel is living with the consequences of past actions. Israel has plundered and pillaged other nations and set up unjust systems that have oppressed and exploited the poor – and now the tables have turned. The boot is on the other foot. The Israelites are getting a taste of their own medicine, not so much as God's punishment, but as the inevitable consequences of the way they have mistreated others.

The science fiction film *Avatar* (director James Cameron, 2009) is set on the fantasy world of Pandora where a team of scientists seeks to understand and befriend the indigenous people, the Na'vi, through the use of avatars. Meanwhile, a greedy corporation will stop at nothing to mine the precious material scattered throughout the forest. When ex-marine Jake Sully falls in love with a beautiful Na'vi woman, he finally understands the interconnectedness of the whole life system of Pandora and the consequences of destroying any one part of it. And the Na'vi are left with no alternative but to trust the alien scientists and fight an epic battle to protect their home. Does this sound familiar?

Somehow, together we need to find a different way and this different way starts with our recognition of the awe and majesty of God.

† The Lord is in his holy temple; let all the earth be silent before him (verse 20).

For further thought

- Each year we hold two minutes' silence on Remembrance Day. Consider holding two minutes' silence today in remembrance of Earth and all Earth's children.
- Make time to watch the film *Avatar*.

October

Saturday 11 October
Confession – the seeds of hope

Habakkuk 3

Though the fig tree does not bud and there are no grapes on the vines, though the olive crop fails and the fields produce no food ... yet I will rejoice in the LORD, I will be joyful in God my Saviour. (part of verses 17-18)

Having spent a week living with the searing call to justice of the prophet Amos and the voicing of lament at the human condition of Habakkuk, it would be easy to leave this week feeling demoralised and paralysed when faced with the newspapers in front of us. But this is not where the story leaves us. Rather, Habakkuk shows us that we need to face and own the human condition. Rather than hiding in fear of God, we should humbly make our confession before God. We have been measured against the plumb-line of God's standards and we know we fall short. Rather than excuses, we are called to confess our part in the mess that humanity has made.

Only when we do this can we lift our heads and get a glimpse of God's rule, in which justice and mercy are the order of the day, and all living beings stand equally before God. It is then that Habakkuk speaks in the voice of a psalmist: 'The Sovereign Lord is my strength; he makes my feet like the feet of a deer, he enables me to tread on the heights' (verse 19). By surrendering our will to God's, by working together to face the issues of injustice that lie behind our news stories, we begin to plant the seeds, the possibility of hope for a new earth. 'Because he has anointed me to proclaim good news to the poor ...' (Luke 4:18).

† God who sets the plumb-line before us, we are sorry, deeply sorry for the mess we, as humanity, have made, and for the part we, as individuals, have played. Forgive us and show us a vision of your rule on Earth ... May we do justice, love mercy, and walk humbly with our God.

For further thought

- This week we have journeyed with Amos and Habakkuk, not the most comfortable of companions to travel with. Do you feel any differently when you hear or read the news? How might you respond?

October

Saints and holy people
1 All called to be saints

This week's notes are by **Catherine Williams**

Catherine Williams is an Anglican priest working as the National Adviser for Vocations for the Ministry Division of the Archbishops' Council, in the Church of England. Her role is to advise and lead the many vocation advisers around the UK who are encouraging and enabling Christians to discern God's call on their lives. She is married to the vicar of Tewkesbury Abbey and has two adult children. In her spare time, Catherine enjoys singing, baking, cinema, and reading and writing poetry.

Sunday 12 October
Called to rejoice

Matthew 5:1-12, 48

Blessed are you when people insult you, persecute you and falsely say all kinds of evil against you because of me. Rejoice and be glad, because great is your reward in heaven, for in the same way they persecuted the prophets who were before you. (verses 11-12)

Over the next few weeks we will be thinking about what it means to be a Christian saint. Often we think of saints as people who are especially holy and have done remarkable acts that mark them out in the Christian community. However, in the New Testament all God's people are referred to as 'saints'. Our churches are fellowships of saints where we as Christians grow in our faith together in order to witness to Christ in our everyday lives.

Our passage today is from the very familiar Sermon on the Mount. Matthew portrays Jesus as the new Moses, teaching the new commandments on the new Mount Sinai. These 'commandments', which mark out who is 'blessed' in God's kingdom, challenge traditional ideas of God's chosen people. The poorest and the least are those who are closest to the kingdom.

'Be perfect … as your heavenly Father is perfect' says Jesus in verse 48. Such saintly living is not an easy option. It brings with it the real possibility of being insulted, persecuted or worse. But it's also a matter for rejoicing, because such attacks demonstrate that the believer is close to God and modelling a challenging new lifestyle that makes sense of God's promised future.

† Lord, during this week help me to hear and respond to your call to saintly living.

Monday 13 October
Called to be salt and light

Matthew 5:13-16

You are the salt of the earth ... You are the light of the world ... Let your light shine ... that may see your good deeds and glorify your Father in heaven. (part of verses 13-16)

Jesus calls his disciples to make a difference wherever they find themselves. Living the Christian life calls for new patterns of behaviour and a fresh engagement with the world that brings transformation for all. Jesus uses everyday, ordinary examples – salt and light – to demonstrate how such a difference can be brought about. Salt is a preservative, a disinfectant and an enhancer. It stops meat going rotten, it heals and makes clean the body, and it brings out the flavour in food. As Christians, like salt, we can help those around us by seeking good, healing and restoring, and building up and bringing out the best in others. Likewise, light enables people to see, banishes darkness and brings all that it touches into focus. The parallels with those who are filled with the light of Christ are obvious. Even a tiny candle flame can make a huge difference in a dark space. The smallest ray of faith can begin to change the lives of others for the better.

But Jesus has a warning to give to those who follow him. Salt is useless if it loses its taste, and a light that is covered up and hidden away gives out light no longer. To be true disciples, we as saints must be prepared to keep our relationship with Jesus alive and fresh. At our baptism we were commissioned to shine with the light of Christ for our whole lives. All our words and actions should be illuminated with Christ's love and goodness, so that those around us may be influenced and turn to God.

† Lord, thank you for calling me to be the salt and light in my community. Shine through me to transform all those I meet. Amen

For further thought

• Where is the salt and light of the kingdom most needed in your community? Ask God to show you how to make a difference there.

Tuesday 14 October
Called to praise the Lord

Psalm 148

Let them praise the name of the LORD, for at his command they were created, and he established them for ever and ever – he issued a decree that will never pass away. (verses 5-6)

Psalm 148 is a call to the whole of creation to join together to praise God. Everything in heaven and earth is urged to shout the Hebrew *Hallelu Yah* – 'Praise the Lord'. Every part of the cosmos is involved in this praise. Angels, stars, sun, moon, mountains, seas, the elements, all vegetation, every creature, and the entire human race are to be part of this dynamic, joy-filled chorus. Nothing and no one is too grand or too lowly to take part in the worshipping community. Creation acknowledges God as creator and commander of all that is, for eternity. Therefore, God's name is to be lifted up and praised, not just by everything that has breath, but by everything that is and has ever been.

As God's saints we are called not only to praise the Lord in all things but also to recognise and encourage the praise of God from others. That includes not just humanity. Our vocation is to enable the whole creation to praise God. The psalmist invites praise from all quarters:

'Praise the LORD from the earth, you great sea creatures and all ocean depths, lightning and hail, snow and clouds, stormy winds that do his bidding.' (verses 7-8)

What a challenge! Are we aware of how all creation praises its creator, or are we in danger of imagining that only people are capable of offering praise to God? Such an expansive vision of a worshipping creation has huge theological, spiritual and ecological implications for the way we live in, respect and tend our world today.

† Lord God, together with all creation I praise your name – *Hallelu Yah!*

For further thought

• Whenever you praise God, try to imagine yourself joining with the whole of creation. How are other parts of the created order offering praise to God?

Called to be radiant

Psalm 34:1-10

Glorify the LORD with me: let us exalt his name together. I sought the LORD, and he answered me; he delivered me from all my fears. Those who look to him are radiant; their faces are never covered with shame. (verses 3-5)

In this psalm it is possible that David is celebrating his escape from the King of Gath recorded in 1 Samuel 21:10-15. Certainly this psalm is a thanksgiving to the Lord, and a celebration of God's saving power. The writer tells of how he searched for God and how in return God heard him, answered his call and saved him. The psalmist urges us to join with him in giving glory to God. Together we, the saints of God, are to sing praises and tell of God's faithfulness and his ongoing deliverance.

Those who look to God in this way are described as *radiant*. We catch a glimpse of God's chosen people shining with his light in a way that is attractive, open and honest. Those who trust in God and follow in his ways need never be ashamed or frightened. We are called rather to *fear the Lord*, which means having an attitude of appropriate reverence and awe, rather than dread or terror.

The early church used this psalm in its liturgy, particularly at celebrations of Holy Communion. Verse 8 reminds us to 'Taste and see that the Lord is good'. In receiving the body and blood of Christ at the Eucharist, and fulfilling the Lord's command to remember him in this way, Christ blesses us and through us reaches out to bless the communities in which we live and worship. As saints of God, Christians are called to be faithful in worship, prayer and service and, when we are, then God's radiance can shine through these acts and touch the lives of many who long to know him.

† Lord, may my words and deeds today shine with your radiant love.

For further thought
- When you next receive Holy Communion remember that through this celebration God is blessing your whole community, not just those who attend the service.

Thursday 16 October
Called to a rich inheritance

Ephesians 1:11-19a

And you also were included in Christ when you heard the message of truth, the gospel of your salvation. When you believed, you were marked in him with a seal, the promised Holy Spirit, who is a deposit guaranteeing our inheritance … (verses 13-14a)

Human beings have a strong tendency to draw boundaries that mark who is 'in' and who is 'out'. We do it because it makes us feel safe and secure, and helps to give us a measure of control over others. St Paul writes to the new Christians at Ephesus with a thrilling message of inclusion. Historically, Israel was described as God's heritage – a chosen people and a holy and precious possession belonging to God. Now in Christ these blessings belong equally to all those who proclaim Jesus as Lord. Both Jewish and Gentile believers are God's saints, called to a rich inheritance – fullness of life in Christ today and life everlasting in the future.

This promise has been marked by the gift of the Holy Spirit in the life of each believer. This precious gift is described as a 'seal' or a 'deposit' – a down payment marking what is to come. The word Paul uses for 'deposit' is, in modern Greek, the word used for an engagement ring. This gives us a wonderful sense of the love God has for each of his people, and the way in which he binds us to himself through the death and resurrection of Christ and the gift of the Holy Spirit. The marriage of Christ to his bride the church will be the culmination of all our relationships with God and with one another. Inclusion in Christ leads to reconciliation with the rest of the created order. Paul prays that God's saints may be open to recognise and celebrate the hope they are called to – a rich inheritance indeed!

† Lord, open the eyes of my heart to the hope you have called me to. Help me to proclaim you as Lord with the whole of my being.

For further thought

- In Christ we are united. Remind yourself of this by spending time getting to know a Christian who is very different from you.

Friday 17 October
Called to build the body

Ephesians 4:10-16

Speaking the truth in love, we will grow to become in every respect the mature body of him who is the head, that is, Christ. From him the whole body ... grows and builds itself up in love, as each part does its work. (part of verses 15-16)

What's your part in the body of Christ? What gifts and skills has God given you in order to help build his body, the church? Paul gives the church at Ephesus a list of possible roles that Christ has given to his people. The list is not exhaustive, and the gifts are not given for self-gratification but to help prepare God's people to go out and be witnesses and ambassadors of Christ in the world. The saints of God, you and I, are called to help build up the body of Christ that is our own church or fellowship. As each of us fulfils the task assigned to us so the body matures and grows together in love and unity, following Christ who is its head. This in itself is a positive witness to the world of how human beings can live and thrive together. But more than this, saints build the body so that the individual members can go out with confident faith to proclaim Christ as Lord to a world hungry to hear God's message of love, peace and hope.

The body of Christ is not static but dynamic. It lives and grows. The church is on a pilgrimage and we haven't arrived yet. Saints are baptised into the death and resurrection of Christ; this means that we must always be open to change. In different times in our lives and in different places God may call us to fulfil different roles in the body and exercise a variety of gifts. What's your part in the body of Christ?

† Lord, thank you for the church I attend. Help all its members play their part in your body. Build us up and send us out to witness to your saving love in our community.

For further thought

• Encourage other members of your church to develop and exercise their part in the body of Christ.

Saturday 18 October
A faith charter

Romans 12:9-21

Bless those who persecute you; bless and do not curse. Rejoice with those who rejoice; mourn with those who mourn. Live in harmony with one another. Do not be proud, but be willing to associate with people of low position. Do not be conceited. Do not repay anyone evil for evil. (part of verses 14-17)

Paul's formulaic charter for the Christian saints in Rome is similar to Jesus' Sermon on the Mount, which began this week's readings. Listed in a series of short pithy sayings that could easily be committed to memory, Paul lays down the way of everyday living that Christians should follow. There are some surprises in his list. In particular, evil is always to be countered by good. It is the work of the saint to take the heat out of disputes, to look for good in challenging situations and not to judge others, however difficult and demanding their behaviour becomes. It is God who judges and the Christian should not anticipate this. If love is to be real, it must be worked out in words and actions that all can appreciate.

Hospitality was of great importance in the ancient world. It could mean the difference between life and death for nomadic people and travellers. Paul develops this hospitality, suggesting that Christians should reach out to all those they encounter, being alongside others in joy and sorrow, sharing with those who are needy and endeavouring to live in peace and harmony with all. Such saintly behaviour needs working at because it doesn't come naturally, and we would be wise to check regularly our thoughts, actions, decisions and patterns of living to make sure they are governed by genuine love and Christ-like obedience to God. Christ dwelling in us and with us longs to bring forth from us holiness and loving behaviour. By remaining close to Christ through faithful prayer and worship, our lives will reflect his goodness.

† Lord, help me to overcome every evil I encounter with good. Teach me to bless those I find difficult and challenging.

For further thought

- Write out Romans 12:9-18 as a charter for saintly living. Refer to this charter often until it becomes second nature to you.

Saints and holy people
2 Inspirational saints

This week's notes are by **Mark Woods**

 Mark Woods is a Baptist minister and journalist. Formerly editor of *The Baptist Times*, he now writes for the *Methodist Recorder* among other publications. He is an avid reader with a particular liking for science fiction and fantasy, and also enjoys running and swimming – neither very energetically. He serves on the leadership team of Leckhampton Baptist Church in Cheltenham, where he regularly preaches and leads worship.

Sunday 19 October
Daring to be different

Daniel 1

Daniel then said to the guard … 'Please test your servants for ten days: Give us nothing but vegetables to eat and water to drink. Then compare our appearance with that of the young men who eat the royal food, and treat your servants in accordance with what you see.' (part of verses 11-13)

Stories in the Bible of great servants of God show us people who are, in principle at least, like us. They are not superheroes, but ordinary people who can rise to extraordinary situations. From their experiences we can learn how we, too, can be faithful in hard times.

Daniel and his three friends are strangers in a strange land, serving in the court of a foreign ruler. Everything possible is done to make them conform. Not only were they educated as Babylonians, but they had to stick to the non-Jewish Babylonian diet. Even their names were taken from them.

It would have been very easy to forget their identity. Many did; the famous 'Ten Lost Tribes' of Israel were absorbed into the surrounding cultures. But Daniel and his companions dared to be different.

To live as a Christian today needs the same sort of steel. In some countries Christians face physical dangers or legal penalties for practising their faith. In many others, even going to church on Sunday is a declaration of difference.

We need to be able to show that, like Daniel and his companions, we are better people because of the Master we follow.

† Loving God, you call us to march to the beat of a different drum. Help me to listen when I am tempted to compromise. Amen

Doing the right thing

Exodus 1:15-21

The king of Egypt said to the Hebrew midwives, whose names were Shiphrah and Puah, 'When you are helping the Hebrew women during childbirth on the delivery stool, if you see that the baby is a boy, kill him; but if it is a girl, let her live.' (verses 15-16)

The greatest evil of slavery is that people are treated as things. Israelites in Egypt were a threat to Pharaoh, or so he believed, so he took steps to deal with them. Shiphrah and Puah were all that stood between the life and death of a nation.

At great personal risk, they disobeyed Pharaoh and let the male children live. It would have been far easier for them to do as they were told.

The two midwives were Hebrews, of the same race as the children they were told to murder. It is easier to feel sympathy with those who are like us than it is to feel for those who are different – though that does not diminish their heroism.

But Christians are also called to stand alongside those who are not like us at all, and that can be a lot harder. In the Second World War, the Churches in Germany mostly failed to do this and to stand up for Jews. Some brave individuals did, though, at the risk – and sometimes the cost – of their lives.

It is not easy to stand up to authority, whether it is the authority of a political leader, a church leader, a boss at work, the opinions of our friends, or public opinion. Sometimes, though, we are presented with very clear choices between right and wrong.

A lot can depend on the decisions we make. One of those saved by Shiphrah and Puah was Moses.

† Loving God, thank you for the example of those who have done the right thing when it was hard. Help me not to be afraid of the powerful, but to stand for what is true. Amen

For further thought

• Am I willing to challenge wrong beliefs and wrong actions, or do I just go along with the crowd?

Tuesday 21 October
Honour for the outcast

Joshua 2:1-14

We have heard how the LORD dried up the water of the Red Sea for you when you came out of Egypt … When we heard of it, our hearts sank and everyone's courage failed because of you, for the LORD your God is God in heaven above and on the earth below. (part of verses 10-11)

Rahab is a complicated person with divided loyalties. Her actions saved herself and her own family but led to the destruction of her city and the deaths of many others.

We can perhaps look to her profession as a prostitute for a clue to her behaviour. She might have been publicly scorned by the respectable people, while visited under cover of darkness by many of those who would be ashamed to admit it. Her loyalty to the city that treated her so badly might have been more fragile than that of other people. Convinced, as the rest of her people were, that the city would fall anyway, she sees a chance of rescue – and a chance to be useful, significant and honoured.

Her hopes and dreams come true. In Hebrews 11 she is in the list of those commended for her faith (verse 31); in James 2 for her righteousness (verse 25). Most remarkable of all, in Matthew 1:5 she is named as an ancestor of Jesus himself.

Many people are drawn to Christian faith because it offers healing for the broken-hearted. Lives that seem to be worthless are redeemed and restored. There is grace for everyone and everyone has a part to play in God's purposes for the world.

What happened at Jericho was terrible, but Rahab's story teaches us that there is hope for everyone – and that, whatever someone's past might be, with God there can be a glorious future.

† Loving God, help me never to look down on people because of what they have done, but to see them with your own eyes and rejoice in their potential. Amen

For further thought

• Does my attitude to other people encourage them to believe that God loves and accepts them just as they are?

Wednesday 22 October
Thinking faith through

Luke 1:1-4

Since I myself have carefully investigated everything from the beginning, I too decided to write an orderly account for you, most excellent Theophilus, so that you may know the certainty of the things you have been taught. (verses 3-4)

Luke was an educated man who knew the importance of checking his sources and getting the story right. He tells Theophilus that he has written 'so that you may know the certainty of the things you have been taught'. In other words, he was giving Theophilus a solid intellectual grounding for the beliefs he had picked up through his regular worship in church.

What we don't know, though, is how Theophilus felt about some of the things Luke left out. We know from other very early sources that there were all sorts of stories about Jesus around in the early church, some of them very odd indeed. By leaving them out, Luke was saying 'I don't think these are true' – potentially very threatening if someone has always believed them, so a brave thing to do.

Nineteen hundred years after Luke wrote, we rely on the four Gospels to tell us about Jesus. But the work of understanding them and applying them to our lives today goes on. Scholars, teachers and preachers have to give the best of their mental and spiritual powers to distinguishing between true and false interpretations. Sometimes this means that we are disturbed by challenges to what we have assumed was true. Conflict and disharmony can result and people can be hurt. The search for truth is costly, and places great responsibilities on us all: the scholars who make it their life's work, like Luke, and the rest of us who sit under their teaching. Grace, patience and a loving spirit are essential as we listen.

† Loving God, help me to be willing to think new thoughts and receive new truths, but keep me always faithful to the scriptures and to your son Jesus Christ. Amen

For further thought

• How much of what I believe do I just believe because other people do, and how much have I really thought about?

October

Thursday 23 October
Simon and Jude: compare and contrast

Luke 6:12-16

One of those days Jesus went out to a mountainside to pray, and spent the night praying to God. When morning came, he called his disciples to him and chose twelve of them, whom he also designated apostles. (verses 12-13)

Luke lists the apostles by name because they are so important in the church's history. Simon Peter we know very well: he is their leader, humanly speaking the 'rock' on which the church would be built. With all his failings, he is a towering figure.

Jude, on the other hand, is shadowy, to say the least. He is mentioned only twice in the New Testament. He is called the 'son of James', but the Greek just says 'of James'; he might be a brother or a cousin. In the lists of the apostles given by Matthew and Mark, he evidently appears as Thaddaeus – even his name is vague! All we have of his later life is a few legends of little historical value. In the Roman Catholic Church he is the patron saint of lost causes, which seems very appropriate.

In today's world there is a culture of celebrity. In the UK recently, young people were surveyed on their ambitions for the future. Most of them wanted to be famous.

Jude is not at all famous. But that is like most disciples of Jesus. We go on quietly doing what we are called to do, without seeking any recognition for it. We do not, or should not, judge individuals by how well known or wealthy or successful they are.

We do not know much about Jude, but when everything that is hidden is revealed, we may find that his work outshines that of many who are far better known.

† Loving God, I know that what matters is what you think of me, not what other people think. Help me to live for your glory, not for other people's praise.

For further thought

• What do I really want to be – famous, or useful?

Friday 24 October
Looking backwards, looking forwards

John 11:17-32

'Lᴏʀᴅ,' Martha said to Jesus, 'if you had been here, my brother would not have died. But I know that even now God will give you whatever you ask.' (verses 21-22)

We are used to comparing Martha and Mary, their different personalities and their different kinds of faith. We usually draw on Luke 10 and his account of the dinner party at which Martha is flustered and Mary calm, and Mary usually comes off better.

Here, though, it is Martha who is the inspiration. They are both women of faith. Their much-loved brother has died and they both believe that, if Jesus had been there, he could have saved his life. Their reaction, though, is very different. Martha says 'I know that even now God will give you whatever you ask.' Mary simply weeps. Martha's faith encompasses the future; Mary's is fixed in the past. Martha has hope, while Mary has only regret.

Of course this might not be entirely fair to Mary. We do not necessarily have the full conversation; all we know is how John chose to tell the story.

But this distinction is very true to life. Some of us are hopeful, trusting God with the future even when the present is very dark indeed. Our faith encompasses resurrection. As Paul wrote to the Thessalonians (1 Thessalonians 4:13), we do not grieve like those who have no hope.

Others are stuck in the past, brooding over what might have been: if we had made different choices, if we had been luckier in life, if Jesus had arrived sooner.

In this story, it is Martha's faith that inspires, rather than Mary's. God is a God of resurrection.

† Loving God, teach me to be hopeful. Give me Martha's faith, and help me to believe that, as you raised Jesus from the dead, you can bring good out of any evil. Amen

For further thought

• Am I too inclined to brood on what is past rather than put my trust in God for the future?

October

Saturday 25 October
Living with the consequences

Acts 6:8-15, 7:54-60

Opposition arose, however, from members of the Synagogue of the Freedmen … who began to argue with Stephen. But they could not stand up against the wisdom the Spirit gave him as he spoke. (part of verses 9-10)

Some scholars think that these opponents of Stephen, as expatriates from a very tight-knit community, were particularly ardent in their faith and determined to preserve its purity. They would listen to no arguments, make no compromises; Stephen was wrong, and if they could not out-talk him, they would resort to force.

So a wise and gifted disciple who would have been invaluable to the early church comes to a tragic end.

The key to understanding his story, though, is to realise that he could not do anything else.

We sometimes like to think that, if only people could be brought together round a table, there can be compromises and everyone can agree. Our differences are because we haven't taken time to grasp someone else's point of view; really we are all the same.

It's true that talk is good, and that many misunderstandings between people of different faiths or among people of the same faith are just that. In the end, though, we have to be willing to say 'I believe that this, not that, is true' – and live with the consequences. Stephen, sadly, died with the consequences.

This story also makes us ask where we fit into it. Are we on Stephen's side, bravely standing up for what we believe no matter what it costs? Or are we on the side of those who are violently hostile to a new idea and prepared to do anything to defeat it?

The Bible rarely leaves us entirely comfortable.

† Loving God, help me to have the courage of my convictions. When I talk with those whose faith is different, let me always remember who I am and whom I serve. Amen

For further thought
• Am I right to be sure I am right, and how do I treat those I think are in the wrong?

Saints and holy people

3 Saints in the early church

This week's notes are by **John Birch**

 John Birch is a Methodist local preacher, worship leader and writer based in South Wales. He hosts *www.faithandworship.com*, which offers prayer and worship resources on the web. He writes prayers and articles and has published two prayer collections. With a keen interest in the early Celtic Church, especially its faith and poetry, he is collaborating with a Canadian composer in putting together a collection of worship songs based on prayers from his website.

Sunday 26 October

The saints who welcome

Romans 16:1-6

I commend to you our sister Phoebe ... I ask you to receive her in the Lord in a way worthy of his people and to give her any help she may need from you, for she has been the benefactor of many people ... (verses 1-2)

When I last filled in a job application form, I had to find two referees to speak up for me: people who knew me both professionally and at a personal level, who could convince a future employer of my undoubted ability, skills and personal qualities!

In the ancient world we find something similar. In the rubbish dumps of Egypt, preserved in the desert sand, are papyrus letters of commendation that would be carried and used when required. Here Paul performs a similar service for Phoebe, who lived in Corinth. He paints a wonderful picture of a generous saint who had helped so many in the church, including himself, and who is travelling to Rome. 'Welcome her, as you would welcome any member of God's family!' says Paul to the churches in Rome.

I have a friend called Douglas who deserves a gold medal for welcoming. When Douglas greets you it's as if he's known you for years, and if you return the following week he will continue the conversation you have just had. I don't know any saints with shining halos round their heads. Most of the ones I have encountered have been like Douglas, ordinary people getting on with serving Christ in the world, and that's the definition I'm using in this week's notes.

† God of grace, accept the offering of our lives, and the talents you have given us, in the service of your kingdom. Amen

October

303

Monday 27 October
The saints who serve

Romans 16:17-27

I, Tertius, who wrote down this letter, greet you in the L<small>ORD</small>. Gaius, whose hospitality I and the whole church here enjoy, sends you his greetings. Erastus, who is the city's director of public works, and our brother Quartus send you their greetings. (verses 22-23)

At a large Christian conference the next speaker was introduced. He was an international banker who had interrupted a busy schedule of meetings in the world's financial capitals in order to speak to a group of Christians staying in a small seaside town.

It was an impressive talk that left me thinking that here was someone who was in the wrong job – he should become a professional Christian speaker where his superb communication skills could be used to motivate the church.

But of course I was wrong! His place is firmly in the financial world because that's where God can best use his gifts, and where his Christian faith will have the greatest influence.

There are Christians working in all areas of life, from politician to refuse collector. Some will be remembered because of their impact on the prosperity of the nation, others may be sadly forgotten by historians. But they won't be forgotten by those whose lives have been touched by them.

In his letter, Paul mentions several people and gives us a tiny glimpse into the life of the Corinthian Church. There's Tertius, a secretary, the high-ranking civil servant Erastus, and Gaius, who seems to have opened his house for the church to use.

Christians are rarely called to give up their occupations, but rather to serve where they are. God works with hearts to change people. God works with people to change the world!

† For Christians in all walks of life, we thank you. Use their gifts and their lives to make a real difference in this world. Amen

For further thought

• Do you ever wonder if there's something better you could do with your life, and fail to consider that God might want you right where you are?

The saints who encourage

1 Corinthians 16:1-24

I was glad when Stephanas, Fortunatus and Achaicus arrived, because they have supplied what was lacking from you. For they refreshed my spirit and yours also. (part of verses 17-18)

Around 40 years ago I was learning to play the guitar. At the same time I was invited to a local church that held a young people's fellowship. The two connected when I was encouraged to help lead worship (despite knowing only four chords, and the presence of two much better musicians than I could ever claim to be).

This encouragement led me to develop my guitar skills, be invited to join a Christian band and eventually play the big stage at a festival. What it did, more importantly, was enable me to enjoy fellowship and friendship with many young Christians and develop my fledgling faith. Forty years on I still lead worship, know a few more chords and try to encourage others, hopefully, through my preaching and writing.

Paul mentions three people in this passage who could be classed as 'encouragers' because they brought good news from the wider church that greatly lifted the spirits of both Paul and the others in Corinth. Of these three, Stephanas is picked out as being particularly noteworthy. His family were the very first converts in Achaia (which is to the north-west of Corinth) who had committed themselves to God's work. In the early church this was how someone became a leader, not by filling in application forms but by showing dedication through service.

Being an encourager of others is a wonderful gift. I shall always be grateful to those who encouraged a very poor musician and a young Christian because they saw in him something that could grow, flourish and bear fruit.

† Help us always to see the potential in others, and encourage them to grow, that others might be blessed by their gifts. Amen

For further thought
• Think about your local fellowship, particularly those young in years or faith. Are there some who would benefit from a little praise and encouragement from you?

October

305

Wednesday 29 October
The saints who give

2 Corinthians 8:1-9

And now, brothers and sisters, we want you to know about the grace that God has given the Macedonian churches. In the midst of a very severe trial, their overflowing joy and their extreme poverty welled up in rich generosity. (verses 1-2)

It is always interesting when newspapers carry stories of billionaires setting up charitable foundations to help others. We can overlook the fact that they remain immensely rich after their generosity; they have made an important commitment to help those who are in need. Generosity is celebrated at the heart of Jewish and Christian faith.

Of course, it is not always the wealthiest who are the most generous, and our experience can often be of those with almost nothing giving sacrificially when they come across someone in need. There is an interesting regulation at the Jewish Feast of Purim that says that, however poor people are, they must find someone poorer and give them a gift.

The Apostle Paul was an enthusiastic supporter of one particular cause, the mother church in Jerusalem, struggling economically and finding it increasingly difficult to care for the elderly, widows and orphans dependent upon its own funds. Paul uses the sacrificial generosity of the Macedonian Christians, who were in extreme poverty themselves, to challenge other churches to examine the level of their own giving.

Giving, of course, is not just about money. Some much-loved saints I have known have been the ones who have given selflessly of their time, gifts and talents for the benefit of others, particularly those who are needy. What we give is between us and God.

Paul says in 2 Corinthians 9:7, 'God loves a cheerful giver'.

† We give thanks for generosity when it improves the lives of others in this world. Bless both giver and receiver. Amen

For further thought

• Paul challenges us to give back to the world out of what we have received. How do you react to that challenge?

Thursday 30 October
Saints are not perfect

Philippians 4:2-3,10-23

I plead with Euodia and I plead with Syntyche to be of the same mind in the LORD. Yes, and I ask you, my true companion, help these women since they have contended at my side in the cause of the gospel, along with Clement and the rest of my co-workers, whose names are in the book of life. (verses 2-3)

I began this series on Sunday by suggesting that saints are ordinary people serving Christ in the world. Well, ordinary people fall out with friends and colleagues now and then. We're not perfect – a fact that is at the heart of the gospel message!

Some people are more sensitive than others, and a few words might be all it takes to upset them. There might be clashes of personality causing friction, and some are naturally impatient, or intolerant of certain opinions. The fact is that, even within the family of God, children squabble and fall out!

Do you ever consider what people might say about you in the future? All history remembers about Euodia and Syntyche is that they are two faithful church members at Philippi who fell out big time!

It was a disagreement that eventually had to be brought to the attention of Paul, and he was keen to see it resolved amicably and quickly. That's excellent advice, because too often we allow disagreements to grow and fester like an open wound. Relationships that are damaged affect the whole fellowship and can never glorify God's name.

Perhaps this should be our model for the resolution of arguments in the church. If they cannot be settled quickly between the parties involved, then the rest of the fellowship should get together to help bring the dispute to an amicable conclusion. It's the family of God working together for the good of all.

I do hope that Euodia and Syntyche resolved their differences!

† Loving God, help your family to pray together, work together and live together in unity, that your name might be glorified. Amen

For further thought

• How does your church resolve personality clashes or differences of opinion?

The saints who pray

Colossians 4:7-18

Epaphras, who is one of you and a servant of Christ Jesus, sends greetings. He is always wrestling in prayer for you, that you may stand firm in all the will of God, mature and fully assured. (verse 12)

Carmarthen is the small Welsh market town where we go to church. To the west, on a small hillside estate, lived a lovely woman called Marian. She was described to me as one of God's real prayer warriors. For years, from her vantage point above the town, she regularly prayed for its people and churches.

She was not discouraged by a lack of visible progress, because she knew that all things happen in God's time, not hers. So Marian continued to pray patiently in faith, believing that God would grow his church!

I think Epaphras was such a prayer warrior. We discover him in the first chapter of Colossians (verse 7) where he was the missionary who first brought the gospel to Colossae. Now we hear that, ever since the Word was sown, he has been praying hard that the Christians there might grow and flourish.

To Paul, this ministry of prayer was vital. He has nothing but praise for this 'servant of Christ Jesus' who is working so hard on behalf of the church.

There is a tendency within many churches to spend a lot of time talking and doing, but not so much time praying. Perhaps we are afraid that sitting and being quiet before God could be misunderstood as inactivity! But Paul corrects us on this point.

If you have a prayer warrior in your church, then you are truly blessed.

† Thank you for prayer warriors, and for all your saints who pray regularly for others. Grant us the patience and faith to know that you listen to our prayers, and answer them! Amen

For further thought

• Does your church prioritise prayer, in meeting together and encouraging individual quiet times, or is there room for improvement?

October

The saints who grow

2 Thessalonians 1:3-12

We ought always to thank God for you, brothers and sisters, and rightly so, because your faith is growing more and more, and the love all of you have for one another is increasing. Therefore, among God's churches we boast about your perseverance and faith in all the persecutions and trials you are enduring. (verses 3-4)

Paul wrote two letters to the church at Thessalonica. It may be that the members hadn't properly understood his teaching in the first letter (not uncommon for a preacher!). So Paul followed it up with a clarification to avoid confusion. It's a nice human touch in the unfolding story of early church growth. Most of us are guilty of misunderstanding at times and, when it is a difficult problem, it can take time and patience to resolve.

Paul handles it with great diplomacy. He picks up on the positives, and takes the opportunity to encourage the church by emphasising how well people were doing. Theirs was a strong and enduring faith, despite the persecution and trials they were facing, and it was a faith that Paul could boast about.

Most of us probably belong to churches that have been established for some time, and have limited experience of God working in a mission or new church plant. Here we have a group of people who have responded to the gospel message with enthusiasm, learning about and experiencing the grace of God individually and, as a community of believers, sharing their faith and lives with one another. It's what church should be, of course!

Paul is proud of them, and thanks God for all that they mean to him. They are like children eager to learn, still requiring some input from Paul, but their growth in faith is something that he is excited to share about on his continuing missionary journeys.

Paul has great hopes for these developing saints!

† Thank you, Father, for all who have recently made a commitment to you within our own church. Help us to help them in their journey of faith. Amen

For further thought

- How many Christians known to us could we boast about because of the strength of their faith? If the number is small, what could we do?

November

Children in the Bible
1 Children in the Old Testament

This week's notes are by **Rachel Montagu** (see page 119).

Sunday 2 November
Even wild sons need love

Genesis 21:12-20

Then she went off and sat down about a bow-shot away, for she thought, 'I cannot watch the boy die.' And as she sat there, she began to sob. (verse 16)

Often the Bible uses parent analogies to describe the relationship between God and Israel: 'As a mother comforts her child, so will I comfort you' (Isaiah 66:13), 'Can a mother forget the baby at her breast?' (Isaiah 49:15), 'As a father has compassion on his children, so the Lord has compassion on those who fear him' (Psalm 103:13). The readings this week show that children are prayed for and loved, as in the case of Samuel, Moses and Ishmael; that they are more spiritually attuned than their seniors (David and Jephthah's daughter); and that they are capable of protecting others and competently advising adults (Miriam, Jephthah's daughter, Naaman's wife's maid).

Sarah thought that using her maid Hagar as a surrogate mother so Abraham would at last have a son solved the problem of her infertility. But once she had Isaac, she could not bear to see Ishmael playing nearby. She told Abraham to send Hagar and Ishmael away.

Ishmael's trial here parallels Isaac's near-sacrifice in the next chapter: someone orders Abraham, Abraham rises early to obey, and an angel speaks just in time to rescue the boy and promises his future well-being.

We can sympathise when Hagar feels unable to stay close and watch her son die of thirst.

Sarah may have tried to dismiss Ishmael once she thought he threatened Isaac's well-being and was surplus to her needs, but God remains faithful to him as Abraham's son, however wild (Genesis 16:12); his name means 'God will hear'.

† Be gracious to us and answer us and hear our prayers, for you are a God who listens to everyone's prayer.

A fine child, nurtured by two mothers

Exodus 2:1-10

... and she became pregnant and gave birth to a son ... But when she could hide him no longer, she got a papyrus basket for him and coated it with tar and pitch. Then she placed the child in it and put it among the reeds along the bank of the Nile. (verses 2-3)

Pharaoh's fears about the increasing Hebrew minority in Egypt led him to decree that all Hebrew boys should be thrown into the Nile – a river that usually brought life and crops, not death. I like the verse saying Moses' mother 'saw he was a fine child' because it reminds me how I kept gazing at my sons in the weeks after their births, fascinated by every expression and movement.

When Moses became too old to hide, his mother found a way for the Nile, which Pharaoh had decreed would kill him, to protect him.

His sister Miriam is later described as Miriam the Prophetess. The Bible does not record her prophecies. Our chapter puzzles us because it says a couple from the tribe of Levi married and had Moses, yet we realise they already have a daughter and older son. Traditional Jewish Bible commentators solve both these difficulties by suggesting Pharaoh's decree so horrified Moses' father that he divorced his wife. Miriam reproached him, prophesying that the divorce prevented the birth of sons, potential victims of Pharaoh's decree, but also daughters. The chapter begins with the remarriage she encouraged.

Pharaoh's daughter was moved by the crying child's plight. We can only wonder how her father reacted to having an adopted Hebrew child brought up in his palace. Many commentators note how hard the children of Israel would have found unlearning the slave mentality they acquired in Egypt. Moses could lead the people because, brought up in Pharaoh's palace, he had learned how to lead and how to take responsibility. So Pharaoh's daughter, by saving Moses, saved his whole people too.

† Truly you are the first and the last, and besides you we have no ruler, redeemer or saviour. Eternal, you redeemed us from Egypt and delivered us from slavery.

For further thought

• Watch *Live and Become* (dir. Rahu Mihaileanu, 2005), a film about a Christian boy airlifted from Ethiopia to Israel as part of Operation Moses. He too is saved by the love of two mothers.

Tuesday 4 November
Don't make foolish vows – ever!

Judges 11:29-40

When Jephthah returned to his home in Mizpah, who should come out to meet him but his daughter, dancing to the sound of tambourines! She was an only child. (part of verse 34)

Jephthah agreed to be general against the Ammonites. Insecure because he was born outside marriage and afraid of failure, he made an incredibly foolish vow. Whatever did he think would meet him? A pet sheep that he could happily sacrifice? His only child dancing to celebrate his victory makes it more poignant but no human being could be sacrificed (Leviticus18:21) nor could most animals. Radak, a mediaeval Jewish commentator, finessed Jephthah's declaration: 'it will be offered if it may be offered, and dedicated to God if not'. Jephthah blamed his daughter: he uses the same Hebrew word Ahab uses to Elijah, 'you troubler'. Ahab and Jephthah both blamed others for problems only they had caused.

Nameless, like many other biblical women, Jephthah's daughter had a voice, speaking with confident faith. She said her father must keep his vow. Her only request was to spend time mourning with her friends.

Some contemporary commentators contrast this story with Isaac's near-sacrifice, asking why no angel saved her, suggesting this proves the Bible's anti-female bias. But the comparison doesn't work: God commanded Abraham to sacrifice Isaac, and then to spare him. Only Jephthah endangered his daughter; human initiative required a human solution. Jephthah and the High Priest both thought the other should move first to annul his vow; their shared arrogance sealed her fate.

The text doesn't explicitly describe her death; some commentators say that she became a dedicated celibate, losing not her life but the possibility of bearing children and giving Jephthah further descendants.

† Pray that you will use speech to enhance and not destroy the lives of those round you.

For further thought

• Many artists have painted this story. If you can access art books or the web, look for a few pictures and decide what each artist wants to convey about the story.

Wednesday 5 November
Pouring out my soul to the Eternal

1 Samuel 1:12-20

Hannah replied, 'I was pouring out my soul to the LORD ... I have been praying here out of my great anguish and grief.' Eli answered, 'Go in peace, and may the God of Israel grant you what you have asked of him.'
(part of verses 15–17)

Hannah's passionate prayer for the child for whom she longs became the example for all prayer in Jewish tradition. Prayer should be, like hers, an outpouring of the heart.

Hannah is one of several barren women whose pain the Bible describes (Genesis 16 and 29 – 30). Isaac prayed that Rebekah would have a child, although Rebekah later approached the Almighty herself (Genesis 25:22). Elkanah, Hannah's husband, was happy that he had a wife to concentrate on him (verse 8), even if this chapter proves neither wife enjoyed this as he did; Elkanah was unlikely to pray that Hannah would become pregnant. In verse 11 she promised that her child would be dedicated to God as a Nazirite (described in Numbers 6 and Judges 13). Once Samuel was born, she waited for several years before coming on pilgrimage again and leaving him in the Temple. Even if they weaned later than we usually do, it may seem extraordinary to us that so young a child – and a child who was so longed-for – was left in the shrine, seeing his parents only once a year (1 Samuel 2:19), even with Eli the priest as a father-figure. I felt reassured when I first noticed that later Samuel rejoined his family in Ramah and that Hannah later had other children (1 Samuel 7:17; 1 Samuel 2:21)! Samuel served God in the shrine at Shiloh, fulfilling his mother's prayer that, if God gave her a child, he should be dedicated to God's service. His role as prophet began when God called to him and gave him a message to pass on (chapter 3). Samuel and Jeremiah were both prophets from when they were very young (Jeremiah 1).

† Our God who is in heaven, have compassion on the young people of our community and the toddlers and babies, and answer us when we call.

For further thought

• Because Hannah sings in delight and thankfulness when she brings Samuel to the Temple, listen to some music that means great joy and thanksgiving to you.

November

313

The boy 'done good'

1 Samuel 17:33-49

Saul replied, 'You are not able to go out against this Philistine and fight him; you are only a young man, and he has been a warrior from his youth.' (verse 33)

When we take up the story today, David has already been called in from shepherding – an excellent training ground for caring leadership, as Moses found before him – to be anointed future king of Israel. Saul did not know this and, when he needed music to soothe his depression, David came and played for him (chapter 16). While the army was campaigning against the Philistines, David's father told him to go to the battle-field to bring his brothers' rations. Daily the giant Goliath challenged one of the Israelite army to meet him in single combat. David heard this and couldn't understand why the army allowed this impudent challenge to go unanswered, to the indignation of his brothers, who suspected his motives in being there. Plus the brothers resented David's implication that they were cowards for not volunteering to fight.

The Bible contrasts the young shepherd with complete trust in God and the pagan warrior. David acknowledged his lack of military experience but believed he did not need armour because he would treat Goliath like one of the animals he killed when they threatened his flock. Goliath considered himself a heroic champion. The huge and elaborate armour to fit his three-metre frame was described in great detail when he first challenged the Israelites. He is represented as the greatest technological achievement of his era, a walking victor in the arms race, but the manner of his death means we see him as an animal. Shepherding proved to be training for battle as well as for leadership, but it is David's faith in God as well as his skill with a sling that makes his victory possible.

† Blessed is the one who delights in the teaching of the Eternal and who meditates on God's teaching day and night.

For further thought

- David's victory is ensured because he uses natural materials wisely. Consider whether there are ways you can reduce your carbon footprint and how you could campaign against the Goliaths who use more than their share of the earth's resources.

Friday 7 November
Singer, king, adulterer, murderer, father

2 Samuel 12:15-23

He answered, 'While the child was still alive, I fasted and wept. I thought, "Who knows? The LORD may be gracious to me and let the child live." But now that he is dead, why should I go on fasting? Can I bring him back again?' (part of verses 22-23)

This is one of several stories in David's life that challenges us today. Kings were appointed so the people would have battle-leaders. But David was lounging at home while his armies were out campaigning when he saw Bathsheba bathing. She became pregnant; to disguise their adultery, he summoned her husband Uriah home from the front. When Uriah refused to sleep with Bathsheba while his fellow-soldiers still fought, David ordered Uriah's death. Nathan the prophet explained to him the enormity of this, using a beautiful parable (12:1-14).

David tried hard to save his child's life by praying and fasting instead of remaining passive as he had often done with his older children (2 Samuel 13). When the child died, he accepted it without letting anger at God keep him from prayer. Many have suggested that belief in life after death became part of Judaism only after the biblical era; this passage is one of many that belies the theory.

The Ten Commandments say that God rewards those who love God for thousands of generations but may punish children for the sins of their parents for three or four generations. Punishment is outweighed by reward in this scheme, and repentance can always avert the decree (1 Kings 21:28-29). Nevertheless, without underestimating the destructiveness of adultery and murder, we may ask why the innocent child suffered for the wrongs his parents perpetrated. This son was born before David repented. We then see David's tenderness, as distinct from his lust, for Bathsheba (verse 4). Their next child, Solomon, was loved by God, survived, and inherited the promise of chapter 7.

† Blessed are you, Eternal our God, who delights in repentance and is gracious and abundant in forgiveness.

For further thought

- David prayed the child would live. His prayer was not answered. David still prayed after the child's death. Let us follow David's example and not lose heart for prayer when we do not get the answer we want, or are angry because we are bereaved.

A captive girl and a healing God

2 Kings 5:1-14

Bands of raiders from Aram had gone out and had taken captive a young girl from Israel, and she served Naaman's wife. She said to her mistress, 'If only my master would see the prophet who is in Samaria! He would cure him of his leprosy.' (verses 2-3)

This story, like others in the Elijah/Elisha series, shows a different role for prophets. Moses and Isaiah preached and taught God's word; Elijah and Elisha, by contrast, move people to faith in God by the miracles they perform. To succeed they must often be very dramatic. All the people saw the trial Elijah staged against Baal's false prophets. The widow with whom Elijah lodged realised he was a prophet only when he returned her son to life, although he had saved her household from starvation for many months (1 Kings 17 – 18). Elisha cured Naaman of leprosy but gets the opportunity only because of the wise child, taken captive, who said the prophet in Samaria would be able to cure him.

When leprosy is described in Exodus, the priest inspected the white spots and declared the leper still infectious or cured but did not attempt to heal. That, like all healing in the Bible, was in God's hands. Some of the earliest prayers recorded in the Bible are prayers for healing (Genesis 20:7, Numbers 12:13). I wonder if the wise girl is also responsible for the plea of 'his servants' that Naaman should do exactly what the prophet commanded.

Elsewhere the Bible assumes captives, even adults, became absorbed into the culture into which they were enslaved (Exodus 12:44). This young girl, presumably bereft of her family, kept her faith and proclaimed her belief in Elisha and God. It is her master, not she, who must now dissemble; he apologised to Elisha that, although he now believed in God, he must still bow down in Rimmon's temple (2 Kings 5:18).

† Blessed are you, Eternal our God, who heals the sick.

For further thought

- Even if we are not Elijah or Elisha, we can still pray for the sick and also help their morale – and therefore perhaps their recovery – by visiting them.

- The Separated Child Foundation and other charities work with isolated young refugees whose situation is a contemporary version of this girl's. Can you help them?

Children in the Bible
2 Children in the New Testament

This week's notes are by **Nathan Eddy** (see page 1).

Sunday 9 November
No children allowed

Luke 1:57-66

Everyone who heard this wondered about it, asking, 'What then is this child going to be?' (verse 66)

I have a secret to tell you – the New Testament is not actually very positive in its estimation of children or families. The stories we will look at this week are justly beloved, but they are few and far between. Marriage and children are generally discouraged by New Testament writers. The challenges facing children and families today are far from their minds.

There is an interesting tension in all this. Jesus without exception held children in very high esteem. But for Jesus nothing comes between the kingdom and his followers – not even children or family obligations. 'Do you think I have come to bring peace on earth?' Jesus asks later in the Gospel. 'No, I tell you, but division. From now on there will be five in one family divided against each other … father against and son … mother against daughter …' (Luke 12:51-52). Hardly family values.

John the Baptist, the subject of today's tender story, is a case in point. John will be an uncompromising prophet of the kingdom. He will live in the wilderness (chapter 1 verse 80) – not the most family-friendly place. The rebellious teenager in me is exhilarated, but I'm not sure what my wife and two daughters would think if I left for the desert.

Jesus loved children, but didn't give parents much advice. Perhaps we should simply live with this tension – raise children (where we are called to) in families that are wide open to the kingdom, not ends in themselves. Perhaps children can even show us the way to the kingdom – let's see.

† Loving God, let nothing come between us and your coming rule – and let the children of the world lead us there.

God the child

Luke 2:21-35

When the time came for the purification rites required by the Law of Moses, Joseph and Mary took [Jesus] to Jerusalem to present him to the LORD. (verse 22)

It's interesting that the church does not have very much to say about children. We have developed sophisticated positions on slavery and human trafficking, abortion, and global trade and social justice; we are more or less silent on children. The most significant recent statement about children was from the United Nations rather than a religious organisation; its Convention on the Rights of a Child became international law in 1990. Where I live, the public library probably does a better job engaging families on Sunday morning than churches! I wonder if there's something we are missing.

In Christ, God became not just a human being, but a child. Luke's nativity stories tell not just of an abstract word made flesh, but of swelling bellies and kicking babies, the joy of expectant mothers, and religious rituals after childbirth. The love of God the Father, often described as mother-like in his care, is made real in a child, here brought to the Temple by his parents like any other Jewish male child. 'Blessed is the mother who gave you birth and nursed you,' a woman calls out to Jesus later in the Gospel (Luke 11:27). In Jesus, through Mary, the very heart of God reaches out in love to a child. Perhaps here we can find a firm ground in our faith for our care for children and their rights.

I wonder if we can see Christ in solidarity with children this week. I wonder if we can see the face of Christ in the faces of the children we meet.

† God of the Christ child, help us value every child in our communities.

For further thought

- So often children are in the news as victims of abuse at the hands of adults. Notice how they appear in the news this week, and consider how God feels.

Tuesday 11 November
Lost and found

Luke 2:41-52

'Why were you searching for me?' he asked. 'Didn't you know I had to be in my Father's house?' (verse 49)

I once lost my eldest daughter on a crowded beach. One moment I thought she was next to me as we walked to the towels; the next minute she was gone. Though only four, luckily she waited for us calmly with the lifeguard while my wife and I rushed around in a panic. Many parents will recognise the anxiety of Joseph and Mary here as they lose (through no fault of their own) the boy Jesus at a festival in the big city. Yikes.

Being found is one of Luke's favourite images for salvation. It's in his Gospel that we find the story of the prodigal son, who returns home to be found again. Here also Jesus announces his mission with the words that 'the Son of Man came to seek and to save the lost' (Luke 19:10). Do you think it is significant that the boy Jesus is found by his parents after three days (verse 46) – the same number of days he will spend dead in the tomb? Even his exchange of questions and answers with his parents here sounds like the conversation at the tomb: 'Why do you look for the living among the dead?' the angels ask at the tomb in 24:5. I wonder if we get so busy looking for Jesus that we miss him seeking us.

Jesus here shows the tug in every parent–child relationship between dependence and independence. This is a precious story, the only one we have of Jesus as something other than an infant or an adult. His business is with God, not ultimately at home with his mother and father; his parents are wise enough to recognise this. One day my wife and I, too, will lose our daughter, in a sense, for good.

† God of young girls and boys, give us the wisdom to love children enough to let them go – and help us trust that they will be found standing with you.

For further thought:
• What do the children around you hope for their lives? What dreams do they have?

Front and centre

Mark 9:33-37

[Jesus] took a little child whom he placed among them. Taking the child in his arms, he said to them, 'Whoever welcomes one of these little children in my name welcomes me ...' (part of verses 36-37)

In Jesus' day, children were non-persons. They were invisible – they had no rights and were completely dependent on their families. By putting them first in this remarkable passage Jesus is saying as much about the priorities of the disciples as he is about children.

It's commonly said that Western societies associate children with innocence or unspoiltness – think of the technicolour images in a children's Bible. But it seems to me that many people I meet don't associate much at all with children. I wonder if in many ways they are as invisible to us as they were in Jesus' day. Anyone who has looked in vain for baby-change facilities in a public place or been pulled this way and that in the middle of a hushed church service by a boisterous toddler will understand!

I'm sometimes left cold by male imagery in the Bible, but in this passage I'm grateful for the image of Jesus and his male followers sitting down with a child in their midst. Jesus didn't have anything to say directly about being a good father or parent, but perhaps he models it here. Men in my community are often absent from child-rearing. They turn up (like me) at the drop-off and pick-up times at nursery, but sometimes not much else. In my church, in co-operation with our local children's centre, we have started a Dads and Tots group to encourage fathers to play with their children. Through attentive childcare, perhaps down on their level as Jesus was, men (and women) can welcome Christ himself.

The danger is that we adults get too busy arguing about who is the greatest, like the disciples, to notice whom Jesus is sitting with.

† Lord of the least, help us to be servants of the children in our communities, that through them you might be among us.

For further thought
• How does your church welcome children? Do they have pride of place?

Such as these

Mark 10:13-16

[Jesus] said to them, 'Let the children come to me, and do not hinder them, for the kingdom of God belongs to such as these.' (part of verse 14)

The image of Jesus blessing children – in Mark, even taking them up into his arms – is one of the most familiar from the Bible. It's famous, but this is one of the very few passages in the New Testament that discuss children explicitly. Theologians throughout church history, for their part, have mostly ignored children altogether, until quite recently. Perhaps this would get Jesus angry all over again. In verse 14 he is 'indignant' here at the disciples' refusal to keep children from coming to him – this is the angriest Jesus gets in the whole Gospel!

It's not clear what exactly Jesus means when he says later in the same verse that the kingdom of God belongs to 'such as these'. Does the kingdom belong literally to children? Jesus could even mean that these children around him will literally be the generation that sees the kingdom of God come. Or are there certain characteristics of children that, if shared by an adult, make that person fit for the kingdom? Perhaps if adults depend on God the way children depend on parents the kingdom is theirs.

I like the first option that puts real children forward, as they are, as inheritors of the kingdom. Often we 'adultise' children and project on to them our own desires for our lives. Often our dealings with children say more about us than them. I want to see children accepted as they are. I imagine them like kids I know – wanting to jump off Jesus' knees rather than pay attention. It's to children 'such as these' that the kingdom belongs.

† God of blessing, help us be a blessing to the children around us – for their sake and yours, not for ours.

For further thought
• I have been helped by British theologian Adrian Thatcher in his book called *Theology and Families* (Massachusetts 2007). What resources can help you in your care for children?

Friday 14 November
You have enough

John 6:5-13

Andrew, Simon Peter's brother, spoke up, 'Here is a boy with five small barley loaves and two small fish, but how far will they go among so many?' (part of verses 8 and 9)

I recently had the pleasure of a five-hour train journey with my six-year-old daughter. Apart from the moment when in a forgetful gesture she tipped over her entire cup of hot chocolate, it was a lovely trip; I wasn't sure it would be. The few books she had, plus some rounds of hangman and word puzzles were enough to keep her interest. It was easier than being in a car – I guess because she had her father's attention, at least some of the time.

The disciples were worried about where the resources would come from to feed the hungry people. Perhaps the wise thing to do would be to send them away – there wasn't enough money to buy them all food, even if there was a shop nearby on that mountainside. But a little lad has a different idea. He has something to share. He knows it will feed someone, at least. He is brave enough to get Andrew's attention.

Although the church is growing very rapidly in some parts of the world, where I live it is shrinking, and has been for several decades. Numbers of members are declining and ageing, and our resources are shrinking. Many are worried and anxious about what to do; people are still hungry – for real food on their tables and for the word of life that Jesus gives.

It took a little boy to help the adults around Jesus see that the resources they had were enough. Children are imaginative, resourceful and resilient. They can be quite happy with very little. If every church in the world closed for lack of money, children will still play, dream and laugh. I wonder what they have to teach us about what we can do with what resources we have.

† God of surprises, we are worried about many things in our world, but children rarely worry for long. Give us their trust that we have all we need, when we offer it to you.

For further thought

- How can you listen to children and take their suggestions seriously today?

Saturday 15 November
A firm foundation

2 Timothy 3:14-17

But as for you, continue in what you have learned and have become convinced of, because you know those from whom you learned it, and how from infancy you have known the Holy Scriptures … (part of verses 14-15)

This is a famous passage – and it has more to do with children than you might believe. Paul, or (as many people think) another author writing later in Paul's name, writes here a kind of farewell letter to Timothy, his co-worker and 'dear son' (2 Timothy 1:2). It's a warm, encouraging, loving letter, written from prison, in which Paul passes on his last encouragement to Timothy before his death.

From a young age Timothy has been immersed in the sincere faith of his family. His mother and grandmother (Eunice and Lois, named in 1:5), and hopefully Timothy's father, raised Timothy 'from infancy' (verse 15) in the holy scriptures of their Jewish faith. These scriptures, what we now know as the Old Testament (the New Testament didn't come together for another 200 years or so) are what is called 'God-breathed' in verse 16 – a word used only here in the Bible. Paul's point here is less about the mechanics of biblical inspiration than it is about the rock-solid foundation that scripture has provided young Timothy. He is ready for good work.

As Paul says, scripture is useful for teaching and rebuking, correcting and training in righteousness. It is also useful in helping children imagine a being who loves them no matter what they do and has created them unique and special. When our children, and the children in our churches, grow up with this bedrock of trust from their parents, grandparents and teachers, we give them the best start we can in life. We prepare them for whatever might come their way, even when we are gone.

† God of all grace, may our reflections in this volume, and all our thoughts, help your holy word support children and young people.

For further thought

• What are some creative ways of sharing Bible stories with children? Share a resource or a tip on Facebook at http://www.facebook.com/freshfromtheword

November

Readings in Matthew 13 – 16
Conversations with Jesus

This week's notes are by **Symon Hill**

Symon Hill is a Christian activist and writer. He is associate director of the Ekklesia think tank and a founding member of Christianity Uncut. His books include *The No-Nonsense Guide to Religion* and *Digital Revolutions: Activism in the Internet Age*, both published by New Internationalist. He can often be found walking, reading crime fiction or arguing about theology in the pub. He lives in London.

Sunday 16 November
Eating with sinners

Matthew 9:9-13

While Jesus was having dinner at Matthew's house, many tax collectors and sinners came and ate with him and his disciples. When the Pharisees saw this, they asked his disciples, 'Why does your teacher eat with tax collectors and sinners? (verses 10–11)

Eating is important. Food plays a major role in many religions. I've had the privilege of eating with Jews on a Friday evening, joyfully sharing bread as they welcome the Sabbath. Muslims eat and thank God late at night when the daylight fast finishes during Ramadan. Sikhs offer meals in the *langar* to anyone who turns up.

Christians have the Eucharist. In the early church, it was a full meal. We now tend to eat smaller portions, but the meaning remains. At the heart of Christian worship is the sharing of food.

Why does Jesus eat with sinners? Not just because the healthy don't need a doctor. Given his later comments, it seems unlikely that he thought the Pharisees were much less sinful than the tax collectors. Jesus defied convention by socialising with people who were not only immoral but who were outcasts from respectable society. Tax collectors and prostitutes were victims as well as perpetrators of sin.

If we're honest, most of us find it easier to eat with people like us. What would it mean to share our food, not merely as an act of charity, but because we are all sinners, and all children of God?

† Gracious God, thank you that the world has enough food to feed everyone in it. Forgive us for failing to share it fairly. Help us to eat with our fellow-sinners, in love and forgiveness.

No one rides a horse on a motorway

Matthew 9:14-17

No one sews a patch of unshrunk cloth on an old garment, for the patch will pull away from the garment, making the tear worse. Neither do people pour new wine into old wineskins. If they do, the skins will burst; the wine will run out, and the wineskins will be ruined. **(part of verses 16-17)**

Jesus and his disciples are still eating. This time, he gives a different reason: celebration. He knows his disciples will lose their appetite when their leader is hanging on a cross. There is a time to celebrate and a time to mourn. God is with us in all our emotions.

In today's reading, Jesus jumps from a discussion about food to talking about newness. How would he make his point in our own culture, unused to wineskins and not always too familiar with repairing clothes by hand? No one puts a VHS tape into a DVD player.

In Jesus, God is present in a new way. Like many people, I'm still tempted to try to fit him into the things with which I'm familiar. The early church struggled over whether Gentile Christians should be obliged to obey the laws of the Torah. Most decided that they shouldn't, although some quickly set up other laws instead. Today, we can easily give in to the temptation to snatch lines of scripture from their contexts and set them up as rules to justify new forms of legalism. It's frightening to think of living by God's Spirit, trusting in prayer and the power of love. Relying on rules and conventions often seems so much easier.

We can't wedge God's kingdom into the habits and attitudes that we find most comfortable. Jesus talks of new wine as he is eating and celebrating with his friends. A new kingdom means new lives. And that's something well worth celebrating.

† Loving God, help me to see where I mistake my own assumptions for your will. Give me courage to follow the scary, exciting, confusing, liberating reality of your new kingdom.

For further thought
• How would our lives be different if we were able to trust more deeply in God's new work in Jesus? How would society be different?

Jesus and John: not much in common?

Matthew 11:11-19

For John came neither eating nor drinking, and they say, 'He has a demon.' The Son of Man came eating and drinking, and they say, 'Here is a glutton and a drunkard, a friend of tax collectors and sinners.' But wisdom is proved right by her deeds. (verses 18-19)

You can't win. Whether you live austerely or enjoy a hearty meal, your opponents will use it against you. It's not often mentioned that Jesus and John the Baptist seem to have led very different lifestyles. Jesus points this out explicitly in this passage, but only after a lengthy defence of John. There is an undertone of anger about how they have both been treated.

When John the Baptist proclaimed that a greater person than him would follow him, he was living off the food he could find outdoors in the desert – locusts and wild honey, as the Gospels put it. Did he imagine that the person he proclaimed would spend so much time tucking into meals with sinners and defending his choice to do so? Yet nowhere in the Gospels does Jesus praise anyone more highly than he praises John the Baptist in this passage.

God's kingdom is proclaimed through the austerity of John and the 'gluttony' of Jesus. Like John, we need to be prepared for the possibility that many of those who work for the kingdom will have different lifestyles from ours. They may not be people with whom we feel comfortable. This doesn't mean that we shouldn't disagree with them or that our lifestyles don't matter. But lifestyle can be as much about personality as principle. When it is about principle, how much can we work through the issues with people who don't share our conclusions? People who seem different will be attacked for their differences, but it is deeds that prove wisdom.

† Loving God, help us to trust you to use all sorts of people in building your kingdom. Forgive us if we imagine that it can be built only by people who share our own attitudes.

For further thought

- Does your church include people with lots of different lifestyles? What can you do to welcome people who worry their lifestyles won't fit in?

Wednesday 19 November
Better for Sodom than for Britain?

Matthew 11:20-24

And you, Capernaum, will you be lifted to the heavens? No, you will go down to Hades. For if the miracles that were performed in you had been performed in Sodom, it would have remained to this day. But I tell you that it will be more bearable for Sodom on the day of judgement than for you.
(verses 23-24)

People in Jesus' time knew about Sodom. A sinful city whose destruction is described in Genesis, it had become a byword for ungodly behaviour. Jesus' listeners may well have thought that he was going over the top. It's easy to think that the sins of our own cities and countries can't be as bad as all that.

It was not until centuries later that 'sodomy' took on its association with homosexuality. One of Sodom's sins was an attempted homosexual gang rape. In reality, most gay and bisexual people find rape just as abhorrent as most straight people do. Many scholars believe that Sodom was considered so sinful not because of homosexuality but because of a lack of hospitality. This may sound trivial to us, but it was seen as a serious sin in biblical cultures. When in Palestine recently, I found it difficult to visit a village, let alone a house, without being offered cups of tea and often vast amounts of food.

Hospitality has become a neglected custom in today's Britain and many Western societies. Of course, hospitality is about more than cups of tea. It's about how we treat refugees, how we perceive 'outsiders', how we relate to people who are different from us. Like Jesus' listeners, we may find it easier to judge the practices and cultures of other countries or groups of people, and to assume that they are worse than us. The sins of our own countries, economies and political systems have become so normal that we barely notice them.

† Loving God, help us to see beyond the assumptions of own culture; to recognise sin that we have overlooked and to notice goodness where we had not expected to find it.

For further thought

• What does the biblical value of hospitality mean for your own life, community, church or country?

Healing and name-calling

Matthew 12:22-32

If I drive out demons by Beelzebul, by whom do your people drive them out? So then, they will be your judges. But if it is by the Spirit of God that I drive out demons, then the kingdom of God has come upon you.
(verses 27-28)

Healing, freedom and love should not be so controversial. Jesus' healings were condemned not because they were ineffective but because of who he was. Some of Jesus' enemies refused to believe that anything he did came from God. Therefore, it must have come from Satan. But Satan does not heal. God heals. All too often actions are judged by who is carrying them out. We refuse to recognise good news from someone we don't like or don't agree with.

To accuse someone of being demon-possessed was one of the worst insults in Jesus' time. It could remove all credibility from the words and actions of the person concerned. The biblical scholar Ched Myers compares it to the way in which the word 'communist' was used to discredit people in the US during the Cold War. Other countries and cultures have their own equivalents. These are the sorts of insults we attract if we dare to proclaim healing and liberation without the approval of political authorities or religious institutions.

Jesus proclaims the power of love to a world more inclined to trust in the powers of violence and money. He has begun the work of 'tying up' those powers and plundering the strong man's house. When people are healed, freed and loved, the kingdom of God has come among us.

† Thank you, Father God, for all the healing, freedom and love in the world, and for all those working to bring more of it.

For further thought

- In what ways does the power of God conflict with the powers of violence and money? How can we act in these individual situations?

Better a lie from a truth-teller

Matthew 12:33-37

Make a tree good and its fruit will be good, or make a tree bad and its fruit will be bad, for a tree is recognised by its fruit. (verse 33)

The German theologian Dietrich Bonhoeffer said that he would prefer a lie told by a truth-teller to a true statement made by a liar. A habitual liar might tell the truth only because it is convenient to do so, but someone grounded in the truth would tell a lie only for a very good reason.

Bonhoeffer was not, of course, encouraging people to lie. He was emphasising that both good and bad behaviour begin with our hearts, our lifestyles and our priorities. He was echoing Jesus' view that we can bring out good from the good stored up in us. If we want to act differently, we need to be different.

Each of us is both a bad and good person, and we are called to lifestyles that build up the good. This too has its dangers: being 'good' can become an end in itself. Do we live environmentally friendly lives because it makes us feel virtuous or because it benefits the planet and its people? Do we show respect for others because it makes us seem nice or because they are all children of God, worthy of our love? Attention to both ourselves and others, private contemplation and public action, are all needed to 'make a tree good'. Dwelling on our own unworthiness is a waste of energy. It also involves too much focus on us. Instead, let's get on with trying to live with a different focus, however long it takes, and the fruit will be good.

† Mother God, help us to live with you as our focus and with love as our goal. Thank you for forgiving us when we fail, and for giving us so many opportunities to try again.

For further thought

• When have you seen 'good fruit' or 'bad fruit' coming from sources you wouldn't expect? Why do you think this is?

November

Saturday 22 November
Crammed with heaven

Matthew 12:38-45

Then some of the Pharisees and teachers of the law said to him, 'Teacher, we want to see a sign from you.' He answered, 'A wicked and adulterous generation asks for a sign!' (verses 38-39a)

Seeking God's will can be so hard. I'm sure I'm not the only one who sometimes wishes that divine guidance would be written in huge letters across the sky. But Jesus rejected the request for a sign.

God wants us to think for ourselves. This is scary. I have been to plenty of churches that are not comfortable with it, and do their best to ensure that their congregations are all taught the 'right' interpretation of the Bible. In contrast, Jesus told parables but rarely explained them. It seems that he wanted his listeners to think through the meanings, whether individually or in discussion with others. I used to think I 'knew' what his teachings meant, after hearing so many sermons about them. But Jesus' teachings are so rich in meaning that the exploration never ends.

As soon as Jesus rejects the demand for a sign, he makes clear that the Pharisees and teachers of the law have been overlooking signs all around them. He praises the people of Nineveh for repenting in response to Jonah. But 'this generation' is not repenting, despite Jesus' own teaching. The teachings and actions of God's messengers should be enough of a sign to help people think differently and to question their own assumptions. Signs, in a sense, are all around us – signs to think about and explore. As Elizabeth Barrett Browning wrote in 'Aurora Leigh' (1856):

> Earth's crammed with Heaven,
> And every common bush afire with God,
> But only he who sees, takes off his shoes.
> The rest sit round it and pluck blackberries …

† Thank you for Jesus' teachings, Lord God. When we find them complicated or frustrating, help us to rely on your power as we seek their meaning for our lives, our society and our economy.

For further thought

- Have you doubted the interpretation given to a Bible passage? Have you discussed your doubts with others? If not, now may be a good time.

Readings in Matthew 13 – 16
2 Teaching and learning

This week's notes are by **Meeli Tankler**

Meeli Tankler lives in Pärnu, Estonia. In her local United Methodist Church she is involved in children's ministry, leads the choir, and serves as a local preacher. In 2013 she earned the Doctor of Ministry degree from Asbury Theological Seminary. She has served as the President of the Baltic Methodist Theological Seminary in Tallinn, Estonia, since 2009. She is married to a Methodist pastor, and is a mother of three grown-up children and a grandmother of four. Her hobbies are choir music, tennis and reading.

Sunday 23 November
Learning to be a family

Matthew 12:46-50

Pointing to his disciples he said: 'Here are my mother and my brothers. For whoever does the will of my Father in heaven is my brother and sister and mother.' (verses 49-50)

As we follow Jesus this week, we have to remember that his teaching comes often with a certain twist. We listen to him supposing that we are able to follow his line of teaching – and suddenly, there is a totally unexpected turn, a whole new perspective before our eyes, a surprisingly fresh insight into some well-known issue, or a turnabout to another topic. But isn't it the real essence of learning – getting to unknown places, discovering perspectives new and fresh! Learning from Jesus is never boring. It is also never too easy because Jesus expects his students to be active learners willing to put the teaching into practice.

The teaching–learning relationship in Jesus' time was somewhat similar to the family situation – the teacher walks and talks, eats and sleeps together with his disciples, and thus the learning occurs both during and outside the 'lecture hours'. This kind of learning experience can bind people together in a special way.

So when Jesus is approached with a family relations issue, he extends the topic into the question about belonging to the family of God. And here his teaching is simple to understand: everyone who is willing to accept God's authority is welcome to belong. No limits here – and also no exceptions.

† Jesus, I do want to belong to your family. Help me to learn, and guide me to obey God's will in my daily life.

Learning the faith from a carpenter's son

Matthew 13:54-58

Coming to his home town, he began teaching the people in their synagogue, and they were amazed. 'Where did this man get this wisdom and these miraculous powers?' they asked. 'Isn't this the carpenter's son?' (verses 54-55a)

Here is a common image of a great teacher: the authority to teach should be backed up by an excellent education or noble origin. As soon as Jesus is recognised as 'the carpenter's son' his authority to teach is questioned. People of his hometown are not willing to respect him as their teacher because he has lived too close to them. He has been one of the boys playing on the streets and, even as they now marvel at his wisdom and his miraculous power, they are still not willing to pay him due respect. In their eyes, he has no authority, and they are not open to receive any teaching from him.

Do we recognise our own prejudices? In today's world we'd rather emphasise academic credentials than someone's origin, but have we not discarded teachers, sent by God, as being not educated enough or not noble enough? And yet, throughout church history, God has repeatedly used simple people as powerful messengers.

In Estonia, the teaching of uneducated sailors began the spiritual awakenings that laid foundation to the Baptist and Methodist Churches in the end of the nineteenth century. On their voyages they had met fervent Christians convincingly living out their faith. Returning home with burning hearts, they eagerly began to share their faith with others. Fortunately, they were heard, and the gospel spread in Estonia.

Jesus, however, could not do his work in his hometown because of the lack of faith. Can Jesus do his work in your hometown today, through people who have been called and commissioned by God to proclaim the good news – whoever they are?

† Lord, help us to be receptive to your teaching, and to accept the teachers you send to us with your living word, regardless of their position or education.

For further thought

• Which teachers have educated you in your faith? In a quiet moment give thanks for them.

God and tradition

Matthew 15:1-9

Jesus replied: 'And why do you break the command of God for the sake of your tradition?' (verse 3)

John Wesley called tradition one of the four pillars of Christian faith. It is one of the four – not the only one or even the main one. Traditions show us how people before us have interpreted and applied God's word in their daily life. And traditions clearly carry on the historical and cultural values of a given community. However, as Pharisees approach Jesus with the question about honouring tradition, he immediately points to the ultimate authority of God's word. It is all about priorities. However good and honourable our human traditions are, they should never contradict the word of God.

In today's lesson, Jesus is asking a hard question. It sounds almost unbelievable: how can it be that the very essence of the religion, the command of God, somehow contradicts the religious tradition? It also leads to the deeper issue of seeing (or not seeing) the connection between the actual meaning of God's word and the practical rules and regulations about religious community life.

Jesus is reminding us also today of the importance of harmony between the practices of our tradition, and the faith in our heart based on God's revelation. Are we really practising what we believe? Let the living word of God speak to us anew today!

† Lord Jesus, teach us to understand the word of God in today's world. Lead us more deeply into it, and help us to find the guidance from this word in our daily life.

For further thought

• What parts of your church's tradition need challenging by a living God?

Wednesday 26 November
A pure heart

Matthew 15:10-20

But the things that come out of a person's mouth come from the heart, and these defile them. (verse 18)

In today's scripture passage, the conversation begins with the issue of washing hands before eating – traditionally connected with religious purity. But Jesus turns this rather casual reproach to his disciples into a profound lesson about the state of the human heart. And thus, instead of speaking about putting food in our mouths with unclean hands (defiling us), he ends up speaking about clean or unclean words that are coming out of our mouths – and our hearts.

I imagine his listeners standing stunned. They have been trying hard to follow all the rules about clean and unclean in their daily living. But now, Jesus is suddenly telling them that these rules are not the most important ones. It is actually the heart deep inside of them that needs purification most urgently. The unclean heart cannot be hidden; the words of the mouth will actually reveal the state of one's heart. And the unclean words may even infect other people.

Here it is, the unexpected twist in Jesus' teaching again. The good news is that the outside world cannot ever 'make' our heart unclean unless we let the unclean things in. And should that happen, there is the wonderful opportunity to ask our Teacher to cleanse our hearts. But we certainly should be on our guard: which words are coming out of your mouth today?

† May these words of my mouth and this meditation of my heart be pleasing in your sight, O Lord, my Rock and my Redeemer. (Psalm 19:14)

For further thought
• What do your words reveal about you today?

Thursday 27 November
Give us a sign!

Matthew 16:1-4

The Pharisees and Sadducees came to Jesus and tested him by asking him to show them a sign from heaven. **(verse 1)**

We live in a world almost addicted to entertainment. The mindset of expecting everything to be amusing and exciting above all is invading even educational institutions and the church. Perhaps it is comforting to know that there is nothing new in this mindset. People in ancient Rome requested a circus (and bread) from their emperor. As we read today, Pharisees and Sadducees requested to see a special show presented by Jesus.

What should we do with this kind of request?

Jesus answers it in a unique way. He takes the word 'sign' used in a certain context and puts it into another context. So instead of performing a thrilling miracle that would attract crowds, he is pointing to the 'signs of the times' that are far more important. As a matter of fact, he is asking here: why are you missing the show that is already going on around you? Why don't you see that God is continually giving signs of his almightiness in many different ways? When we have eyes to see and ears to listen, we begin to experience God's powerful presence in the world. No special effects are needed any more.

God is not in the entertainment business, and we shouldn't be either. But the lessons of faith do not need to be boring. We should learn to pass on the message about God's love in a way that broadens people's range of sight, and opens their hearts to notice the fascinating and spectacular things God is already doing in our world.

† Dear God, there are times when we would really like to have a special sign from heaven in order to strengthen our faith. Teach us instead to notice the signs you are already continually providing for us, and to rely more on your faithfulness.

For further thought
• Notice God in the ordinary today.

The yeast not used in bread

Matthew 16:5-12

'Be on your guard against the yeast of the Pharisees and Sadducees.'...
Then they understood that that he was not telling them to guard against
the yeast used in bread, but against the teaching of the Pharisees and
Sadducees. (verses 6b, 12)

We can be lazy learners now and then. Some days we might not pay attention to every word; we pick and choose the pieces of a given lesson, and we sincerely believe that we can substitute the missing pieces with our own thoughts and ideas. Well, this is not always a good idea. Especially with a teacher like Jesus. Because the illustrations and metaphors he is using need our undivided attention.

Here the disciples clearly mistook Jesus' yeast metaphor as a reproach for not bringing enough provision for the voyage. But Jesus will use their misunderstanding as an opportunity for another lesson about trusting God's providence. As soon as he becomes aware of their discussion about bread, he reminds them of the five loaves for the five thousand, and also the basketsful of leftovers. No need to worry about our daily bread – as their own experiences can testify!

The real lesson, however, is about being careful and not trusting every theory and thought we are offered in the name of the Lord. This warning is even more relevant in our days. Do we listen carefully enough when Jesus is trying to catch our attention? The metaphor here is a good one – a false teaching can really begin to impact us in subtle ways until our whole mindset is changed. As the false prophets and preachers offer their thoughts, we need to be prayerfully on our guard.

† Jesus, we ask for your wise guidance when we learn and read and listen. In our world of information overload, teach us to discern the right from wong, and protect us from 'the yeast' of false teachings about God's kingdom.

For further thought

• Where is Jesus trying to get your attention?

The Teacher's exam

Matthew 16:24-28

Whoever wants to be my disciple must deny themselves and take up their cross and follow me. For whoever wants to save their life will lose it, but whoever loses their life for me will find it. (verses 24-25)

This is the end of our weeklong learning from Jesus. Normally, a class ends with an exam. In our case, there also seems to be an exam. The teaching has been presented to us, and now is the time to put the whole thing into the practice.

The disciples in today's story have listened to Jesus much longer than just a week. They have asked questions, commented on the teaching, and sometimes also offered their opinion about it. They seem to have learned their lesson. Just recently, Peter has openly confessed his faith, saying that Jesus is indeed the Son of the living God (verse 16). Jesus calls him blessed.

But almost immediately after that powerful confession, Peter also makes an open suggestion that Jesus – the Messiah – should certainly not go through suffering and death (verse 22). And perhaps just this bold suggestion from Peter, estimated by Jesus as a serious failure in mastering the lessons, leads Jesus to his challenge: 'Whoever wants to be my disciple' …

Here is our exam. What have we learned during this week? If we have really learned the lesson about Jesus being the Messiah, and about the divine call to follow him, then the message about the cross should neither surprise nor frighten us. Jesus does not expect us to understand this difficult lesson in its fullness. I believe that today we are challenged just to demonstrate our trust and faith. Do we trust Jesus enough to follow him regardless of circumstances?

† Lord Jesus, help us to become your real followers. We do need more faith and trust, and you have said that the faith is God's gift. Teach us to be more open to this gift in our life.

For further thought

• What do you need to let go of in order that you might find your life in Christ?

November

God in translation
1 Rainbows, visitors and wrestling matches

This week's notes are by **Robert Parkinson** (see page 140).

Sunday 30 November (Advent Sunday)
In God's image

Genesis 1:26-31

Then God said, 'Let us make mankind in our image, in our likeness, so that they may rule over the fish in the sea and the birds in the sky … and over all the creatures that move along the ground.' So God created mankind in his own image, in the image of God he created them; male and female he created them. (part of verses 26-27)

That human beings are created in the image of God is one of the great ideas of the Bible. Still, it is not entirely clear what it means. In what way are humans made in God's likeness? What aspect of human being resembles that of God? Is it that, like God, humans can think and reason? Is it that they can create and organise? Is it that they are capable of sustaining relationships with each other, with the world and with God? Is it that humans are created to be free? Perhaps it is all these aspects and others besides.

The concept says something about the uniqueness of humanity. All the animals are said to be 'living creatures' but only human beings are made in the image of God. They are given a unique responsibility: to care for each other and for God's world. Yet, as the biblical story unfolds, human beings will struggle to live up to their vocation. They will fail God, each other, and the world, but God will not desert them. The Bible readings for this week all testify to this as they anticipate the coming of Jesus, 'the radiance of God's glory and the exact representation of his being' (Hebrews 1:3).

† Creator God, as human beings we are all made in your image; help us to discover traces of God in men and women everywhere. Amen

Monday 1 December
Where are you?

Genesis 3:8-21

*Then the man and his wife heard the sound of the L*ORD *God as he was walking in the garden in the cool of the day, and they hid from the L*ORD *God among the trees of the garden. But the L*ORD *God called to the man, 'Where are you?'* (verses 8-9)

In the Eden story, God is portrayed with human characteristics. In the evenings, for example, God likes to take a stroll in the garden with the man he has made. Today, however, everything is different. The man and the woman have eaten of the fruit forbidden by God. They are ashamed. They are afraid. For God had said that, if the man ate of the fruit of the tree, he would die. When they hear God setting out for his evening walk, they hide in the bushes but God goes looking for them. 'Where are you?' God cries. Soon discovered, the man and woman begin their litany of excuses and evasions before God pronounces judgement on them. Still, that 'Where are you?' of God seems full of pathos and significance.

The humans assume that God is looking for trouble but this is by no means certain. Perhaps God is looking for their repentance and restoration. What matters most is that God is doing the looking. God goes in search of humankind. This is an act of grace if also one of judgement. Even when all seems lost, when human beings have turned their backs on God's requirements, God does not give up on them but seeks them out.

Is not the coming of Jesus an extension of the same seeking-heart of a loving God? Perhaps we might think of Jesus as God's 'Where are you?' issued to the whole of humanity.

† Loving God, thank you that you search for me even when I hide from you. Help me then to follow you and never give up on others.

For further thought
• Have you ever felt like hiding from God? Where are you in relation to God today?

Rainbow's promise

Genesis 9:8-17

I have set my rainbow in the clouds, and it will be a sign of the covenant between me and the earth … Never again will the waters become a flood to destroy all life. (verses 13, 15b)

The rainbow is the sign of a covenant between God and the whole of creation. That is to say, God enters into covenant here not with a chosen people but with everybody and everything! God's covenant partners are variously designated as 'Noah', 'Noah's descendants', 'all the living creatures that came out of the ark', 'the earth' itself, and 'all life on earth'. This is about as comprehensive as it can get. What is more, this covenant is one-sided. Requirements for human beings are laid down in the first part of the chapter, but God's promise never to destroy the earth again by flood does not depend on their fulfilment.

I was visiting a nature reserve recently. It was rainy day at the end of a wet summer. A few of us were in the hide both sheltering and watching birds. Suddenly the sun shone and a magnificent rainbow formed over the expanse of the nature reserve in front of us. Photographers began snapping away and all agreed that it was a beautiful sight. A dark and dismal day was suddenly brighter, illumined by the light and colour of the rainbow. I do not know whether anybody else there thought of Genesis 9, but I did. The rainbow reminded me of the God we may encounter even in darkness. It can remind us all that God's mercy triumphs over judgement and that God is working for the good of the whole world.

† 'O joy that seeks for me through pain, I cannot close my heart to thee; I trace the rainbow through the rain, and feel the promise is not vain that morn shall tearless be.' ('O love that wilt not let me go', George Matheson, 1842–1906)

For further thought

- A major cause of flooding today is climate change. Can you learn more about it? Can you reduce your harmful impact on the environment?

God in disguise

Genesis 18:1-16

The Lord appeared to Abraham near the great trees of Mamre while he was sitting at the entrance to his tent in the heat of the day. (verse 1)

As if to prove that God does not only appear to people in idyllic gardens at the cool of the day, he is encountered by Abraham in the desert in the heat of the day. What is more, if the text did not tell us, we might struggle to believe that God had appeared at all. Even the text seems unsure about it all. Was it the Lord or three men that came to Abraham, or were there three messengers and one of them was the Lord?

We do not know at what point Abraham realised he was meeting with the Lord. We do know he was ready and waiting when the three visitors showed up. Abraham was receptive to their visit and, with Sarah, welcomed the messengers as honoured guests.

Could it be that God comes to us all in disguise? Could it be that only those who sit at the door of their tent and wait will see the Lord? Could it be that in the practice of hospitality we encounter God? Perhaps the Letter to the Hebrews has this story in mind when it says, 'Do not forget to show hospitality to strangers, for by so doing some people have shown hospitality to angels without knowing it' (Hebrews 13:2).

Two strangers in Bethlehem would need a similar hospitality many years after the time of Abraham and Sarah. The two would become three; and the little child would bring light to the world.

† Loving God, help us to practise hospitality and to find you in the people we welcome.

For further thought

• Is there more you can do to welcome those who seek refuge and help?

Thursday 4 December
Wrestling with God

Genesis 32:22-31

So Jacob called the place Peniel, saying, 'It is because I saw God face to face, and yet my life was spared.' The sun rose above him as he passed Peniel, and he was limping because of his hip. (verses 30-31)

Alone and in the dark, Jacob is suddenly confronted by someone who wrestles with him all night long. Introduced to us as 'a man', this character turns out in some way to represent God. Jacob wrestles with God, sees the face of God, and survives. He journeys onward, limping into a new day. Another encounter awaits him – with his estranged brother Esau who is turning out to be a better man than Jacob ever was. Nevertheless, Jacob the trickster and the cheat is becoming Israel, man of God and man of peace.

Strange as this story is, many have come to discover that the life of faith has something of the character of wrestling about it. We wrestle with God as we ask and hope for something that God does not seem willing to grant. We wrestle as we struggle to become the kind of people God wants us to be. We wrestle when God calls us to do something that we know is right but we are afraid to do. The process of believing and becoming is fraught with difficulty as we struggle to accept or to embrace the purposes of God. It appears that, if God is to be for us, God must sometimes be against us.

A surprising aspect of this story is that Jacob wins! Prevailing with God, he extracts a blessing from his assailant. God, it seems, plays hard to get but blesses those who wrestle and do not give up.

† O God, help us to be persistent in prayer even when it feels as if we are wrestling with you.

For further thought
- Have you ever felt as though you were wrestling with God?
- Do you think Jesus was wrestling with God in Gethsemane?
- Can you think of other biblical passages that are reminiscent of Jacob at the Jabbok?

Friday 5 December
Paying attention

Exodus 3:1-6

Moses thought, 'I will go over and see this strange sight – why the bush does not burn up.' When the LORD saw that he had gone over to look, God called to him from within the bush … (verses 3-4a)

Does this passage seem to suggest that God had been there in the bush for quite some time? Does it not read as if God had been waiting for someone to notice that the bush was strangely burning without being burned up? Was God waiting, longing perhaps, for someone, anyone, to pay enough attention to stop, go over and look at the wonderful sight? Who knows? God might have lit the bush hours, days, weeks or years earlier. Finally, someone of the stature of Moses comes along. While tending the flock, Moses notices the burning bush and is inquisitive enough to take a second look. Delighted, God calls out to Moses from the bush.

Of course, we cannot know whether the burning bush was lit solely for Moses but we surely ought to be impressed by his holy inquisitiveness. I wonder – if I had been there, would I have noticed the burning bush and would I have taken a closer look?

It took a few exceptional people to notice something special about the birth of a child in Bethlehem many years later. He would cause a stir when he began to preach and work wonders, but even then only a few people opened their ears and hearts to his words and followed him. Today, the Spirit of Christ is still at work. The question is: are we paying attention? Do we see; do we hear and take notice?

† God of the burning bush, open our eyes and our hearts to the wonder of your presence in ordinary and extraordinary occurrences.

For further thought

• Take a few moments to reflect on what has been happening in your life over the past week. Is God trying to get your attention in some way?

Saturday 6 December
A blind seer and a talking donkey

Numbers 22:22-35

Then the LORD opened the donkey's mouth, and it said to Balaam, 'What have I done to you to make you beat me these three times?' ... Then the LORD opened Balaam's eyes and he saw the angel of the LORD standing in the road with his sword drawn. (verses 28, 31)

Stories of a God who walks in the garden, of burning bushes, talking animals and angelic visitors, go beyond the bounds of historical description. Yet, whether we think of them as dreams, visions, parables or legends, they can all speak to us if we will let them.

On reading this strange story, I wonder which is the greater miracle, the opening of the mouth of Balaam's donkey or the opening of Balaam's eyes. I am intrigued by the ironic reversal of the roles of Balaam and his donkey. Initially, Balaam the Seer sees nothing of the angel's presence – but his donkey sees all. Balaam is cruel: his donkey is kind. Balaam is confused and agitated: the donkey is calm, considerate and, after God opens its mouth, becomes a persuasive witness. The donkey is all that Balaam ought to be: Balaam is the ass. The seer has one thing going for him – his willingness to learn. So Balaam listens to his donkey and to the angel and changes his ways.

Human beings have always been indebted to animals. Scientists routinely study the behaviour of animals in order to discover solutions to human problems. The invention of the aeroplane, for example, would surely never have occurred if it were not for the inspiration of birds in flight.

Though made in the image of God, human beings remain part of the created world. They depend on the natural world for their survival and are at their best when living in harmony with their environment.

† Life-giving God, let us never be so proud as to imagine that we are independent of the world around us. Help us always to respect the natural world and to observe in it your ways.

For further thought

• If animals (your pets, for example) could speak, what would they say to you? What would they say about you?

God in translation

2 Sounds and silence

This week's notes are by **Anastasia Somerville-Wong**

 Dr Anastasia Somerville-Wong is the author of *A Progressive Christianity in Liturgy, Poetry and Prose* (Pilgrim Press, 2013) and other articles and poems. In addition to her writing, Anastasia lectures part-time in history and theology, and works independently as a researcher and consultant, helping non-profit organisations to develop community-building initiatives in the areas of arts and culture, education and sustainable development.

Sunday 7 December
In a quiet heart, in quiet wilderness

Deuteronomy 8:2-3

Remember how the LORD your God led you all the way in the wilderness these forty years, to humble and test you in order to know what was in your heart, whether or not you would keep his commands. (verse 2)

As we journey through our lives, we arrive at different places physically and spiritually, and we encounter God in different ways. In carefree youth, we might experience God in an ecstasy of dance and song, or in the awesome power of wind and wave. As we mature, we may grow sensitive to God's presence, not so much amid noise and commotion but in the stillness of silent contemplation and prayer, and in the gentler rhythms and complex patterns of nature.

There have been times when, like the Hebrews of the Exodus story, I have carried God's commands in my heart through a place or time that could be compared to a barren and hostile wilderness. I know it can be tempting to let standards slide, or even to give up on life when we are worn down by circumstances we cannot control, and when God seems to have abandoned us. However, if we look to the inner life, we will find new depths of untapped resources; a wellspring of God's eternal spirit within us.

The resilience of our trust in spite of disappointment, the strength of the conscience in spite of temptation, the endurance of our hope in spite of despair, these are the measure of God's presence in adversity.

† Loving God, when the way ahead is dark and wrought with danger, catch our eyes with a flicker of your flame within us – a reminder that we never walk alone.

In stone

Exodus 24:12-18; 31:18

When the Lord finished speaking to Moses on Mount Sinai, he gave him the two tablets of the covenant law, the tablets of stone inscribed by the finger of God. (31:18)

Despite the inadequacies of human language, God comes to us in translations that resound with beauty, in phrases heavy with meaning beyond the words that make them up. God comes to us in the timbres of the human voice and in shapes and symbols silently read.

When we think of the 'Word of God', we often think of the words written in our Bibles. However, literacy was only for the priestly and powerful in the ancient world and few had access to important manuscripts. For centuries, stories, statutes and precepts were passed down orally with varying renditions. People believed God addressed them afresh in their own contexts, so they had no qualms in re-interpreting, embellishing and rewriting their history to convey a particular message. The story of Moses was written to explain the Jewish people's origins and the special relationship they had with their God. This God was primarily a law-giver, with jurisdiction over the Jewish people and their region, creating the moral framework required for them to live in peace with one another, and to preserve their distinctive culture. However, as their vision grew, the reach of the one unknowable God would extend throughout the world.

Many of us neglect to listen for God in the many languages of the modern world. We prefer to criticise the present and romanticise the past, harking back to some imagined utopia. It is even harder to embrace a future we cannot control, even though we know at a deeper level that it will find us out in the end.

† Living God, help us to take courage to discern in literature and the speech of the wise the marks of the still-speaking God.

For further thought
• Take time each day this week to put aside your assumptions and agendas, and simply listen, read and observe the presence and workings of God in the world.

Tuesday 9 December
In whispers and bread

1 Kings 19:1-16

All at once an angel touched him and said, 'Get up and eat.' He looked around, and there by his head was some bread baked over hot coals, and a jar of water. He ate and drank and then lay down again. The angel of the LORD came back a second time and touched him and said, 'Get up and eat, for the journey is too much for you.' (verses 5b-7)

Has anyone fed you when you were hungry, clothed you when you were naked, housed you when you were homeless, or visited you when you were in hospital or prison? Did anyone persist with you while you were broken? Could these have been the angels you never knew you met, married or befriended?

Angels in the Bible are overlooked as much as their real-life counterparts. They are regarded as mere vessels that bring messages from God to chosen individuals. However, their role should not be underestimated. In this story, it is the angel whose sympathy for Elijah's exhausted body and spirit, whose tender care and encouragement, brought him back from the brink of failure and death.

Sometimes it is the simplest things such as freshly baked bread that give us strength to carry on when we feel defeated, just as it is often the simplest things that spur us on to fulfil our potential, such as a few kind words. It costs us very little even to turn a life around, and yet so often we let such opportunities pass by, or we say or do something unhelpful instead.

The rich often lack the generosity of angels because they are preoccupied with increasing and protecting their possessions. They become suspicious of others and impatient with those who are of no obvious use to them. People who live modestly have less to lose and everything to gain. They are unafraid to be hospitable to strangers, and are rewarded as they entertain the angels.

† God of compassion, send us your angels in times of distress, and teach us to be angels in our turn, that we might bring warmth, relief and comfort to others.

For further thought

- Listen and watch for the needs of those around you, taking any opportunities that arise to assist them practically or to say something encouraging.

Timeless wisdom and endless creativity

Job 38:1-18

Have you journeyed to the springs of the sea or walked in the recesses of the deep? Have the gates of death been shown to you? Have you seen the gates of the deepest darkness? Have you comprehended the vast expanses of the earth? Tell me, if you know all this. (verses 16-18)

Knowing what we do not know and what we cannot do at any given time is the essence of what it means to be wise. There are many people who are clever in various ways but their lack of wisdom means they fail to appreciate the bigger picture, and act in a rash, judgemental, short-sighted or blinkered fashion. The accumulated stories and sayings known as wisdom literature remind us of the transcendent God whose thoughts are not our thoughts and whose ways are not our ways; the God who is beyond us. They point to the mystery of God, to what God is not, so we do not imagine a God who is only a reflection of ourselves.

The book of Job was written as an attempt by Hebrew sages to grapple with what theologians call 'the problem of pain', in order to reconcile a loving God with the evils in the world. Job is a good man brought low by suffering and tragedy. He ends up despairing of his life and taunted by his friends. He refuses to curse God, however, and is eventually vindicated and restored to a life of blessing. Job has faith in the character of God, in spite of the hopelessness in his own life. His lament is answered when God reassures him that God has a plan and purpose for the whole of creation, including Job. God draws his attention to the vastness and magnificence of the universe, and brings new perspective on his troubles.

† God of mysteries, open our eyes to the wonders of your ceaseless creation and a broader view of your purposes. Give us patience in times of sorrow, strengthening our trust in your goodness and love.

For further thought

• Cultivate wisdom as well as cleverness by looking beyond your own life and interests to appreciate the other: other subjects and other minds.

Thursday 11 December
In prophecy, parable and song

Isaiah 5:1-7a

What more could have been done for my vineyard than I have done for it? When I looked for good grapes, why did it yield only bad? Now I will tell you what I am going to do to my vineyard: I will take away its hedge, and it will be destroyed ... (verses 4-5a)

The Old Testament prophets captured divine beauty in elegant poetry and narrative. They also warned their people that social injustice, moral degradation and unfaithfulness to God would lead to their destruction. It is up to us to keep alive opportunities for modern people to encounter God in story-telling, poetry and song, and in perceptive interpretations of the times.

Priests or ministers perform sacred rituals, facilitating the relationship between humanity and the divine, and preserving traditional teachings and practices, while prophets claim to speak for God in the deliverance of new knowledge or truth to their contemporaries. Jesus was a prophet who risked everything to speak truth to the corrupt powers and authorities of his day. He taught a radical compassion that posed a threat to the religious purity systems and hierarchies. Yet he also taught with authority from the scriptures in the Temple courts, passing on ancient wisdom. Within him, as within all of us, was the tension between the priestly and prophetic.

As the early churches sought respectability amidst the dominant cultures of their time, they largely lost the prophetic voice of the Jesus movement. Modern churches claim to admire people like Gandhi or Martin Luther King Jr who, like Jesus, gave their lives for a just cause, but they have often been quick to bow down to empire, government or dictator and kept silent in the face of injustice. However, we cannot hide behind priestly robes or rituals without being complicit in the evil deeds of our societies and those who lead them. We cannot, like Pontius Pilate, simply wash our hands.

† God of justice, keep us watchful within and beyond church walls, and ready to stand up for the truth where it is obscured and the rights of the vulnerable where they are denied.

For further thought

• Discuss ways you and your church could help counter an injustice of our day such as poverty, human trafficking, gender inequality, or environmental destruction.

In visions and callings

Isaiah 6:1-8

Then I heard the voice of the LORD saying, 'Whom shall I send? And who will go for us?' And I said, 'Here am I. Send me!' (verse 8)

It is surprisingly hard to determine what route one should take through life. Many wish for a vision and calling as clear as Isaiah's and would hope to respond as willingly. Others immerse themselves in life's fleeting pleasures, running from a call that might prove challenging and costly.

I have often wrestled with my own calling, wondering whether to seek ordination, or maintain a prophetic voice, unrestrained by loyalties to a particular denomination. Jesus was no cleric. He spent much of his time speaking out against religious elites and their abuses of power. Thomas Jefferson wrote, 'In every country, in every age, the priest has been hostile to liberty. He is always in alliance with whatever despot, abetting his abuses in return for protection to his own' (letter to Horatio G. Spafford, 17 March, 1814). Despite the truth in this statement, many lesser-known priests have played vital roles in community building and caring for ordinary people through the best and worst of times. Whistleblowers and radicals, consumed by their particular struggles, had little time for these routine but invaluable tasks.

It is difficult to gain legitimacy without the backing of an established tradition or institution but, wherever people are organised into groups, they become partisan and exclusive. Life is balanced between unhealthy extremes and each of us must find our own way through. Opportunities will come for personal fulfilment, whatever your background and expertise, at the same time as meeting needs and improving the lives of others. Some have more opportunities than others, but even the smallest, when seized, can bring about the greatest transformation.

† God of all-ways, give us discernment and courage to choose our paths wisely and to share your love and hope along the way.

For further thought

• Consider what opportunities may be available to you to serve God and others that you have not yet explored.

Saturday 13 December
In life, love and salvation

Isaiah 25:6-9

On this mountain he will destroy the shroud that enfolds all peoples, the sheet that covers all nations; he will swallow up death forever. The Sovereign Lord will wipe away the tears from all faces; he will remove his people's disgrace from all the earth. (verses 7-8)

The words of the prophets resound with hope that the sufferings of their people will one day be healed by the compassion of God. They express the need of all human beings to be brought out of the darkness of mourning and loss, and of ignorance and aimlessness, to be released from the chains of past mistakes and present temptations, and rescued from their enemies. This is the liberation and enlightenment that we all seek, and which the ancients would have understood to be our salvation.

The prophets of the Old Testament were in no doubt as to what they needed to be saved from because they were struggling to live exemplary lives of faith, in perilous and uncertain times. However, the threats posed by ignorance, sin, complacency and conflict in our time are nonetheless real, even though they may seem more distant to those living in safety and freedom in the developed world. After all, it takes very little to spark the end of one empire and the beginning of another.

We can't afford to lose sight of God's vision for a world where peace and prosperity reign. We can't neglect to nurture the seeds of the kingdom of God that are already growing among us. Despite the general malaise that has engulfed the world with the recent economic crises, Christians live in hope because we cannot forget what God has done for us in the past. Like Isaiah and Job, we have learnt to trust in God's unchanging character.

† Saviour God, teach us to live the spiritual life, working together towards the realisation of your vision for a world healed and at peace, even when it seems to us an impossible dream.

For further thought
• Share with a friend your own experiences of God's saving power and how it has transformed your life.

God in translation

3 The holy one and a withering plant

This week's notes are by **Helen Van Koevering**

 Living in Southern Africa for 17 years has challenged Helen, raised in England, to live differently, and to see God at work in a different context. Apart from being the mother of three teenagers and the wife of the diocesan bishop, Helen presently works as an ordained priest and the Director of Ministry with the Anglican Diocese of Niassa in northern Mozambique, a diocese that has doubled in members and congregations since 2004.

Sunday 14 December
Renewing Creator and withering plants

Isaiah 40:18-31

No sooner are they planted, no sooner are they sown, no sooner do they take root in the ground, then he blows on them and they wither ... but those who hope in the Lord will renew their strength... (part of verses 24 and 31a)

Isaiah popularised the name of God as the Holy One in laying out for us his doctrine of faith. God, the Holy One, brings order out of chaos, revealing God's creative and redemptive nature in the continuing transformation of the whole created universe. The image of the plant withering under God's breath enables us to lift up our eyes and see our capacity for transformation through God's eternal concern.

This week's readings offer us prophetic images of the ordinary to help us see the extraordinary life of the Holy One whose eternity of being sweeps the divine presence and power across all time and throughout the world. God knows, has always known, and God's creative power will always renew God's people as they look to him and wait on him. 'Waiting for the Lord' is to understand Isaiah's description of faith as intensifying our sense of helplessness alongside our appreciation of God's redeeming power and promise. 'Waiting' is what we do now in Advent, even in our busy preparations and early celebrations – waiting for Immanuel, God with us, and remembering that our lives are in God's creative, redeeming hands.

† Life-giving Lord, the creative and redeeming Holy One of Israel, transform us to see your order in our chaos, and your power in our weakness, today and always. Amen

Monday 15 December
Nurturing life and flourishing grass

Isaiah 66:12-14

… you will feed and be carried on her arm and dandled on her knees. As a mother comforts her child, so will I comfort you, and you will be comforted over Jerusalem. When you see this, your heart will rejoice and you will flourish like grass. (verses 12b-14a)

A mother learns, as her child grows and matures, that her mothering changes. The dependency of the newborn brings awe-filled nursing and pain-forgetting presence. Toddler energy takes life-giving strength. Teenagers bring out mothering comfort responding to all the tears and dreams, joys and trials of those years. And the place of mothering will draw the adult child home long after the letting go of mothering love watched the child leave. Love nurtures life at every stage, brings comfort where it is needed, flourishing where it can.

Just as place speaks of mothering comfort and brings that knowing of 'home' to our lives, so the place of Jerusalem spoke to the people of Israel of the comforting, 'at home' presence of God with them. As it was with them, so it is with us today. Grass growing in the cracks of long-standing walls, broken pavements, amongst the rubbish as well as in the flower beds, speaks of God's nurturing and comforting life in this world with us. Grass can flourish in even the toughest, forgotten places, those thin spears of gentle green life revealing incredible resilience. Grass needs only a little soil. It is the first to reveal new life after the first seasonal rains in dry places, promising more to come, and announcing the hope of new crops. Grass adds beauty to familiar places.

Whether the signs of the coming Christmas are all around us in material terms or not, our eyes of faith and home-desiring hearts see new and different signs of God's living mercy, hope and love in this world and with us.

† Lord, open my eyes to your nurturing life and loving hope. Fill my home-coming heart with your comfort and presence. Amen

For further thought

• Wherever we might be this Christmas, let us be open to God's Son, sent to our world for the comfort, joy, flourishing, and life of all creation.

Tuesday 16 December
Awesome Sovereign and the writing hand

Daniel 5:1-9

Suddenly the fingers of a human hand appeared and wrote on the plaster of the wall, near the lampstand in the royal palace. The king watched the hand as it wrote. (verse 5)

The unexpected and the inexplicable can fill lives either fear or awe. It has been said that the centre of global Christianity is now Africa south of the Sahara. Church leaders of Africa know the challenges of high and rapid church growth in new places, and the struggle to create training and discipling programmes to support a Christianity that is not 'a mile wide and an inch thick'. In some parts of Africa, many still walk with a foot in their roots of African traditional religion and in the new life of Christianity. Fear of spiritual realities, fear of the unknown and fear of powerful evil remain. Apart from weakening Christian communities, these fears can break up families, cause hardship with costly ceremonies to appease spirits, be seen in mental and social disturbances, even lead to crime and death.

This story about King Belshazzar would be read very differently in rural Africa than in cosmopolitan city centres. The fear may change from spiritual forces to social or economic failure and loss of control, from the unknown causes of sickness to the known incurable disease, from poverty to lonely old age, but fear remains. Look ahead in this chapter to Daniel's interpretation of the writing on the wall, and see that pride, misdirected praise, and dishonouring of life were behind King Belshazzar's fear. Fear led to his death before repentance could bring humbling, awe-freeing transformation – not only in the king's life, but in his kingdom.

† Awesome Creator, remind us of your presence. May the knowledge of your Son who came to set us free, and the indwelling work of the Spirit, reveal your grace today. Amen

For further thought
- Pray for those around you living in fear and needing to know the awesome presence of God in their lives.

Merciful grace and the shady bush

Jonah 4:5-11

You are concerned about this plant, though you did not tend it or make it grow ... should I not have concern for the great city of Nineveh ...?
(verse 10)

God's question to Jonah reminds us of current environmental concerns and our response as Christians. Our overconsumption and materialist values may lead us to forget either God's mercy or protective grace in a spirituality of individual salvation and dominion over the world. On the other hand, our love for nature may push us towards protecting the planet. The poorest, dependent on the environment and squeezed by the powerful's greater share of resources, suffer first and worst. The rich learn to 'reduce, reuse, recycle'; the poor are restricted to living less sustainably. But is it really such a clear 'poor or planet' argument?

Jonah was happy that a bush provided him with shade as he waited to see Nineveh destroyed. Then God allowed that bush to wither, and spared Nineveh punishment. Jonah's angry reaction to the loss of the shady bush is the same as his reaction to God not bringing calamity on Nineveh; he lacks understanding of God's mercy and grace. God's aim is care for all creation, not Nineveh's punishment and destruction.

Our Creator God cares for both the planet and the people, saves both and calls us to work for the flourishing of all and God's shalom kingdom – where all people and all nature are held in embracing love.

† Compassionate Creator, show us how to live in your kingdom shalom. Amen

For further thought

• In what way could you and your community be involved in showing God's care and shalom for where you live?

Thursday 18 December
Everlasting compassion and human cords

Hosea 11:1-4

I led them with cords of human kindness, with ties of love. To them I was like one who lifts a little child to the cheek, and I bent down to feed them. (verse 4)

Call it a *capulana*, *chitenje*, or a *zambia* – the most common form of transport in Africa is neither the minibus nor the car, nor even the bicycle, but this colourful length of cotton cloth used to bind and carry babies on their mothers' bodies!

In truth, this cloth is multi-purpose, and can be at times a table or bed covering, a towel, a skirt or head wrap, or a carry bag for anything from anywhere to everywhere. Feast days and festivals are celebrated with commemorative *capulanas*. It's an ideal gift for any woman of any age and the first item to be grabbed in any emergency. But it is also what is used to wrap babies securely to their mother-carer – to be where she is, to be part of all she does, and to be close to the source of nourishment and care, whether sleeping or looking out on the world from a higher place. The face, voice and smile of the baby's beloved are within reach and vision.

What a wonderfully intimate image of God in today's verses! As a good parent delights in the baby just for being, so God reveals himself in humanity, healing the separation and distance, bringing us close through recognising who is in the acts of human compassion and bonds of relationship that surround and sustain us. God is translated to us in bonds of loving kindness.

† God, you are our loving parent and we rest gratefully in your arms. Amen

For further thought
• Thank all those in your life who have shown you loving care.

The righteous way and the plumb-line

Amos 7:7-9

Look, I am setting a plumb-line among of my people Israel; I will spare them no longer. (part of verse 8)

The prophet Amos spoke at a time of prosperity yet social and religious corruption for Israel. Four themes are important to Amos: judgement by the covenant-making Yahweh of the nation of Israel, with particularly harsh words for leaders; social justice; hypocritical religion with no concern for neighbours; and the loss of God's guidance in his day.

Amos recounts five visions, with the plumb-line vision as the third, in which God asks Amos what he sees and then explains the significance. In the first two visions, God relents because of Amos' intercession but, in the final three, punishment seems certain. As a plumb-line tests the straightness of a wall and whether it needs to be demolished or repaired, so God's word tests and reveals what is not and what should be.

God's way is guided by God's word, whether heard in the words of a prophet, read in scripture or seen in the life of Jesus. Jesus gave yet clearer guidance about God's way for us: 'love one another as I have loved you'. In that love, God's judgement becomes mercy, injustice becomes righteousness, hypocrisy becomes truth and God's word is heard in our world.

† God of truth, nothing is new in our day. May we be bearers of your mercy, righteousness and truth, guided by your word. Amen

For further thought

- Advocacy for truth, justice and peace are important in the church's mission. How are you and your community involved in such advocacy where you are?

Saturday 20 December
The glorious voice and the thunderstorm

Psalm 29:3-9

The voice of the LORD is powerful; the voice of the LORD is majestic.
(verse 4)

There is a fearsome beauty in the power of a thunderstorm. In the tropics, after many months of dry, energy-sapping heat, that first clap of thunder and wild darkening of the sky calls forth a deep response. Where life and crops depend on the rainy season, the thunderstorm brings relief and promise in its power. Storms may cause damage to property and inconveniently cut electrical services, and their sounds may strike fear into animals and children but, when experienced from a safe window, the storm's power is beautifully enthralling.

The thunderstorm described in Psalm 29 rises out of the Mediterranean Sea and sweeps inland with devastating effects across Lebanon and the mountain ranges around Mount Hermon, and ends in the Syrian desert east of Kadesh on the Orontes river. Myth enters into dramas such as this, and affirms that our God, who dethrones all other powers and fearful forces, is king of the universe. God's voice heard in the sounds of the terrifying storm paradoxically speaks of the kingdom's powerful peace and security. Rather than seeing power as to be feared, held on to or sought after, God's voice in the thunderstorm shows how power is rightly inhabited – how power, and those who have it, can be used to bring peace, prosperity, unity, blessing. The power of God reveals the beauty of his majesty and the reality of his rule in our world.

† Lord of all beauty and power, you speak to us even in a thunderstorm. Help us live to your praise and glory, for ever.

For further thought
• How do you inhabit the power that you have?

God in translation
4 The ultimate translation

This week's notes are by **Kate Hughes**

 Kate Hughes spent 14 years working for the Church in Southern Africa. Since her return to the UK in 1990, she has worked as a freelance book editor, specialising in theology. She now lives on a small council estate in Coventry and is involved in her local community and preaches regularly at her local Anglican church.

Sunday 21 December
The sign of a baby

Isaiah 7:10-14

The LORD himself will give you a sign: the virgin will conceive and give birth to a son, and will call him Immanuel. (verse 14)

God's greatest act of translation is the event we look forward to in Advent: God's nature translated into a human being. All the essentials of God are there, in the easiest possible way for us to grasp, because God created human beings in his image and the baby born on Christmas Day is God. This week we shall be exploring the events surrounding this greatest translation and some reflections on it.

God had used the sign of a baby before. King Ahaz of Judah and his people are being attacked by the kings of Aram and Israel and God sends Isaiah to reassure Ahaz that his enemies will be defeated. Through Isaiah, God then tells Ahaz to ask for a sign to validate the prophet's words, and Ahaz goes all humble: 'I can't do that with God!' (verse 12). Isaiah's exasperated answer (verse 13): 'Just for once, simply do what you're told!' And God gives him a sign anyway: 'The virgin will conceive and give birth to a son, and will call him Immanuel.' (part of verse 14)

The name Immanuel reappears in Matthew 1:23, which quotes this verse from Isaiah and gives the meaning of the name: the ultimate translation, God with us.

† Thank you God that, once and always, you are Immanuel.

Monday 22 December
The sign of new life

Luke 1:39-45

As soon as the sound of your greeting reached my ears, the baby in my womb leaped for joy. **(verse 44)**

One of the things we have learnt from our Advent readings is that God can use anything to communicate with human beings. Anything – rainbows, storms, silence, donkeys, visitors, even a dying caster oil plant. Far from being a divine watchmaker, as some earlier theologians thought of him, who creates the world, sets it going like winding up a watch and then walks away, God is still involved with his world, communicating with the beings he has created, translating himself into ways we can understand, so that everything can potentially connect us to God. As the poet Gerard Manley Hopkins wrote, in 'God's Grandeur', 'The world is charged with the grandeur of God,/It will flame out, like shining from shook foil.' Here, as in yesterday's reading, God uses a baby to announce his presence (verse 44).

Elizabeth was six months pregnant, so this wasn't the first time her baby, the future John the Baptist, had moved. But for both Elizabeth and her pregnant cousin Mary it was a reminder from God that new life was on the way, salvation was on the way, the ultimate translation was about to be given. A normal part of a healthy pregnancy, but also a reminder of the wonder of God's activity in his world.

† Lord, help us to see and hear your speaking to us through everyday, ordinary things and events.

For further thought
• What everyday things does God use to speak to you?

Working through bureaucracy

Luke 2:1-7

While they were there, the time came for the baby to be born, and [Mary] gave birth to her firstborn, a son. She wrapped him in cloths and placed him in a manger, because there was no guest room available for them. (verses 6-7)

Every ten years in England an official census counts every person resident in England on census night and asks questions about their circumstances. The census that took place in Palestine 2,000 years ago was in some ways simpler – apparently it just counted heads – but was in practice much more complicated, as it required everyone to go back to the place where they were born or their family came from. So Joseph and Mary had to go back to Joseph's hometown of Bethlehem, together with many other people.

Some Christmas hymns speak of Bethlehem lying still beneath the stars, a silent place for this special coming of God. In reality, it must have been chaos. Full inns, with people drinking, eating and talking through the night. Newcomers arriving at all hours. Shouting, laughter, probably some swearing too, donkeys braying, disturbed dogs barking. And in the midst of all this, God speaks. In circumstances dictated by Roman bureaucracy, in a town bursting at the seams, in a cave used as a stable, with all the pain and mess of giving birth, God tells us so much about himself. He can use external circumstances, chaos, dirt, displacement, pain, an ordinary young woman and a manger to speak his most important word to his creation.

† God, we worship you as almighty and lifted up, but you willingly get down to our level and get your hands dirty in order to draw close to us. Thank you.

For further thought
• What do the circumstances of Jesus' birth tell you about God?

Wednesday 24 December
This will be a sign to you

Luke 2:8-20

Today in the town of David a Saviour has been born to you; he is the Messiah, the LORD. This will be a sign to you: you will find a baby wrapped in cloths and lying in a manger. (**verses 11-12**)

This baby born in a stable at Bethlehem is a multiple sign: a sign of God's nature, God's willingness to translate himself into something that people can understand. And a sign for the shepherds of how God will reveal his glory in the world. God will do glorious things – it is a saviour who is born (verse 11), the long-awaited Messiah – but he will do them through a man that people can see, touch, speak to, and put to death.

St Irenaeus, a second-century bishop, said that the glory of God is man (or woman) fully alive. Jesus is the man above all who is fully alive, alive as God created all his people to be. He is the sign of what God's glory is truly like, a glory that is willing to die if that is the only way he can deliver human beings from the bondage of sin. It is a glory that does not come with triumphalist armies to destroy its enemies, but overcomes evil in the quietness of a tomb and the stillness of death, and in resurrection is revealed first to a woman in a garden. The shepherds glimpsed the glory of the Lord in a vision of angels. But they were directed to find the true translation of God's glory, a newborn baby with his parents in a stable.

† Thank you, God, for your ultimate translation of yourself into the baby that the shepherds worshipped.

For further thought

• In what way does Jesus illustrate Irenaeus' saying that the glory of God is man fully alive?

Thursday 25 December (Christmas Day)
Accepting the Word

John 1:1-14

He came to that which was his own, but his own did not receive him.
(verse 11)

I think the verse selected here, verse 11 of the first chapter of John, is one of the saddest verses in the Bible.

We have glimpsed, this Advent, some of the efforts that God makes to communicate with people in ways suited to their human nature. And we have seen in this week's readings the crown of these efforts, in the birth of Jesus. But for all God's work in revealing himself to his chosen people across the centuries, they still, in the end, could not hear his words. They did not recognise the longed-for Messiah, perhaps because he was God, not a warrior-king who would deliver the Jewish nation from its oppressors. Even in translation, they failed to understand what God was saying to them.

But it is not just the Jews who have failed to recognise God's Word made flesh. We all fail to listen to God, to recognise when he speaks to us, especially if he uses rather unexpected means of communication. Do we recognise the voice of God if the word of encouragement, guidance, judgement, love comes to us from someone we dislike, from a child or a subordinate, or someone who isn't a Christian? As followers of Christ and lovers of God, we are now his people, his own.

Today, commit yourself to receiving God in whatever way he comes to you, so that he can never say of you that 'I came to you as one of my own, but you did not receive me.'

† On this Christmas Day, come, Lord Jesus.

For further thought

- Thank God today for all the presents he has given you, and give him the present of yourself.

Sharing the good news

Hebrews 1:1-3a

In the past God spoke to our ancestors through the prophets at many times and in various ways, but in these last days he has spoken to us by his Son. (verses 1-2a)

Reading the scriptures, it was obvious that God had been speaking to his people in many different ways. But now God was here himself, present in the human body of the man Jesus, who shared the very nature of God and revealed it to all who were willing to listen to the Word of God.

In these early days of the church, the good news of Jesus had to be handed on by word of mouth; the gospel was gossiped and preached, the stories of those who had been with Jesus passed on from congregation to congregation. This was something new, exciting, life changing, world changing. And this is still the good news that we have to share. If being able to recognise God revealed in his Son has changed us and made sense of our lives and our world, we need to share this with others. We may not be called to go to other lands as a missionary but, like the first Christians, we can pass the news on by word of mouth, by our every word and action towards those we meet in our daily lives. They will judge Christianity by us. God translated himself in Jesus and also translates himself in us so that others can glimpse him and be drawn to know him.

† Lord, if I am to be a channel through which you can communicate with those who do not yet know you, I am going to need your help. Thank you for always being with us.

For further thought

• Look honestly at how you translate God into words and actions in your own life. Where could you do better?

Saturday 27 December
The ultimate translation

Hebrews 2:14-18

Because he himself suffered when he was tempted, he is able to help those who are being tempted. (verse 18)

These verses underline the extent of God's translation of himself in the person of Jesus, and why he needed to do it. Jesus was God, but he was also a real human being who felt heat and cold, got tired and hungry, had a crowded and busy life and had to make difficult choices. Although our own lives may seem very different from his, we all have points of identification with Jesus. We all have a way in to listening to him, thinking about his life, pondering his words and actions. Because Jesus was like us in being human, we can go beyond him to the God he points us to. He is indeed God's ultimate translation.

Today's reading highlights some of the ways we can identify with Jesus. 'Tempted' here would be better translated 'tested'. We are always being tested, often in quite small things: keeping our temper, being generous with our time, treating others with respect, making time for prayer, being loving to ourselves as well as others. Jesus also experienced these testing moments: when his disciples argued amongst themselves, it would have been so easy to lose his temper; when he was tired at the end of a busy day, why not refuse to help the latecomer who was desperate for healing for his child? And was there any way he could avoid the cross? If Jesus, with God's help, could get through the testing times, so can we.

† Lord, when I am tested may I look to you and be helped.

For further thought
• Why do you think that knowing that Jesus was tested can help us when we are being tested?

God in translation
5 What we have heard and seen, looked at and touched

This week's notes are by **Kate Hughes** (see page 359).

Sunday 28 December
The sign of a star

Matthew 2:4-12

On coming to the house, they saw the child with his mother Mary, and they bowed down and worshipped him. (verse 11a)

In these last few days of 2014, we shall be moving on from the birth of Jesus to see how God continued to make himself known to his world.

If today's foreign visitors really were magi, astronomers, God chose exactly the right means of getting them to set out on a long journey. A moving star – just the thing to make them give chase. So God translated himself into something that would catch the eye of a magi/astronomer, in order to lead them to the ultimate translation, Christ.

I wonder how they felt when the star stopped. Jesus was now a child, no longer a baby, so presumably he and his parents were living in a house or lodgings in Bethlehem. So the star stopped over an ordinary house, occupied by an ordinary family. Was that really what the magi had come all this way for? But these astronomers trusted their beloved stars. If a star led them somewhere, that place must be special. And so they went in and recognised the child himself as a sign from God.

† Lord, help us to be sensitive to all the signs you give us, so that, like the magi, we may seek and find you.

The sign to Paul

Acts 22:3-21

The God of our ancestors has chosen you to know his will and to see the Righteous One and to hear words from his mouth. (verse 14)

The sign to the magi rounds off the Gospel accounts of God's revelation of himself through a baby and young child. Now we shall see how God continues to speak to his people by translating himself into terms that catch their attention and help them to hear him and change. We begin with Paul.

For Paul, God translates himself into sight and words in a dramatic encounter on the road down to Damascus, an encounter that totally changed his life. Given his background, which he describes in the first part of his speech to the crowd from the steps of the Temple, perhaps nothing less than a direct sign from God would have been enough to make Saul change direction. In this instance, Saul is blinded by light and addressed by Jesus himself (his account of the words of Ananias in today's text imply that he also saw the figure of Jesus). Even before the voice identifies itself, Saul addresses it as 'Lord' (verse 8). Ever afterwards Saul maintained that he had had an actual encounter with the risen Lord, as real as the resurrection appearances to the disciples and others described in the Gospels (see 1 Corinthians 15:3-8). God's ultimate translation of himself has given human beings a permanent way to recognise him and communicate with him in the person of Jesus.

† Gracious God, we may not have spectacular Damascus road encounters with you, but thank you that we can still get to know you through your translation in your Son.

For further thought
• What difference has getting to know Jesus as the way to the Father made in your life?

The sign to Peter

Acts 11:1-18

So if God gave them the same gift as he gave us, who believe in the LORD Jesus Christ, who was I to think that I could stand in God's way! (verse 17)

This is another dramatic intervention that changed a life. The Peter who out of fear refused to eat with Gentiles in Antioch (Galatians 2:12) has his behaviour directly challenged by God. He knew who was speaking to him, who had sent the vision of a sheet holding unclean animals, birds and reptiles, guaranteed to make Peter draw back in horror. As with Paul yesterday, even before the voice identifies itself, Peter calls it 'Lord'. This was again God speaking through his final translation, Jesus. Peter was not only calling the food unclean that he might have to eat at a Gentile's table; he was by implication calling the Gentiles unclean, so the Lord tells him not to call *anything* made by God unclean. And this vision is confirmed when God sends his Spirit upon the Gentile household of Cornelius just as he did upon Peter and the other disciples at Pentecost.

The changed Peter goes to a Gentile's house without hesitation, begins to tell them about Jesus, rejoices when the Spirit comes on them, and baptises them. God has indeed in these last days 'spoken to us by his Son' (Hebrews 1:2).

† Thank you, God, that your salvation is available to all those you have created.

For further thought

- Is there any group in your life (a different denomination, another religion, those with different values or lifestyle) about whom you need to learn the same lesson as Peter?
- How can you change, as he did?

Wednesday 31 December
God in translation

1 John 1:1-3

That which was from the beginning, which we have heard, which we have seen with our eyes, which we have looked at and our hands have touched – this we proclaim concerning the Word of life. (verse 1)

If this letter was written by John the disciple and Gospel writer (though no one knows for sure), he had indeed heard, seen, looked at and touched God's ultimate Word, Jesus. John could remember being there at the feeding of the 5,000, at the Transfiguration, at the bringing back to life of Jairus' daughter and Lazarus, at the Crucifixion and the Resurrection appearances. We can't remember these events. We have never met the human being who lived and died in Palestine 2,000 years ago, even though some have encountered the risen and ascended Jesus. However, although we may not be able physically to see and touch the human Jesus, every experience we have of God that reaffirms the portrait of God seen in Jesus confirms the truth of God's ultimate translation of himself. When we read the Gospel accounts of Jesus, we see what God is like, how he relates to his people and his creation, what he expects of us, how we should be serving him, what help is available to us.

When we read the Gospel accounts of Jesus we see how God has acted to break our bondage to sin, how much it cost him, and how much he loves us.

God, as we have seen, translates himself for us in many different ways. Jesus is indeed his ultimate translation.

† Thank you, Father, that we go into the new year secure in the knowledge of your love for us, revealed in Jesus.

For further thought

• Looking back over your year of Bible reading with *Fresh from the Word*, how do you think your relationship with God has grown?

IBRA International Fund: would you help us?

Since the International Bible Reading Association was founded in 1882 our UK readers have been making donations to the IBRA International Fund (previously named the Missionary Fund), with the aim of supporting our overseas readers through the network of IBRA partners.

Our partners are based in 16 countries but the benefit flows over borders to at least 32 countries all over the world. Partners work tirelessly and often without pay to organise the translation, printing and distribution of IBRA Bible study notes and lists into many different languages from Ewe, Yoruba and Twi to Portuguese, Samoan and Telugu!

For over 130 years IBRA readers' donations have helped to support them and we guarantee that 100 per cent of your donations go to support our international brothers and sisters in Christ.

This money enables those who live in remote and isolated areas of the world not only to have access to Bible reading materials, but also to be part of a global Christian community. The comfort and encouragement brought by the knowledge that hundreds of thousands of Christians are reading the same Bible passages worldwide creates a feeling of unity on a global scale.

How your donations make a difference!

- **£5.00** prints 6 translated copies of *Fresh From the Word* in Ghana
- **£10.00** buys 14 translated copies for India
- **£25.00** sends 5 copies of *Fresh From the Word* (including the postage and packaging) to Nigeria
- **£50.00** would fund 1000 IBRA reading lists to be translated into Spanish, printed and distributed in Argentina.

We have been unable to fund the printing of the Spanish lists for the last couple of years. Digital versions are available but in many areas of South America there are poor facilities for printing and churches may lack the funds to do this.

Our aim is to promote the daily reading of the Bible and to support readers in understanding and applying its message to their daily lives. We know that this work is appreciated as we get many letters of thanks, such as:

> I have found the [Bible study notes] immensely helpful over the years, a constant stimulus to fresh thinking, providing valuable insights to what is happening and what people are thinking both in our own Churches and in the World Church.
>
> **GB, a reader in Orkney**

> ...I just want to inform you that whilst in prison I came across your notes through my inmate... I was always wanting to find servants of the living God who were going to make me grow in my Christian life. Your messages have touched my heart. I thank God for changing my heart; I had no regard to God as my Abba Father. Today I am who I am by the grace of God.
>
> **AM, 26 years old**

Will you work with us and help us to enable Christians from different parts of the world to grow in knowledge and appreciation of the Word of God by making a donation of £5, £10 or even £50 to keep reaching people across the world with the word of God? The whole of your donation will support people overseas.

If you would like to make a donation, please use the envelope inserted in this book, send a cheque to IBRA, 1020 Bristol Road, Birmingham B29 6LB, or go online to shop.christianeducation.org.uk and click the donate button at the top of the page.

International Bible Reading Association Partners

A worldwide service of Christian Education at work in five continents

HEADQUARTERS
1020 Bristol Road
Selly Oak
Birmingham
B29 6LB
United Kingdom

www.christianeducation.org.uk
ibra@christianeducation.org.uk

and the following agencies:

NEW ZEALAND AND AUSTRALIA
Epworth Bookshop
157B Karori Road
Marsden Village
Karori
Wellington 6012

Mailing address:
PO Box 17255
Karori
Wellington 6147

sales@epworthbooks.org.nz

SAMOA
Congregational Christian Church
Central Office
Level 5, John Williams Building
Tamaligi
Apia

isalavao@cccs.org.ws

AMERICAN SAMOA
Congregational Christian Church in American
Samoa
PO Box 1537
1 Kananafou Street
Pago Pago
96799

reupenaalo@yahoo.com

FIJI
Methodist Bookstore
PO Box 354
Suva
Fiji

mbookstorefiji@yahoo.com

GHANA
IBRA Secretary
Asempa Publishers & IBRA
Box GP 919
Accra

asempa@iburstgh.com

NIGERIA
David Hinderer House
The Cathedral Church of St David
Kudeti
PMB 5298 Dugbe
Ibadan
Oyo State

SOUTH AND CENTRAL AFRICA
IBRA South Africa
6 Roosmaryn Street
Durbanville 7550

biblereading@evmot.com

DEMOCRATIC REPUBLIC OF THE CONGO
Communauté Baptiste du Fleuve Congo
Avenue Kalemie no 8
Kinshasa
BP 205 & 397
Kinshasa 1

ecc_cbfc@yahoo.fr

CAMEROON
Redemptive Baptist Church
PO Box 65
Limbe
Fako Division
South West Region

evande777@yahoo.com

INDIA
All India Sunday School Association
Plot No 8,
Threemurthy Colony
6th Cross, Mahendra Hills
PB no 2099
Secunderabad – 500 026
Andhra Pradesh

sundayschoolindia@yahoo.co.in

Fellowship of Professional Workers
Samanvay
Deepthi Chambers
Vijayapuri
Hyderabad – 500 017
Andhra Pradesh

fellowship2w@gmail.com

Fresh From the Word 2015
Order and donation form

International Bible Reading Association

	Quantity	Price	Total
ISBN 978-1-905893-81-2 AA140201 **Fresh From the Word 2015** P&P (UK only) please see table below		£9.00	
P&P (Western Europe only) If ordering 3 or more copies please contact us for revised postage.		£5.00	
P&P (Rest of the world only) If ordering 3 or more copies please contact us for revised postage.		£6.00	
Donation Yes, I would like to make a donation to IBRA's International Fund to help support our international community of readers.		£5.00	
		£10.00	
		£25.00	
		£50.00	
		Other	
Total			

UK P&P Rates	
Order value up to £25	£2.50
Order value up to £25.01 - £75.00	£5.00
Order value up to £75.01 - £100	£7.50
Order value over £100	free

Ebook versions are available from our website: shop.christianeducation.org.uk

Gift Aid declaration *giftaid it*

If you wish to gift aid your donation please tick the box below.

I am a UK tax payer and would like IBRA to reclaim the Gift Aid on my donation, increasing my donation by 25p for every £1 I give.

☐ I want IBRA to claim back tax on this gift and any future gifts until I notify you otherwise. I confirm I have paid or will pay an amount of Income Tax and/or Capital Gains Tax for each tax year that is at least equal to the amount of tax that all the charities or CASCS that I donate to will reclaim on my gifts for the tax year.

Thank you so much for your generous donation, it will make a real difference and change lives around the world.

Please fill in your details on the reverse of this page and send back to IBRA.

Please fill in your order on the reverse

Name: _____

Address: _____

_____

_____

Postcode: _____ Tel: _____

Email: _____

Your order will be dispatched when all books are available. Payments in pounds sterling, please.

☐ **I have made a donation**

☐ **I would like to know more about leaving a legacy to IBRA**

☐ **I enclose a cheque (made payable to IBRA)**

☐ **Please charge my MASTERCARD/VISA/SWITCH**

Card Number: ⬜⬜⬜⬜⬜⬜⬜⬜⬜⬜⬜⬜⬜⬜⬜⬜ **Issue Number:** ⬜⬜

Start Date: ⬜⬜ ⬜⬜   **Expiry Date:** ⬜⬜ ⬜⬜

Security number (last three digits on back): ⬜⬜⬜

Signature: _____

Please return this form to:

IBRA
1020 Bristol Road
Selly Oak
Birmingham B29 6LB
UK

You can also order through your local IBRA rep or from:
- website: shop.christianeducation.org.uk
- email: sales@christianeducation.org.uk
- call: 0121 472 4242

Registered Charity number: 211542

The INTERNATIONAL BIBLE READING ASSOCIATION is a Registered Charity